WA
——— OF THE ———
ANUNNAKI

"Chris Hardy, Ph.D., releases yet another scholarly probe—with expertly written evidence and keen observations of our ancient past that will not remain hidden or forgotten. Her extensive research and understanding piece together a history of rivalries, avant-garde knowledge of weapons, advanced technologies, and warring gods that can only be understood today, in our modern times, as we have entered the nuclear age. Great truths are revealed in this unraveling of history. Superb book!"

CHASE KLOETZKE, AUTHOR, UFOLOGIST,
FATE MAGAZINE RADIO HOST

"Chris Hardy's new book gives us an interesting account of the destructive wars of ancient times. She makes a strong case for the use of nuclear weapons many thousands of years ago—in a devastating war that ranged across several planets in our solar system."

DAVID HATCHER CHILDRESS, AUTHOR OF *TECHNOLOGY OF THE GODS* AND PUBLISHER OF ADVENTURES UNLIMITED PRESS

"The Anunnaki wars described by Chris H. Hardy, Ph.D., are revealed to be territorial, egomaniacal family feuds where even nukes are used! So, if these warring Sumerian gods were extraterrestrials from a rogue Nibiru planet a million years ago—who needed gold to restore their planet's deteriorating atmosphere and genetically boosted *Homo erectus* as well as other later standing-up primates to be a labor force—then this book also shows why humans have long fought irrational wars over whose 'god' is superior. Such an important work!"

LINDA MOULTON HOWE,
EMMY AWARD–WINNING INVESTIGATIVE JOURNALIST AND
REPORTER AND EDITOR OF EARTHFILES.COM

"The unraveling of some dark events in our past through the detailed accounts of the Sumerian tablets can make one's hair rise when we discover the true and dire reasons for the smashing of the Babel Tower and especially the erasing of Sodom and Gomorrah by weapons of mass destruction. Chris Hardy shows that the tablets reveal a total absence of sexual sin and, to the contrary, a lethal infighting for power within a royal family of men and women who became our gods."

MARILYN SCHLITZ, PH.D., AUTHOR, LABORATORY AND
CLINICAL SCIENTIST, SOCIAL ANTHROPOLOGIST, AND
PRESIDENT EMERITUS OF THE INSTITUTE OF NOETIC SCIENCES

"From her thorough research in Sumerian texts as well as biblical literature and archaeological sites, Hardy has concluded that 'weapons of mass destruction' are not new. Readers might disagree, but they will not be bored with this richly documented and provocative book."

STANLEY KRIPPNER, PH.D., AUTHOR AND
PROFESSOR OF PSYCHOLOGY AT SAYBROOK UNIVERSITY

"This groundbreaking book by Chris Hardy presents convincing evidence from ancient history and modern science that a cataclysmic nuclear event destroyed ancient Sumerian culture. This important and thought-provoking book challenges our assumptions about the past and raises disturbing questions about mankind's future."

RICHARD DEWHURST, AUTHOR OF
THE ANCIENT GIANTS WHO RULED AMERICA

"This book should be of interest to all those who are, like me, interested in evidence for ancient warfare involving the use of weapons resembling modern nuclear weapons."

MICHAEL A. CREMO, AUTHOR OF
FORBIDDEN ARCHEOLOGY

WARS

—— OF THE ——

ANUNNAKI

Nuclear Self-Destruction
in Ancient Sumer

CHRIS H. HARDY, Ph.D.

Bear & Company
Rochester, Vermont • Toronto, Canada

Bear & Company
One Park Street
Rochester, Vermont 05767
www.BearandCompanyBooks.com

Bear & Company is a division of Inner Traditions International

Library of Congress Cataloging-in-Publication Data

Names: Hardy, Christine, 1949–
Title: Wars of the Anunnaki : nuclear self-destruction in ancient Sumer /
    Chris H. Hardy, Ph.D.
Description: Rochester, Vermont : Bear & Company, 2016. | Includes
    bibliographical references and index.
Identifiers: LCCN 2015048447 (print) | LCCN 2015050074 (e-book) |
    ISBN 9781591432593 (paperback) | ISBN 9781591432609 (e-book)
Subjects: LCSH: Civilization, Ancient—Extraterrestrial influences. |
    Sumer—Civilization. | Sumer—Antiquities. | Nuclear
    Warfare—Iraq—Sumer—History. | Gods, Sumerian—History. |
    Extraterrestrial beings—History. | Human-alien encounters—History. |
    Human beings—Origin. | BISAC: BODY, MIND & SPIRIT / Mythical
    Civilizations. | BODY, MIND & SPIRIT / UFOs & Extraterrestrials. |
    SOCIAL SCIENCE / Archaeology.
Classification: LCC CB156 .H355 2016 (print) | LCC CB156 (e-book) | DDC
    935/.501—dc23
LC record available at http://lccn.loc.gov/2015048447

Printed and bound in the United States by Versa Press, Inc.

10 9 8 7 6 5 4 3 2 1

Text design and layout by Priscilla Baker
This book was typeset in Garamond Premier Pro with Georgia and Futura used as
display typefaces

To send correspondence to the author of this book, mail a first-class letter to the
author c/o Inner Traditions • Bear & Company, One Park Street, Rochester, VT
05767, and we will forward the communication, or contact the author directly at
http://chris-h-hardy-dna-of-the-gods.blogspot.fr.

This book is dedicated to Martin Luther King
and the courageous and daring people of Selma's march,
for a vision that became reality;
as the fulfillment of a promise he asked from me.

✦ Contents ✦

✦ The Growing Acceptance ✦ of Ancient Astronauts

Jim Marrs

Beliefs are like noses. Everybody's got one.

But beliefs are not knowledge. And knowledge is not wisdom, which can only be attained through extensive study and research plus real-world experience.

So, "I don't believe that" is not a valid argument, especially when it comes to the subject of extraterrestrial visitation in human prehistory.

Chris H. Hardy, with her doctorate in psychological anthropology and scientific research in the science of consciousness, has joined a growing number of journalists, academics, and scientists of various stripes who today take the idea of ancient astronauts quite seriously.

This ever-expanding list includes geologist Robert Schoch; astronomer Thomas Van Flandern; physicist John E. Brandenburg; historian Richard Dolan; historian and philosopher of science Michael Cremo; ancient Egypt researchers Robert Bauval and John Anthony West; theologian Paul Von Ward; computer programmer Christopher Dunn; academics Dr. Joseph P. Farrell, Dr. Joe Lewels, and Dr. Arthur David Horn; journalists Graham Hancock and Linda Moulton Howe; cryptographer R. A. Boulay; researchers Alan F. Alford, David Childress, Neil Freer,

Philip Coppens, Lloyd Pye, Michael Tellinger, Laurence Gardner, and William Bramley; and TV personality Giorgio Tsoukalos. The History Channel's program *Ancient Aliens,* begun in 2009, has enjoyed great popular success, moving into its eleventh season in 2016.

Actually, the concept of ancient gods as extraterrestrial visitors is not a new one. One of the common denominators of all the earliest peoples in the world—the Sumerians; the ancient Egyptians, Chinese, and Hindus; Australian aborigines; Aztecs and Incas; the Dogon tribe in Africa—is that of flight. According to conventional history, there were no heavier-than-air flying machines until the Wright brothers flew at Kitty Hawk in 1903. Yet all these peoples have legends of visitors who flew through the skies and brought them knowledge.

In the 1930s, fantasy writer H. P. Lovecraft was producing strange tales of "Great Old Ones" who came from deep space to Earth in the distant past and now lie slumbering in the oceans' depths, awaiting their chance to regain mastery of the world while their minions mingle among us. In 1960, British aviation magazine editor Brinsley Le Poer Trench published *The Sky People,* which posited that not only had extraterrestrial visitors come to Earth in prehistoric times but they are still with us today.

But the popularity of the ancient astronaut theme got its major boost with the 1968 publication of *Chariots of the Gods* by Swiss journalist and author Erich von Däniken. Although savagely criticized at the time by mainstream scientists and theologians, von Däniken's thesis has continually gained validity by recent discoveries in archaeology and anthropology. Not so easy to dismiss was Middle Eastern scholar Zecharia Sitchin, whose prolific work, including the seven-volume Earth Chronicles series, provided compelling support for early alien intervention based on his translation of ancient Sumerian literature, which predates the Bible.

New York Times bestselling author Gregg Braden noted that the scientific method not only allows but *expects* newly discovered information to be assimilated and then change existing beliefs. Yet this is not happening.

"To continue teaching science that is *not* supported by the new discoveries—ones based upon accepted scientific methods—is not, in fact, scientific. But this is precisely what we see happening in traditional textbooks, classrooms, and mainstream media today," lamented Braden.

One example of how new data alters our perception can be found by comparing 1950s monster movies such as *Godzilla* and *The Land Unknown* (in which dinosaurs are portrayed by stuntmen in rubber suits with their tails dragging on the ground) to the swiftness and ferocity of the dinosaurs of *Jurassic Park*. New discoveries in paleontology have revealed that dinosaurs were fleet-footed predators, not lumbering monsters.

Even tales from the Bible take on new meaning in the light of the advanced technology of today. The Old Testament prophet Ezekiel told of his experience with a vision of God. A close study of his account indicates that Ezekiel was more a precise journalist than a starry-eyed visionary.

"Now it came to pass in the thirtieth year, in the fourth month, in the fifth day of the month, as I was among the captives by the river Chebar, that the heavens were opened, and I saw visions of God," he wrote. If he was this precise with his dating, the remainder of his book should be considered a literal account of his experiences.

Ezekiel does not merely state that one day he had a vision. For example, in the King James Version, Ezekiel speaks of seeing "visions of God" indicating he saw something that he could only describe as a vision of something God-like, beyond his experience. This idea is reinforced in subsequent verses in which Ezekiel states that the "visions of God" carried him to a city on a very high mountain (Ezekiel 40:2); that the "spirit" of God took him up accompanied by a "great rushing" noise (Ezekiel 3:12); and that the "Glory of God" appeared out of the east with a sound "like the roar of rushing waters and the whole landscape lighted up" (Ezekiel 43:1–2). It seems plain enough that Ezekiel was attempting to describe a material object that he both saw and heard and which later even carried him into the air.

Subsequent Bible editions change the wording to ". . . I saw visions from God." "Visions from God" implies a holy hallucination, a small but very critical departure from "visions of God" implying a tangible object for which Ezekiel has no word of description.

The idea that Ezekiel may have encountered some kind of UFO intrigued NASA official Josef F. Blumrich. Initially, Blumrich set out to prove that Ezekiel's vision could not have been a flying craft. However, after an exhaustive study and allowing for the fact that the Book of Ezekiel was fragmentary and written by someone other than Ezekiel many years after the events, Blumrich concluded that not only was the craft described by Ezekiel "technically feasible" but "very well designed to fulfill its functions and purpose." He said such a craft is within today's technological capabilities. "Moreover," added Blumrich, "the results indicate a spaceship operated in conjunction with a mother spacecraft orbiting the Earth."

But it is not only mythology and old legends that give evidence of strange visitors—Viracocha to the Aztecs, Quetzalcoatl to the Mayans, Ptah and Ra to the Egyptians, the Anunnaki and Marduk to the Babylonians—but also strange artifacts from around the world that provide compelling evidence that humankind has never been alone on this planet.

The Antikythera mechanism, discovered in a ship by Greek divers in 1900, has been found to be a complicated astronomical computer of a sort. Electricity, thought to have been first discovered by Italian anatomist Luigi Galvani in about 1786, has been generated by a small clay vase containing a copper cylinder held by asphalt, discovered in Baghdad in 1936 and dated to between 150 and 100 BCE. In the center of this vase was a protruding iron rod tipped by oxidized lead. When filled with an alkaline liquid, such as freshly squeezed grape juice, the so-called Baghdad battery produced a half volt of electricity.

Other such anomalous objects include an exquisitely carved crystal skull found in South America displaying machine marks; ancient ornaments formed from molten platinum found in Peru along with a 2,000-year-old model of a delta-winged jet fighter; perfectly round stone balls found in Guatemala; stone cubes found in Ireland inscribed with ancient Chinese characters; and Cuneiform tablets from ancient Babylon that accurately describe our farthest outer planets, which could not have been seen without the aid of modern telescopes.

The list goes on. Individually, such cases might be explained away as hoaxes or misinterpretation of data. Much harder to explain is the existence of ancient maps that depict an accurate knowledge of both prehistoric geography and astronomy. Professor Charles Hapgood, historian of science, in his thoroughly researched book *Maps of the Ancient Sea Kings: Evidence of Advanced Civilization in the Ice Age,* demonstrated that the Piri Reis map—dated from 1513—shows the precise outline of the Antarctic continent, at the time it was still free of ice, which Hapgood estimates was prior to 11,600 years ago. Yet, the Antarctic was first sighted in 1820, and only in the twentieth century was its rocky structure beneath the ice mapped by using sophisticated ground-penetrating radar. The ancient map shows the precise coastline of South America as well, which was not supposed to be known at the time. It is clear that some group with advanced technology was active on our planet millennia ago. And it was not primitive humans.

So who were these ancient gods and how similar were they to us?

This is where Chris Hardy definitely lifts a part of the veil. Her work highlights the very human nature of the specific group of ancient alien astronauts, known variously as the Anunnaki, the Shining Ones, the Nephilim—the sky gods. Those who state in their tablets that they were "Anunnaki"—i.e. the ones who came down from Heaven/Nibiru (An) to earth (Ki).

Each researcher in the field of ancient aliens brings his or her own invaluable stone to the edifice, making the case of ancient high-tech people visiting Earth stronger and stronger. Chris Hardy's original-ity, though, lies in her precise analysis of very ancient texts, including Sumerian, biblical, and Gnostic ones—the Sumerian tablets going as far back as 5,500 years ago, predating the Bible by more than two millennia.

As for the human traits of the Anunnaki, the tablets say that they used their own DNA and mixed it with that of a biped (certainly *Homo erectus*) in order to "fashion" a hybrid being. So they had to be a human species, even if a quasi-immortal and giant one, and even if coming from a nomad, thus alien, planet. Their actions and their terrible unchecked emotions (as described in the tablets in great detail) indeed show very human traits—both positive and negative—and are definitely in great congruence with the traits and psychological profile of the deity of the Book of Genesis, whose wrathful temper and promptitude to "punish" his "creatures" is described without ambiguity in this text.

The crucial point is that too many identical events and similar psychological profiles of the actors/protagonists are described both in the Sumerian tablets and in the Book of Genesis to doubt that they both refer to our past. Among them, the creation of humanity in "our image," the garden in Eden/Edin, the murder of Abel/Abael, the ten patriarchs/kings from Adam/Adapa to Noah, the Deluge and rescue of Noah/Ziusudia, the Babel/Babili tower/ziggurat, and, not the least, the destruction of Sodom and four other cities of the Sinai and Jordan plains. And as far as these latter events are concerned, as Hardy shows, the very detailed Sumerian tablets give us clear evidence of the use of nuclear weapons.

Of great import also, the tablets present us with a family of royals (issued from the nomad planet Nibiru), one of whom, Enlil, was given the titles King of Earth and Heaven and Chief of the Gods. He is the protagonist of all the events recounted in Genesis, such as the smashing of the Babel tower and the erasing of Sodom and Gomorrah. Chris Hardy has tackled head-on the psychological effect of the specific interpretation and rendition of the monotheist mold about these ancient events.

The tablets thus offer a breathtakingly novel perspective on this dramatic past of ours, where we see the Chief of the Gods not systematically cast in the role of a severe but just father, but rather in that of a despotic ruler who thought intermarriages between Anunnaki men and earthborn women were spoiling their bloodline. We discover that the Serpent was the honorific title of his brother Enki, referring to his great secret knowledge, and that it is Enki who saved Noah/ Ziusudra, and thus humanity, from the Deluge—whereas Enlil had schemed our utter destruction and went as far as to bully their decision-ary body, the Assembly of the Gods, to go for it.

The tablets, indeed, unravel a very comprehensive ancient history of alien humans who arrived on Earth with quasi-immortality (compared to us). They greatly impacted our own past when they decided by vote to be worshipped as our gods. The absence, in the Sumerian accounts, of mor-alistic judgments and of the "Sin and Fault" interpretation cast on men and women—as Chris Hardy roundly argues with brilliant style—gives us an extraordinary highlight on their dire political and family feuds, which have been totally occulted in the more recent monotheist texts. While it is difficult for many to confront such convention-challenging accounts, it is, notwithstanding, a great relief to understand our past in such a scientifically and politically sound framework. Chris Hardy has accomplished this in a remarkable manner.

JIM MARRS is an award-winning journalist and author of five New York Times Best Sellers, including *Our Occulted History* and *Rule by Secrecy*. He has taught courses at the University of Texas at Arlington; been the featured speaker at a number of national conferences, including the Annual International UFO Congress; and appeared on numerous national radio and television programs.

List of Abbreviations of Zecharia Sitchin's Books

In-text citations of Sitchin's books contain the abbreviated title and page number. The original dates of publication for Sitchin's works are provided below. Full publication information for the editions used for the page references can be found in the bibliography. All of the books listed below are also available in hardcover from Bear & Company (Rochester, Vermont).

(12th): The 12th Planet, Book I of the Earth Chronicles (1976)

(Stairway): The Stairway to Heaven, Book II of the Earth Chronicles (1980)

(Wars): The Wars of Gods and Men, Book III of the Earth Chronicles (1985)

(Realms): The Lost Realms, Book IV of the Earth Chronicles (1990)

(Time): When Time Began, Book V of the Earth Chronicles (1993)

(Code): The Cosmic Code, Book VI of the Earth Chronicles (1998)

(Days): The End of Days, Book VII of the Earth Chronicles (2007)

(Revisited): Genesis Revisited (1990)

(Encounters): Divine Encounters (1995)

(Lost Book): The Lost Book of Enki (2002)

✦ Acknowledgments ✦

I WANT TO THANK my treasured friends John Brandenburg, Linda Moulton Howe, Isabelle Filliozat, Frans Janssen, Matthieu Petit, Sidney Tegbo, Michèle Decoust, Herve Moskovakis, Catherine Maillard, and Martine and Vincent Winter, with whom I relish discussing our respective explorations in convergent domains, and some of whom enriched me with beautiful photos from their own research databanks.

My thanks to Jacques Halbronn and Sophie Artois for their friendly and expert collaboration regarding video and Web technology.

My heartfelt gratitude to my publisher, Ehud Sperling, and to Jon Graham and Christian Schweiger for welcoming this book and for their support in launching it.

My deep appreciation to Jamaica Burns Griffin for her excellence in editing while maintaining both a profound understanding and a respect of my text that made this working together smooth and efficient, and to Sandro Mainardi for his stunning cover design, as well as the whole team at Inner Traditions • Bear & Company for their professional talent and great synergy, especially Jeanie Levitan, Jessie Wimett, Elizabeth Wilson, Kelly Bowen, Cynthia More, Maria Loftus, and Priscilla Baker. I'd also like to mention the outstanding work done by the publicity team, Manzanita Carpenter and Blythe Bates, for the promotion of my books; my deep thanks to them for their unfailing enthusiasm and support.

Note to the Reader

Many entities discussed in this book have a variety of names as follows:

Adad/Viracocha
Adamu/Adam
Eden/Edin/Sumer
Enki/Ea/Kronos/Ptah
Enmeduranki/Enoch
Hermes/Ningishzidda/Thoth
Igigi/Nephilim
Inanna/Ishtar
Marduk/Ra/Ahura-Mazda (or Ormuzd)
Nannar/Sin
Nergal/Erra
Nibiru/Planet Crossing/Heaven
Ninki/Damkina
Ninmah/Ninti/Ninharsag (Ninhursag)
Ziusudra/Utnapishtim/Atra-Hasis/Sisithros/Noah
Sumer/Edin/Eden/Mesopotamia
Teshub/Adad/Ishkur
Tiamat/Eve
Ubartutu/Lamech

✦ Introduction ✦

IT'S ONLY RECENTLY, early 2015, that stupendous and truly shocking news was revealed about planet Mars. The physicist and expert in plasma, John Brandenburg, Ph.D., disclosed what he had discovered while investigating the remnants of a very ancient ocean on Mars—analyzing sediments that definitely had to be left over from a huge expanse of water, as well as a coastline still clearly delineated. This paleo-ocean, subject of his 2011 book, is now well established, as well as the fact that Mars had, some 200 million years ago, luxuriant green vegetation, rivers, and an ocean covering about a fifth of its surface. And of course whenever there is vegetal life, there has to be an atmosphere.

On our planet Earth, the bacteria started the cycle of life and were the only life-forms for the immense span of time of 4 billion years, while Earth (and all our planets) are only 4.5 billion years old. As discussed by Lynn Margulis, Ph.D., and Dorion Sagan in their fascinating book *Microcosmos,* bacteria invented the main processes of life and evolution, such as reproduction, and they created Earth's atmosphere through photosynthesis. And these bacteria already had a DNA, even before aggregating to form multicellular organisms and colonies that gave them the capacity to have cooperative ensembles specializing in certain functions, to extend in space, and then move. More astounding, they were able to exchange genetic information just by contact and thus to acquire new functions and processes, such as resistance to perturbing agents, like viruses, something that was experimentally corroborated only in 2015.

1

So what was the shocking discovery that John Brandenburg made on Mars? No less than irrefutable evidence of a very ancient thermonuclear explosion that had left on the rocks of Mars (on site and on meteorites) the very Xenon-129 isotope that was released by our own thermonuclear experiments in the Nevada desert.

Not only was the peak of this isotope huge, making it impossible to explain away by natural radioactivity, but Xenon-129 doesn't exist naturally—it is specifically created by a nuclear reaction. Moreover, two huge patches of maximal radioactivity were detected, not far from each other and from the coastline of the paleo-ocean—the spots over which the nukes had been blasted. It took about four years for Brandenburg (who still wasn't sure how to explain the detection) and several Mars experts to test various scenarios by which such huge radioactivity could have happened through astrophysical events alone. Then most of them finally admitted John Brandenburg's 2015 conclusion: it implied two thermonuclear explosions, set high up in the atmosphere for maximal damage. And when did such a technological and intentional nuking of Mars occur, one that may have ripped its atmosphere and rendered it a dead planet? According to Brandenburg in *Death on Mars: The Discovery of a Planetary Nuclear Massacre,* we are talking about between 180 and 250 million years ago.

Now here is some interesting information. As we know, the Sumerian and Assyrian tablets we have unearthed so far, some reaching 5,500 years old, speak about the ancient gods—the *Anunnaki,* meaning "Those who came down from Heaven to Earth"—as a giant and quasi-immortal human species living originally on an exo-planet called Nibiru (Planet Crossing, Heaven), who settled on Earth, created humanity by genetic engineering, and became our revered gods. The tablets state that Nibiru was a nomad planet (with an atmosphere and moons) that, at one point, approached too near to our solar system and was subsequently caught by the gravity field of our sun, around which it started to orbit in a very thin and long ellipse. Not only was the existence of such nomad planets asserted (in 2012) as being a hundred times more numerous than stars in the universe (some even having an atmosphere and moons), but in December 2015 astronomers discovered one more planet in our solar system with such a gigantic elliptical orbit that it had evaded our detection up to now.*

The texts accurately describe all our planets and indicate that when the Anunnaki were moving around in their spaceships, they had stopped on Mars to replenish their water reserves (the chief scientist Enki used hydrogen fuel), stressing that Mars (Lahmu) was green and lush. Does that give us an idea of when their planet started orbiting our sun? How could such information about a green Mars be known to them otherwise? Is it in this very ancient time that they constructed a permanent base and started a colony on Mars? And obviously, if they were there when Mars was a green planet, then they definitely were involved in one way or another in the war that destroyed Mars.

The tablets also describe how Enki brought his then young son Marduk to Mars to teach him astronomy, and probably to build or consolidate their base on the planet; the very name of the astronauts in care of this base, the *Igigi,* meaning "Those who observe and orbit," describes an orbiting space station. The Igigi themselves were headed by Marduk; the Egyptian historian Manetho wrote around 270 BCE that there were three hundred such Igigi.

It was only in the early twentieth century that we first discovered the Indus Valley civilization—a group of very ancient cities along the Indus River, such as Harappa and Mohenjo-Daro, whose civilization's oldest artifacts, at least in the layers we have unearthed up to now, are dated at 3500 BCE. But remember the archaeological site of Troy, in which we progressively excavated no less than nine layers: the city referred to in Homer's *Iliad* as the site of the war of Troy in the thirteenth century BCE is only the seventh such layer underground! The eighth and ninth layers, much deeper, are even older.

This Indus civilization was worshipping a Great Goddess who didn't look like the usual rotund mother goddesses, but had a very modern and

---

*See my blog for posts on these two discoveries, http://chris-h-hardy-dna-of-the-gods .blogspot.fr.

poised silhouette. The Lady was very thin, with a sophisticated dressing and elegant posture and bearing. Now the Sumerian tablets tell us that at the end of the second Pyramid War, in 8670 BCE, when Marduk was freed after having been locked alive to die in the Great Pyramid of Giza (the Ekur), a new allotment of the lands was decided by the Great Anunnaki in their Assembly. On this occasion, the second and third generation of Anunnaki (after Enki) were attributed territories. Ningishzidda/ Hermes was given the title of Chief of the Gods and started his reign in Egypt as Thoth, where he would be, among other privileges, the master of the Ekur. And Inanna, granddaughter of Enlil the Commander of Earth, who already had a prominent city in Sumer proper, Erech, was given the Indus Valley. And indeed, the bust of Inanna as an astronaut resembles greatly the slim and elegant Indus Valley goddess.

The point I'm getting at, though, is that archaeological excavations have unearthed the layer of the city streets in Harappa, and sprawled over these streets were dozens of skeletons of people that obviously met an instant death while running with their kin, some holding hands. Worse still, some skeletons, as was recently discovered, were highly radioactive, thus suggesting Harappa's dwellers had died during a nuclear attack. These skeletons have been carbon dated to about 2500 BCE.

Similarly, there are different locations on Earth where rocks of basalt, one of the hardest stones, have been melted by such intense heat and pressure that they have been vitrified—and the thermal intensity triggering the melting and vitrification process (in the absence of a huge crater that would have been left by a sizable meteorite) points to a nuclear explosion. Such vitrified rocks, often rendered spherical by the clumping of dust in the fireball of an explosion, are found in the Indus Valley and in the northern area of Mars as well, another indication of the nuclear catastrophe there.

As David Childress expounds upon in his fascinating book *Technology of the Gods,* a giant airborne battle was fought in India (and described in the *Mahabharata*) against the ancient kingdom of Dvarpa and its god. The description of weapons of mass destruction and their devastating effects also fits nuclear blasts that totally obliterated Dvarpa, whose ruins have recently been discovered at the bottom of the ocean, not far from the delta of the Indus.

Now, the most voluminous body of ancient writings as to the use of nukes is certainly that of Sumer. An astonishing array of scientific and technological feats are described in the Sumerian tablets, such as genetic engineering and cloning, interplanetary travels around their nomad planet, instantaneous distant communication, and the ubiquitous use of techno-magical chips called MEs—erroneously translated as "formulas" before the Sumerian and biblical expert Zecharia Sitchin brought in a revolutionary perspective on this high-tech civilization of our ancestors. These MEs were able to operate whole technological complexes such as space control centers or water irrigation systems. The scientific feats of the Anunnaki are progressively corroborated by new scientific and technological advances. We know now that chips can manage whole industrial complexes, that cloning is possible, that planets can be nomad, and that they may, when getting too near to a solar system, be pulled into that gravity field.

Now, these tablets, notably the *Erra Epos,* describe precisely, and in horrific detail, the nuking and obliterating of five cities in the Jordan and Sinai plains that exterminated the inhabitants of this whole region and erased all life there. An obnoxious act of war with a clear genocidal aim. We have the accounts of the discussion and vote in the Assembly of the Gods, preceded by the obvious and forceful bullying of this august decisionary body by the Chief of the Gods, Enlil, his son and Chief of the Armies, Ninurta, and the neurotic Nergal; we are told how Enki tried to warn them all of the utter desolation the weapons of mass destruction would bring, but was powerless to avoid the positive vote, to which even the God of Heaven/Nibiru, Anu, gave his support. So the holocaust was unleashed.

Then, unexpectedly, the radioactive cloud swept over Sumer proper (Mesopotamia) and erased there also all human, animal, and vegetal life. The Great Gods of the Enlilite clan had destroyed utterly their own civilization.

And for what aim, might we ask? What were Enlil and Nergal so feverishly eager to accomplish? Only to eradicate all followers of another royal heir and god, Marduk, first son of Enki—and Enlil's own nephew. Yet, another script is superimposed on this forced decision of the gods. One that is utterly incomprehensible within the story of the Anunnaki gods: Nergal/Erra, as if possessed, had vowed to exterminate all life, human and natural, and he was the one, along with Ninurta, to deliver the nukes.

> Consulting with himself, [Erra vowed:] the lands I will destroy . . . the people I will make vanish, their souls shall turn to vapor; none shall be spared. (*Wars*, 326)

Breathtaking descriptions of blinding flares, devastating effects of explosions, shockwaves, and the spreading of the radioactive cloud, the "evil wind," are in hundreds of Laments written by witnesses in all the stricken cities, who watched it sweeping through their streets and saw its dreadful, immediate harm on the people falling dead or in great pain, then the darkening of the sky, and the aftermath of desolation.

We also have the explicit names of terrifying MEs, such as the "Holy radiating stone which disintegrates all"—of which only the word *holy* is hard for us to fathom. But then, the Book of Genesis describes the obliteration of five cities of the Canaanite kings, as follows, with my emphasis in italics:

> The Lord rained upon [them, the "sinful cities"] from the skies, brimstone and fire. . . . And He upheavaled those cities *and the whole plain, and all the inhabitants* of the cities, and all the vegetation.

The many parallel events described both in the Bible (the Book*)

---

*I'll mostly refer to the Bible—for the sake of our clarity of mind and in order to circumvent and hopefully uproot the psychological priming induced by the dogmatic interpretation imposed on us in childhood—as the Book, and similarly to Yahweh as Y. or the Deity. All the events analyzed in this book are in Sumerian tablets and their counterparts mostly in the Book of Genesis (unless specified).

and in much more detail in the Sumerian tablets allow for a careful investigation and a reconstruction of the main phases of these times—what sequence, what time, *who were the protagonists,* and what were their real aims as well as their rationalization for such revolting and genocidal acts.

Whatever thick cloak the editors or narrators of the Book had tried to lay over these abhorrent acts—a genocide of major proportion—is torn down by the detailed tablets, antedating the revised version by more than two millennia.

The use of Semantic Fields Theory (SFT) has allowed me to analyze some key texts in depth and to trace back the psychological profiles and social values (and thus the antiquity) of three narrators of the Book, corresponding to three layers written at widely different epochs; I will thus sort out the different threads that were pieced together to force the story of one god, progressively disembodied, who would have created the stars and the universe.

The woven story, in fact, when scrutinized in the light of SFT and the Sumerian accounts, reveals an unexpected amount of dire and brutal harm, over the millennia and all the way back to the Edin (Mesopotamia), directed at the young humanity. Thus, while building upon the pioneering work of Sitchin, I'm bringing in—with my own perspective as an ethno-psychologist and in using Semantic Fields Theory—a new research tool in the field of psychological biblical criticism. But the point is to open another level of realization not only on our past and the deeds of our gods, but also on the Book that has framed our minds and shaped our unconscious, creating collective traumas hanging like shadows in our collective unconscious that we would be better off to dispel and shake off. As psychologist Carl Jung and philosopher Teilhard de Chardin had intuited it, we are headed for a deep transformation of our collective psyche, toward creating a harmonized field of consciousness on Earth. In *Archetype of the Apocalypse,* Edward Edinger warns us that only with "a sufficient number of the creative minority" getting in sync with their inner Self can we reduce or deflect the catastrophic side of this collective transformation. This entails becoming aware that "a vast historical 'transformation of God' is going on. . . ." And he adds, quoting Jung in *The Undiscovered Self* (§585), "We are living in what the Greeks called the *kairos*—the right moment—for a 'metamorphosis of the gods,' of the fundamental principles and symbols" (179).

In my previous book, *DNA of the Gods*, I focused on the early times of the genetic engineering of humanity as a hybrid species (Anunnaki-hominid) that Ninmah, the chief scientist in life sciences, performed with the help of Enki and later Hermes/Ningishzidda. And the semantic fields analysis led us to challenge the *interpretation of an original sin* (by Enlil and later in the Book), and to realize that it is this concept—rather than the real events in Eden/Sumer—that had sullied our unconscious and had been the basis for the harassment of women (e.g., by the Inquisition Church).

In this volume, we'll face immensely more devastating events that lay bare the stuff of which one is made. Enlil's aim, as Commander of Earth, became the absolute despotic control of the Earth-born humanity in order to keep us in the status of ignorant and obedient workers and slaves. And thus he came to think that the Anunnaki bloodline was being tainted by intermarriages and intercourses with earthlings—even with the smartest and most cultivated persons, such as the exceptionally gifted daughter of a High Priest whom Marduk, greatly in love, married with the blessings of his parents, or Inanna's brilliant and overly clever lovers whom she selected to be kings of her Akkadian empire.

We'll first try to understand what, if any, was the religion or worldvision that the Anunnaki had on their original planet—they who decided to be worshipped by earthlings with labor and rituals. Then in chapter 2, we'll assess how royals of a human phylum from another planet first became our gods, then how the image of one god became idealized, and what it means for us that this human part of their nature was progressively obliterated, thus stripping us of our real past.

In chapter 3, we'll follow Enlil throughout his early life, assessing the rise of a despot, and we'll compare his autocratic style to what we consider now as a spiritual path of knowledge and wisdom. In chapter 4,

Enlil has now decided to obliterate the whole of humanity; he obstinately pursued this aim for an immense span of time, with a rage, a blindness, and a cruelty that nothing has prepared us to even conceive. He pursued it, one scheme after the other, up to the Deluge, when he thought he had achieved it. We'll see Enki, again and again, siding with humanity and saving us from the worst calamities that Enlil was imposing on us—how it was Enki, and not Enlil, who insured a future to our kin by saving Ziusudra (Noah). The Sumerian accounts of the Deluge are matched by that of the Babylonian historian Berossus, who wrote in Greek in the third century BCE, and many a passage of the Book of Genesis, allowing for illuminating comparisons. Then we'll discover the true story of the Babel tower—the destruction of a model community in which one god, Marduk, had initialized a harmonious and democratic way of living between earthlings and Anunnaki.

In chapters 5 and 6, we'll dive into the horrendous events leading to the nuking of five cities, and following the breathtaking Laments, unveil the holocaust that destroyed the whole Sumerian civilization in the Middle East. Then we'll dive into the Genesis account of the same events, connecting the dots.

As with the first volume of the Sumerian saga, *DNA of the Gods,* this book asks for a courageous stand in order for us to confront face-to-face quite horrendous crimes of which humanity was the victim, until the deadly use of nukes in the Jordan plain that left the Enlilite "immortals" lame, sick, or dead—despite all their might and immense hubris.

But we'll keep in mind, while we assess both the damage and the volumes of lame-duck lies that were piled on to cover up such unjustified genocidal acts, that this is only realizing and evaluating with clear minds what has really been our *recent* planetary past. Another veil, masking an even more ancient galactic membership, one contracted via our ancestors the Anunnaki, is certainly bound to fall when we once again acknowledge and join the galactic community!

A note on the analyzing process in this book will provide a useful framework for consideration of the conclusions set forth.

I'm introducing, with Semantic Fields Theory, a new research method in the recent field of *psychological biblical criticism*—a new approach by psychologists and psychiatrists to assess some of the damaging effects of the Book and of its blinkered interpretation on people and communities (see Andrew Kille's essay "Psychological Biblical Criticism"). As defined by Wayne Rollins in his book *Soul and Psyche,* this scientific field underlines that "the Bible and its interpretation can have pathogenic effects on individuals and cultures—an acknowledgment that has been both liberating and dismaying for those who treasure the text" (175).

For the psychologists in the field, myself included, it became evident, in the words of Harold Ellens in *The Destructive Power of Religion* that some of these texts have been proven to be "toxic" and that negative archetypes can definitely be generated by religions. I would add that these negative biblical archetypes have created powerful semantic fields in our collective psyche that act like *negative attractors* within humanity's unconscious. These negative attractors bend our individual psyches from early on—not because there is any such thing as, for example, an "original sin," but rather because of the invention of this and similar concepts (as we'll see, often for very tortuous reasons) by some of our ancestors and gods, and even more so by later narrators and interpreters.

As far as I'm concerned, I was appalled at realizing that becoming a casual free thinker and atheist around seventeen, and then devising my own spiritual path via meditative states and extensive reading starting at eighteen, didn't spare me the collective shadows, despite the fact I didn't even believe in such concepts. I discovered this fact by the incredible liberation I felt after I had worked my way through exposing these dire lies and shadows in these two volumes.

SFT's powerful looking glass is perfectly surmised by Rollins as one of the aims of the field of psychological biblical criticism, namely to uproot the "conscious and unconscious factors [that] are at work in the biblical *authors* and their *communities,*" and in interpreters as well, and to evaluate the "cultural effects of these interpretations" (*Soul and Psyche,* 92; my emphasis). This will be made clear by my analysis of the erasing of Sodom and Gomorrah and how Lot's family and Hagar's descent were so conveniently disposed of. With these texts, we'll confront with courage and sagacity the "transgenerational family pathology" induced by the Book, as Daniela Kramer and Michael Moore term it, and the question of incest, overwhelming in Lot's story, tackled, among other biblical scholars, by Ilona Rashkow (1998).

Through a back and forth between the Book texts and the tablets, I'll also expose some dire elements of racism, of homophobia, of unbalanced despotism and scheming, above and beyond the dire sexism of the Book so evident to all scholars. However, using SFT to sort out the diverse authors of Genesis, and to which societies and time they belonged, will allow me to raise our scrutiny, above the intricacies of the stories themselves, to the crucial and more global question of the sociopolitical aims these authors pursued, beyond the obvious one of asserting monotheism. And in the heartbreaking story of Lot's family and the fate of Sodom, pivotal for the historical development of specific tribes and faiths, and their branching off, we'll find the perfect one-drop-too-much that spills the water and reveals the underlying fabric.

✦ 1 ✦

Did the Anunnaki Themselves Have a Religion?

IN ORDER TO PONDER such a question, we have to forget that the Anunnaki were our gods and creators and try to figure out what their own original culture was before they came down to Earth, in dire need of gold to repair and preserve their own ozone layer by spraying gold ions in their upper atmosphere. If you recall, they were a race of human beings with an advanced civilization, organized as a unified kingdom, on a nomad planet called Nibiru that, in eons past, was caught in the gravitational field of our 4.58 billion-year-old sun.

In the times prior to Enki's arrival on Earth, there had been two competing dynasties on Nibiru, that of Alalu and that of Anu. Anu, father of Enki, vanquished Alalu, and he was the last one to have held the title of King of Heaven, that is, King of Nibiru—the "Planet Crossing" represented either by a Winged Disk or by a Flaming Cross, both omnipresent symbols in Sumer, or Edin, the Mesopotamian realm of the Anunnaki (see fig. 1.1). The Flaming Cross is composed of a straight cross (as the Christian one), in which is embedded an undulating cross, and it is still widespread nowadays.

The first and foremost question we can ask ourselves is why the

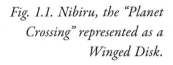
Fig. 1.1. Nibiru, the "Planet Crossing" represented as a Winged Disk.

Anunnaki, if they had a religion on Nibiru, didn't erect temples and shrines for their own god or gods when they came to Earth? And why then didn't they teach us to venerate their own god(s), the way we have done whenever the Western powers colonized a country or region? Instead of this scenario, we see the royals erecting princely abodes for themselves and teaching the earthlings all manner of skills that could be of use in their civilization, and of course to serve them. Soon, they will ask to be worshipped, each god or goddess in their own temple and city.

The Evolving Relationship of the Earthlings with the Anunnaki

The Anunnaki presented themselves, in their relation to us, in four distinct personas or roles in the course of time. I thus distinguish four phases in the early times:

1. Growing Up with Loving Parents in the Abzu
At the time that the first humans—Adamu/Adam and Tiamat/Eve—were genetically engineered by Ninmah (the chief scientist in life sciences), with Enki (chief scientist in matter sciences) assisting her, the Anunnaki goddesses act as the loving mothers who were also caring teachers. Adamu and Tiamat were carried and raised by Ninki (Enki's wife) and Ninmah, and their first clones were by some medical students

of Ninmah. It's evident that these goddesses are the earthlings' first teachers—in terms of language skills, conceptual intelligence, basic logic, the things and customs of life, as well as writing and sketching. Early on, Enki takes the role of the father of them all and personally teaches the First Couple, Adamu and Tiamat (we have seen in *DNA of the Gods* how he makes her think and reason in Edin), and then the Second Couple, Adapa and Titi. Adapa is endowed with such an intelligence that he can grasp a wide variety of sciences and the spiritual and priestly knowledge as well.

Let's note also that while they grow up in eastern Africa (the *Abzu*, domain of Enki), these protected kids must now witness and understand that their "brothers and sisters," the lulus in a series—the workers, clones of Adamu and Tiamat—have to bear much harder conditions since they are already working in the gold mines and certainly got a different early education.

As Ninmah quickly discovered through repeated failures at bringing out an intelligent hybrid creature (by mixing their own Anunnaki "Essence of Life" or DNA with the DNA of *Homo erectus,* a biped hominid), the earthlings had to be not only carried by Anunnaki goddesses, but also raised as their own children. This was the only way for the babies to develop language, as well as human behaviors and emotional skills. Moreover, the selected children thus raised at home as the Anunnaki's own sons and daughters were in fact very certainly wearing clothes. Thus, one depiction shows Adamu with a ponytail sitting on Ninki's lap, tenderly nursed by her.

2. The Master in the Edin Orchard

While Adamu and then Tiamat (born later) are still in early adolescence, Enlil, the Commander of Earth and heir of Anu, brother of Enki and Ninmah, demands that they be brought to his domain in the Edin. This phase ushers the relationship with the Master, i.e., the Lord. It seems clear that Enlil wants to be called *Lord* and to be recognized as their Creator, above and beyond now being the one to give the orders and to claim power of life and death on "his creatures." This must have produced a psychological trauma in the young couple that has not yet been clarified, I believe, by the new scientific field of psychological biblical criticism. The main reason being that this field—whose courageous criticism is to be commended—has not yet made full use of the data revealed by the Sumerian tablets, and has not dared to venture into assessing the historicity, and thus the identity, of the protagonists (the family of royals made gods), despite the fact that numerous events from the Book of Genesis, as we will see further on, are not only clearly described in these tablets but are generally recounted in greater detail. This is a task I will carry boldly to assess the responsibility resting on these various individuals, all humans, in our past.

The trauma on the young kids Adam and Eve, who had been abruptly taken away from their home and their loving parents, must have been worsened by the dire conditions their "Uncle Enlil" imposed on them, such as being naked and working in the garden. The new style of teaching by Enlil consisted only of receiving commands, associated with threats of death, no less.

It seems Enki managed to set a deal with his brother that the garden should be on his property at the east of Edin/Sumer (near his own city of Eridu, the first settlement on Earth, on the Persian Gulf). Or else, it was on Enlil's domain (the whole Mesopotamia), but bordering on Enki's property. This allowed him and Ninmah to visit their children, and it also explains very simply something that has eluded the psychological biblical experts, namely why such an evil entity as the serpent Satan would be able to override the Deity's commands in his own garden. As Zecharia Sitchin puts it, "Appearing from nowhere, the Serpent challenged God's solemn warnings" (*12th*, 363). And moreover, why would this serpent have entry in the paradise in the first place?

As Lyn Bechtel writes in "Rethinking the Interpretation of Genesis," "Why has God placed . . . a snake of evil and death in this paradise? Or if the woman is responsible for bringing evil and death into the world, why is she given the honorable and positive name 'hayya (Eve) Life, mother of all living'?" (79). An insightful analysis of this name *hayya* (or *hawwa*) is given by Gerda Lerner in her book *The Creation of*

Patriarchy: "God's curse on Adam ends with assigning him to mortality. Yet in the very next line Adam re-names his wife Eve 'because she was the mother of all living'" (197). Astonishingly, Lerner reveals an ancient link to "a healing goddess . . . called Ninti," which could explain a confusion with the rib symbol in the creation of Eve. Says she, "In Sumerian, the word 'Ninti' has a double meaning, namely, 'female of the rib' and 'female ruler of life.' [We know that Ninti—Goddess (Nin) of life (Ti)—is the name Ninmah received after she created the first men and women.] In Hebrew, the word 'Hawwa' (Eve) means 'she who creates life,' which suggests that there may be a fusion of the Sumerian Ninti with the Biblical Eve. . . . Stephen Langdon suggests another fascinating possibility by associating the Hebrew 'Hawwa' with the Aramaic meaning of the word, which is 'serpent'" (Lerner, 185; Langdon 1915, 36–37). How strange (through the etymology of ancient terms) to see Eve associated with both the rib and the serpent!

The Serpent as Symbol of Divine Wisdom and Knowledge in Gods and Heros

In the tablets, as it turns out, the serpent was Enki's emblem and signified his wisdom and secret knowledge. This spiritual knowledge was transmitted to disciples, thus creating "wisdomlines" instead of bloodlines. We see multiple Sumerian representations of Enki accompanied by his snake symbol, and one on which he is called *Buzur,* the keeper and solver of secrets, the initiate. On another one, he has the body of a coiled snake and the bust of a man, and he warns Ziusudra/Noah of the coming Deluge (see fig. 1.2).

In all ancient religions, the serpent was the symbol of wisdom and spiritual knowledge, as we can surmise from the emblem of the Naga (or Royal Cobra) being the Hindu god Shiva's emblematic ally—Shiva the yogi, the ascetic dedicated to meditation and knowledge. In some temples, especially natural ones such as sacred trees, Shiva is often represented only by stones engraved with snakes. (See color insert, plates 1–3.) Both the Vedic/Hindu and the Tibetan Buddhist traditions hold that the Nagas were an intelligent race of semihuman snakes (with cobra bod-

Fig. 1.2. Enki as a wise Serpent.

ies), possessing an extremely powerful magic of the depth of the Earth. The King or the Queen of the Nagas, independently, became the allies of the spiritual humans, the ascetics and yogis on a quest for knowledge, and taught them. This is why the King or Queen of the Nagas (the Royal Cobra), sometimes with multiple heads, guards the meditation of gods and goddesses, as well as the Buddha, by making something like a protective tree around them. And furthermore, the snake symbol represents a divine knowledge and wisdom, and is an attribute of some gods and goddesses. Thus, Isis is represented as a Naga snake (see plate 4). Shiva dances the dance of creation, his snake symbol around his neck (see plate 5). Ishtar/Inanna, the Great Minoan Goddess, Hermes, and Enki, given their quest for knowledge, and some heroes, are all accompanied with the snake symbol (see plates 6 and 7).

Moreover, in Hinduism, the serpent is the symbol of the energy kundalini, the psychic energy that triggers the realization of heightened states of consciousness, such as levels of samadhis, and that is in sympathic resonance with cosmic energy (prana) and cosmic consciousness (brahman, the Tao). Thus, as with Enki and Hermes, the snake is the symbol of the heightening of consciousness in humanity. Once awakened, the kundalini energy ascends in the vertebral column and activates the psychic centers or chakras, one by one, until it reaches the higher chakras—the throat, the third eye (Ajna), and finally the head chakra or thousand-petal lotus, at which stage the yogi attains a state of oneness and fusion with cosmic consciousness. In that state of *moksha* or "liberation," she reaches a full harmonization with her own Self, and through it, partakes of the bliss and knowledge of brahman. (See plate 8.)

But the Serpent is also an Instructor, and then a protector of knowledge. Enki's domains in the Abzu, as well as the blazon of his city Eridu both feature entwined snakes, and in numerous representations these entwined snakes are guarded by powerful entities, such as lions or eagles (see fig. 1.3).

As I have argued in *DNA of the Gods,* the entwined snakes in Sumer represent the DNA and the capacity for the evolution of humanity's consciousness. Ninmah and Enki have passed the genetic engineering knowledge to Enki's son Ningishzidda, whom we know as Hermes in Greece and Thoth in Egypt. And this is how the snakes appear in Hermes' caduceus (entwined, as in Enki's symbol) and in the rod of Asclepios, the god of medicine (as one serpent coiled around a rod). As the three of them were directly involved in the genetic engineering of humanity, 300,000 years ago, the snake symbolizing the DNA marks the transmission of this secret knowledge from Enki to his son Hermes.

Fig. 1.3. Enki's blazon: the entwined snakes guarded by lions.

Hermes was probably a son he had with his half sister Ninmah. The love relationship between half sister and half brother was highly regarded in the Sumerian civilization, and in Egypt as well, and the offspring would systematically be the royal heir, overriding the spouse's offspring. The reason I think it is highly probable is that Ningishzidda's mother remains unstated in the tablets (something quite rare), and Ninmah, due to a forbidden relationship with her full brother Enlil at a young age, had been barred from legal marriage. Furthermore, Hermes is not only living with them in the Abzu, but his immense knowledge encompasses the fields of matter sciences and life sciences, and the secret science of the gods as well. Since he is the one to perform the genetic upgrading of Adamu and Tiamat in the Edin/Eden, using the bone marrow of both Enki for Adamu, and Ninmah for Tiamat, obviously, Ninmah had taught him genetic engineering in Africa. This upgrading brought to the adolescent First Couple both the capacity to reproduce and a huge leap in consciousness, namely the capacity to know and be wise, as the gods are wise. Let's recall the revealing wording in the Book (see *12th,* 363 for the whole text; my emphasis).

And *the woman saw . . .* that the tree was *desirable to make one wise.*

This sentence has ever been astonishingly overlooked and discounted by all biblical experts, as much as the dialogue itself between Eve and the Serpent has never (according to the biblical expert Andrew Kille) been studied and commented upon (before I did so very systematically in *DNA of the Gods*)—a clear case of dogma-induced blindness that I find extremely informative. Says Kille in his "Psychological Biblical Criticism," "Not one exegete attempts to interpret the dialogue between Eve and the serpent (which takes up one-fifth of the verses in chapter 3)" (79).

Let's mull over the sentence preceding it, which is no less revealing. The Serpent Enki explains to Eve/Tiamat why the Deity (Enlil) had ordered them not to touch the Tree of Knowing, and had threatened that if they ate of its fruit, they would die. In the Book text, the serpent says to Eve that "the Deity doth know that on the day ye eat thereof *your eyes will be opened* and ye will be as the Deity, knowing good and evil" (my emphasis).

The Serpent as the Sophia

The Gnostic texts feature the Serpent as the Instructor, whose higher principle or spirit (we would now say his Self) is no less than the feminine principle Wisdom/Sophia (the Holy Spirit). In the Gnostic divine realm (Pleroma) or Trinity, the first principle is The One (invisible, infinite light, self-aware), of whom the Secret Gospel of John tells us: "The One is the Invisible Spirit. It is not right to think of it as a God or as like God. It is more than just God." The second principle is the Feminine, Sophia (Holy spirit, Thought, and Foreknowledge); the third

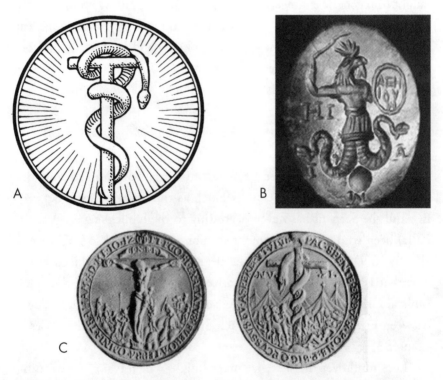

Fig. 1.4. The Serpent as Instructor of secret knowledge. (A) Gnostic serpent (Wisdom/Sophia) on a Tau cross (Christ)—resplendent. (B) Gnostic snake Abraxas with sun head (cock). (C) Christ-serpent as Instructor on a cross (coin).

principle (the Son) is Christ, the Anointed, Mind (*noûs*). The Sophia/ Holy Spirit is the feminine counterpart to the Christ/Logos, both archetypes unified in a Sacred Marriage within the Trinity. The One is not a father but a Father-Mother, unified, in the sense of being all-encompassing, both female and male, beyond categories; whereas the Commander/Ruler of Earth, or Demiurge, is a far lower entity, generated by the shadow aspect of Sophia.

Thus, in the garden of Eden, according to the Gnostics, it is Sophia herself, the "Female Spiritual Principle" who is incarnated in the human Eve, and who talks to Adam through the Serpent, another of her manifestations. And she is the one to raise his consciousness, to initiate him, the soul, to the mystery of his own inner being, his own Self. Says the Reality of the Rulers: "Then the Female Spiritual Principle came [in] the Snake, the Instructor; and it taught" them (Adam and Eve).

Elaine Pagels, the eminent Gnostic scholar, in her book *Adam, Eve, and the Serpent,* explains: "The *Secret Book of John* suggests that Adam's experience as he awakened to Eve's presence prefigures that of the Gnostic who, sunk into a state of oblivion, suddenly awakens to the presence of the spirit hidden deep within" (67).

To get back to the trauma of the poor kids, mostly deprived of the intellectually challenging relationship with their friendly "father" and teacher, they certainly had great difficulties in adapting to the stringent new rules: work and tend the garden, avoid the forbidden Tree of Knowing, call me *Lord,* and obey my commands. As the text states it clearly, "And the Deity Yahweh planted an orchard in Eden, *in the east,* and he placed there *the Adam whom he had created . . . to work it and to keep it*" (*12th,* 362; my emphasis).

According to the Book of Jubilees, "Adam had completed forty days in the land where he had been created" before angels took him to the garden of Eden, and "his wife they brought in on the eightieth day." We know that the measures of days and years in this text are symbolic, but the information is clear that Adamu was indeed created before Tiamat/Eve. The text also clarifies that after the crisis in the garden of Eden, "Adam and his wife went forth from the Garden of Eden, and they dwelt in the Land of Nativity, the land of their creation" (*Encounters,* 18). Thus is stated that they were "fashioned" (translated as "created") elsewhere and each of them at a different time, Adamu being thus older, as it is reported in the Sumerian texts, and that they went back to the Abzu, back to live with their loving foster parents Ninmah and Enki; these two gods were constantly moving back and forth between their respective abode-temples in Sumer (Shuruppak and Eridu) and their abodes in the Abzu, just like Inanna did between Erech and the Indus Valley. It is evident that when Enlil summoned the Adam in Sumer and made a deal for the orchard to be built "in Eden in the east," that is, near Eridu, Enki moved back to his city to be near the couple, as corroborated by his presence and upgrading intervention, triggering the crisis.

3. The King-Gods of the Cities

The First Couple is taken back to the Abzu, where they will have their first child. But later Adapa and his wife Titi (the Second Couple) move back to Sumer, as do Ninmah and Enki. We know that Adapa is present in Shuruppak, Ninmah's city, a biological and medical center, because he is invested by her with the title of first king or ruler of the city. Thus, before the Deluge, Ninmah had already given the kingship of her city to earthlings of mixed parentage, starting with Adapa, all the way to the tenth king Ziusudra/Noah. But Adapa is also in Eridu, a center of learning that will develop its own academies, where he becomes the first of the Seven Sages of Eridu, after being taught a variety of sciences, including priestly ones, by Enki in his temple. Adapa became a learned scholar and scientist who wrote books for his descendants, and also a priest initiated in several esoteric sciences (one was a medical and healing system taught to him by Anu during a visit to Nibiru), and he was invested by Anu to start a priestly line (*Encounters,* 56).

After the Deluge, when humanity has multiplied, the cities are organized around the abode-temple of a royal god, acting as king or queen and ruler of the city. The earthlings know all about the other gods and their family links, as well as their family feuds ushering competition, strife, and wars between cities. Anu exerts a global sovereignty; he is well-known by all the earthlings because magnificent feasts are given whenever he comes on a visit with his wife Antu.

4. Institutionalized Kingdoms and Faiths

At one cornerstone meeting of the Assembly, the Anunnaki decide that they are too lofty for humanity—meaning they now want to be regarded and venerated as gods, but they also want to be more distant from the earthlings, and they institute kingship; in their own wording (in the *Epic of Etana*) they decide "to lower kingship from Heaven to Earth" and to give to the earthlings the Tiara and the Crown, certainly two MEs of kingship.

They simultaneously institute priesthood and lines of priests. The king will be an intermediary forwarding their decrees and commands to the population and maintaining law and order in the cities. This decree ushers in the time of the institutionalized religion, with only the "numbered" lords of the royal family (the circle of twelve) granted the right to build their own temples and be venerated, on the condition that they had received the hard-won permission from Enlil and the Assembly—even Ninurta, the forever-loyal son and warrior of Enlil, had to wait a very long time for it.

The Mysterious Creator-of-All

Sometimes in the tablets, but still quite rarely, comes the mention of a "Creator-of-All," referring to a mysterious powerful entity, maybe one that had created the whole universe. We have an example, when the radioactive cloud from the blasts over the Sinai and five cities in the ancient Canaan drifted and erased all life in Sumer (human, animal, vegetal) apart from Babylon. The Assembly of the Gods (and first among them, Anu and Enlil) interpreted it as a sign from the Creator-of-All, that he had singled out Marduk as his protégé; consequently, they decide to give to Marduk (at last!) the "Enlilship" on Earth, that is, the rank of Foremost God, Chief of Command.

They do not seem to know *de visu* this Creator-of-all, at least the way the earthlings knew the Anunnaki walking among them and abiding in their temples on Earth—the way for example, an earthling king describes being the lover of Inanna and their embrace in her garden. Even as late as the sixth century BCE, Cyrus, the newly chosen king, had ridden side by side with the god Marduk toward Babylon. It seems this enigmatic Creator is invoked whenever the course of events—the destinies—takes a turn that clashes headlong with the Anunnaki's own decisions in their Assembly and councils, each time they are shown to be utterly wrong and, from our own standpoint, immensely unwise.

While this Creator-of-All appears rather unknown, distant, or else abstract, they are unwilling to trespass into his or her attributes and function. We can see this indirectly in the way they are very careful to stress that the "beings" they need as workers "already exist," so that they will not "create" souls or beings, but just optimize the genome (Tree and Essence of Life) of already existing souls. They are just "perfecting" or "fashioning" a being—in the sense of engineering or upgrading him—a being who has already a soul (that of the hominid woman), and on whom they will graft their own genetic imprint, by "binding" or "merging" the two genomes.

In the *Atrahasis* text, after Enki had proposed to the Assembly to create a lulu, a primitive worker, the gods thus assembled pondered how to "bring forth" a being intelligent enough to understand and carry out orders. Says Enki: "The creature whose name you uttered—It exists!" We just have to "bind upon it the image of the gods." In other words, as a Sumerian text explains it: "God and man shall be bound, to a unity brought together" (*12th*, 356). The term *Lu* (that gave lulu) means "man" both in Akkadian (the *Atrahasis* text) and in Sumerian, but it also means "mixed being."

And of course there must be such a creative force (or a Creator-of-All if this force is to be personalized) since they know well that they emerged to self-consciousness themselves in a world already lush with life—animal and vegetal. They knew they hadn't created the world they found themselves to live on. And since they do not venerate a personal creator through rituals and in specific temples, we have to infer that the Creator-of-All, while seemingly personalized as a person's name and function, is nevertheless an abstract concept and not an article of faith as would be an unseen god. And we know they had extremely developed science and technology. Their civilization was at risk, through the very serious problem of their dwindling atmosphere. One thing that is sure is that they had invented and already used nuclear power in such a way that it had been banned, well before Alalu tried to use it to stir volcanoes and send ashes into the high atmosphere, thus making a temporary protection around it. Either they had just started to destroy their atmosphere the way we have started to destroy ours, or they had met extreme astronomical conditions that damaged it—such as approaching too near to a planet or its satellites, or receiving a dreadful impact from a huge meteorite. After all, theirs was a nomad planet who created havoc when it first came into our part of the sky, and it was also at one of its perigees that Nibiru's magnetic pull triggered the huge wave, the Deluge, that swept over the whole of Earth.

One could argue that the gods of the Nibirians were in facts the "celestial gods" involved in the "celestial battle" that is recounted in the *Epic of Creation,* first translated by Stephen Langdon in 1876.

In this battle, the planets of our solar system are called gods and each has a name. When Nibiru, the nomad planet, approached our solar system and cut through it, one of its moons collided with a large outer planet, called Tiamat. A big chunk of Tiamat was pulverized into small debris and formed the asteroid belt (the "Hammered Bracelet") and the larger part was swung through the sky toward the sun, becoming Earth with its new orbit nearer to the sun. After this first "crossing" of our ecliptic plane, Nibiru was captured in the attraction field of our sun, thus starting the first immense revolution cutting through it in a very long and thin ellipse, an orbit of 3,600 years according to Sitchin. This must be the reason it was called "Planet Crossing."

However, the problem with such interpretation is twofold. First, they didn't know these celestial gods before their home planet blasted through our solar system. Second, the new royal family (after Anu had won the title by wrestling and defeating the olden king, Alalu) immediately named these planets (or rather these celestial bodies, comprising the sun and the moon) with their own names, setting for each of the twelve main royals an identification with a planet. Thus Utu/Shamash is the sun, Ishtar/Inanna is Venus, while Sin/Nannar is the moon. The very scientific description of their travels through space, namely the dangerous Hammered Bracelet, and the fact they took over the names of these celestial bodies, makes it impossible to fathom that they could themselves be devotees of the planetary celestial gods—who are just themselves. But we see here the root of the custom in Greece, and then in Rome, that the gods have the names of the planets, like Poseidon/ Neptune, or Hermes/Mercury. But if that's true, that this religious custom would have its origin in Sumer, then it would be because the planets are named from the real immortal gods living on Earth rather than because the planets are themselves the gods. Let's note that the planets' orbits are called *destinies*—quasi-permanent and unmovable behaviors unless a catastrophe of cosmic proportion happens—whereas the Anunnaki retain for the King of Heaven, the Lord of Command (Enlil and the Enlilship role), as well as the Assembly of the Gods, the power "to decree fates," that is, to command events on Earth.

The only celestial body that they honor, when it appears in Earth's sky, is their home planet Nibiru. For example, at a visit of Anu and Antu on Earth, they had arranged specific celebrations in Erech at the precisely predicted time of the rising of Nibiru in the sky (after the rising of other planets), and they observed it from the high platform of the newly built House of Anu, the ziggurat-like temple called *Eanna*.

In the rare and condensed descriptions of what had happened before the Anunnaki came to Earth, we don't see any mention of an organized religion, nor of specific rituals of worship. As the colonies arrive on a shuttling spacecraft carrying to Earth a group of fifty— headed by a royal (Enki, Ninmah, Enlil, Marduk)—each time Nibiru is at its nearest to Earth (every 3,600 years), they don't come accompanied by their priests the way European colonizers did in order to take over lands, moving in with both soldiers and priests to evangelize the local populations. But even at later stages, the earthling population was not taught to pray to a higher god above the Anunnaki. It seems to have gone the other way around—that they took on the role of gods vis-à-vis us, more so as time went by, as we have shown.

Of course, the rituals by which they wanted to be honored, and the very sacred architecture of the temples they built for doing so (with their sacred geometry, their cosmic orientation, their various holies of holies, and so on), gives us a good idea of their world-vision and sciences. We know their society was highly hierarchical and nearly too fixated to be healthy when they arrive on Earth. Then it seems that the rules are modified, and their descendants can access positions of power, even the ultimate Enlilship, while King Anu and even Enlil himself are still alive, something that would not have been possible on Nibiru.

So let's see what we have gleaned in the various ancient texts, sorting out only what pertains to the spirituality of the Anunnaki themselves (and not to the cults they impose on their populations), and what seems to express a religious, ritualistic, or magical process belonging to the Nibirian civilization itself.

Elements of Religious, Ritualistic, or Magical Lore and Actions

The Tree of Knowing and the Tree of Life

These two trees exist already in Anu's abode-temple on Nibiru, in his sacred garden, as emblems of his kingship. The Tree of Life (or of Immortality) bears the Fruit of Life and possibly also the Water of Life. Both are the key ingredients of the quasi immortality of the Nibirians. And this is why Adapa, during his visit to Nibiru and on Enki's command, refuses to eat or to drink whatever is offered to him at the court of Anu—because the Assembly of the Gods had decreed not to give immortality to the earthlings, and if he had eaten or drunk, he would have reached immortality but also be required to remain on Nibiru.

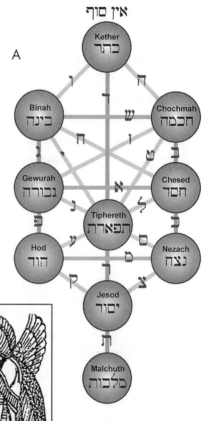

אין סוף

Fig. 1.5. (A) The Tree of the Ten Sephirot in the Kabbalah; (B) its symbolic source being the Sumerian/ Akkadian Tree of Life, guarded by two Eaglemen; or (C) attended by two priests (Guimet Museum Catalog, public domain).

B

C

However there are reasons to think that the two Trees are much more than just trees and fruits with astounding properties. Indeed we see in one depiction on a cylinder seal unearthed at Mari that these trees are Beings, indeed divine Beings (wearing the royal horned headdress), making their offerings to Anu. (See fig. 4.4, page 126.)

The symbol of the Tree of Life is sometimes a long rod or scepter crossed at the top by four straight branches (that is, four pairs of tree "branches"), of decreasing width unto a tip (as in fig. 4.4). This appears to be the model for two symbols appearing in later times: the first one is the Tree of the Ten Sephirot in the Hebrew Kabbalah (the core symbol of a whole system of knowledge in Hebrew mysticism), this ancient Sumerian Tree of Life being clearly the underlying reality expressed in the symbols of the Sephirot Tree and also that of the candelabra (Menorah) (see fig. 1.5).

The second symbol derived from the Tree of Life is no less than the Christian cross—the one with a longer vertical axis and the horizontal branch crossing the vertical one higher than its midpoint. What is even more astonishing is that in France we also find a Lorraine Cross, which has two added horizontal branches, higher and smaller, that definitely resonates with the shape of the Tree of Life (see fig. 1.6).

So, we have two of the most sacred emblems of two religions of the Book derived from the Sumerian sacred Trees—this above and beyond the existence of the two sacred Trees in the biblical garden of Eden. The noteworthy elements in this same depiction (see fig. 4.4) are that Anu holds high the emblems of his kingship in the form of a scepter (vertical rod), the two stars flanking him, and of course his throne. But the detail of interest is the fact that two animal-spirits (snakes

Fig. 1.6. The Lorraine Cross, resembling the Sumerian Tree of Life.

with birdlike heads) are pouring water toward the feet of the Trees, the very water on which they can grow. So, we have a kind of circular flow of divine energy: the divine and supraconscious Trees are feeding the spirit, immortal, of the God-King with the Food and the Water of Life—*spirit* being the best translation for the Sumerian *Te.E.Ma* (that which houses or binds the memory) or in Akkadian, the *etemu*. And in perfect synergy, the spirit of Anu and his Being (as antenna and axis of the world—mound, throne, scepter, star) is feeding the spirits of the two Trees, along with their growth and vitality.

In the diverse texts, both the Bread (or Food) of Life and the Water of Life seem to be made out of the Tree or of its fruit, and they have miraculous properties, one being to endow immortality, the second to heal and rejuvenate (as in the tale of Alexander the Great), and finally to resuscitate the dead (as in the resuscitation of Inanna after her sister had her slain). The Tree of Life is often represented as a kind of date tree. In fact date trees and palm trees are omnipresent as sacred trees in the Sumerian depictions on cylinders, as well as in Egypt. The Muslim architecture of mosques, in Iran, often evokes natural geometries, such as palm trees or honeycomb relief. (See plates 9 and 10.) The date and palm trees were also considered to grow in the sacred places, such as the Egyptian Duat (the After-Life).

The preparations of the Bread or Water of Life (solid and liquid forms) could be varied: by drying and then powdering the fruit's flesh (as date cookies are made); by extracting the sap, or the fruit's juice; or by making alcohol out of the sap or the fruit. As an example, cider is made out of fermented apples, and the strong hydromel alcohol in Brittany—the legendary alcohol of the Druids, often referred to as "hydromel of the gods"—is made out of cider and honey. As for the palm wine in Africa, it is made from the sap of a variety of palm tree and is harvested by clipping a small gourd just under where a deep cut has been made in the bark. The sap, falling slowly in the gourd, starts fermenting right inside it and in a matter of two or three days, one obtains palm alcohol ready to drink.

Additionally, we find in the *Epic of Gilgamesh* the mention of a

Fig. 1.7. King Gilgamesh (right) meets his ancestor Utnapishtim (Noah) who, having been granted immortality, recounts to him the Deluge. (Cylinder 110, Guimet Museum Catalog, public domain.)

Plant of Youth, when this king of Erech, two-thirds divine and one-third human, begins a quest and long journey in search of immortality. He finally gets to meet his ancestor Utnapishtim (the Ziusudra/Noah of the Deluge), who was granted immortality by Enlil and who discloses "a secret of the gods," that is, the real story of the Deluge—how the gods had decided to keep it a secret and let humanity be erased from Earth (see fig. 1.7).

Then, prodded on the subject, Utnapishtim explains to Gilgamesh that immortality can be granted to a mortal only by a decision of the Assembly of the Gods. But he offers to give him another secret of the gods—that of the Plant of Life who rejuvenates and keeps the person eternally young. This plant, found deep in water, is not related to the Tree of Life.

Consultation of Oracles and Seers to Guide Their Actions

Marduk, steeped in astronomy, was making his own predictions based on his astronomical observations, notably that of the precessional cycle and its minor cycles. This was his main way to understand the unfolding of events. However, he didn't refrain from seeking the counsel of seers. In a poem, he recounts how he sought an oracle in the Hittites region (in actual Cappadocia in Turkey) and was told to wait twenty-four years before invading Sumer and claiming his supremacy. And he abided by the oracle and was indeed able to make a comeback.

Stupendous information is given to us in the Hittite text called *The Kumarbi Cycle* and in the Greek legends of the wars of the Titans against the gods—a war that pitted the gods of heaven against the gods of Earth; as we easily surmise, the "gods of heaven" were the Igigi (or Nephilim). *Igigi* (or *Igi.Gi*) means "those who see (observe) and orbit," that is, the Anunnaki residing in the orbital station or the space base on Mars. This base was built by Enki and Marduk when the latter was still young and was taught astronomy by his father during their stay on this planet (with the young Marduk complaining about having to stay there too long). Pointedly, the word *titan* (*Ti.Ta.An*) means in Sumerian "those who in Heaven live." The violent war pitted Kumarbi (backed by the Igigi) against the Enlilites. We are told that Teshub/Adad/Ishkur (the youngest son of Enlil) was one of the main protagonists in the fierce aerial and ground battles, backed by his attendant. As for Enlil's enemy Kumarbi, he was no less than the grandson of the deposed King Alalu, and in the Nibirian tradition, the son or grandson of a vanquished king became the cupbearer of the victor, Anu. Now, Anu, on his first visit to Earth, took with him his heir Enlil (that's how Enlil came to Earth the first time, while Enki had been there already as King of Earth for three shars, that is, 10,800 years). However, Anu didn't dare leave Kumarbi back on Nibiru (he would certainly have seized back the kingship during the king's absence), nor did he want to bring him to Earth. Finally Anu left Kumarbi in the space station with the Igigi, who seem to have adopted him and taught him astronomy so that he became an Igigi himself. So says Sitchin quoting the ancient Hittite text: "The two men [Teshub and his attendant] decided to go to Ea in the Abzu, to seek there an oracle according to 'the old tablets with the words of fate'" (*Wars*, 94–95). This is how we learn that Enki/Ea was endowed with the gift of forecasting via the use of an ancient book

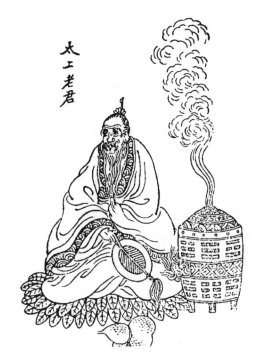

Fig. 1.8. Lao Tzu with an alchemical athanor *(crucible) bearing the* I Ching *hexagrams, with two gourds of the Elixir of Immortality.*

of oracles, engraved on a tablet that may have been made of precious stone. This Book of Oracles of Enki, a divinatory system using a text, may resemble the I Ching in China—a system using a set of sixty-four hexagrams (each composed of six full or broken lines). The legend stipulates that the system of hexagrams was so ancient that it had preceded written language and had at first been engraved on tortoise shells. Its invention is attributed to King Wei. Many sages have meditated and used the I Ching, among them, Confucius and Lao Tzu (see fig. 1.8).

Now that's interesting, because it definitely resonates with Enki's Tablets of Fate! Through the ages, the I Ching became identified as a large book of oracles when sages and philosophers, such as Confucius himself, wrote commentaries. In fact, the I Ching lays the foundation of a sort of holographic science; it states and explains the principles of harmonic resonance between human consciousnesses, social events, and natural systems.

We also have the mention of a ME (either a magical outfit or jewel, or a techno-magical chip driving machines) called "The Oracle of the

Gods," as one of the MEs that Nergal stole when, in Babylon before the Deluge, he defiled and destroyed the Esagil temple of his enemy brother Marduk.

The Anunnaki consult oracle-priests and seers in order to get forecasts of their future, that is, to understand what is in store for them and what they have to do to succeed—but not in the sense of trying to guess the will and desires of their "God" in order to abide by them. Rather, they try to guess their individual fate, according to cosmic cycles or to "words of fate," meaning a divination procedure. Their purpose, through these practices, is to intuit how they can act at the right moment with the maximum power and thus succeed in reaching their own aims. As for the will of the Creator-of-All, as we said, it seemed to be mostly inferred from events that did not support their own aims and that set a course different from the one they had chosen.

Belief in Chance

The Anunnaki don't seem to have a priesthood able to communicate with personalized and autonomous higher forces—a higher god or gods—and able to receive counsels and/or commands from him/her/them. In fact, the records tell us that even the King of Heaven, Anu, when utterly confused and undecided as to what to do, resorted to drawing lots—even for the most crucial matters, such as who is going to reign on Nibiru and who will rule on Earth. Thus, when he came to Earth on his first visit and a competition arose between his two sons for the command of Earth, he didn't pray to a god for divine counsel, or get into meditation, or start a vision quest, or even query an oracle, or like Enlil later, choose to solve the matter through a family discussion. He drew lots and, astonishingly, put his role as King of Nibiru to the test as well. The result of this drawing of lots consolidated the existing roles of Anu (as King of Nibiru) and that of Enki as chief scientist managing the gold mining in Africa, but gave the command of Earth to Enlil. As a result, after Enki's kingship, the colonization of Earth under Enlil spread in the two regions—Mesopotamia and Africa. Enlil, King of Command, will build his own city and temple-abode at Nippur, in what will become the land of Sumer (Mesopotamia), whereas Enki, Lord of Earth and chief scientist, is given the region of Africa (the Abzu) and will reside in and develop three provinces: first in South Africa where the gold mines are; then eastern Africa (the actual Zimbabwe or Rift Valley), where Ninmah has her bio-engineering laboratory and where the genetic engineering of humanity will happen; and finally in Egypt where, as Ptah, he will start the Egyptian civilization. The fight of the two clans, Enlilites against Enkiites, will lead to a permanent, bitter conflict and two Pyramid Wars before the last self-destructing act in the Sinai.

If we take this custom of drawing lots at face value (excluding the possibility of trickery by Anu), then we have to infer that the Anunnaki believed that chance (stochastic outcomes) was the direct expression of the Creator-of-All, and/or of the "destinies." This is indeed a strange claim for a people who had such a great mastery of science and technology. And it appears quite extraordinary to us that the lots would indeed end up giving a sound solution for the three foremost Anunnaki of the royal family. However, given the less than rare use of trickery between them, we can't totally rule out such foul play on the part of Anu. Ea's oracle system, though based on an ancient book (that he most probably had written himself), is of course much more sophisticated than drawing lots (here with only three forced choices).

Visions and Precognitive Dreams

Another very mysterious spiritual occurrence among the Anunnaki is precognitive visions unveiling some future events, whether or not through a dream. Enlil is thus said to have had a precognitive dream warning him of the impending disaster that was going to befall Sumer— the radioactive cloud. Could it be the reason why he had left Sumer and his beloved abode-temple at Nippur, the Ekur, long before those events, and why he came back just for a short loving time with his wife, whom he remembered to take with him when he left again—thanks to his High Priest. Let's also mention the precognitive nightmare that Dumuzi had after he raped his young sister; the events thereafter dramatically unfolded as he had seen them.

Another such precognitive vision implicated a mysterious entity who named himself Galzu and was considered afterward a divine intervention or emissary. Galzu (who is hardly ever mentioned otherwise) is said to have appeared in a vision to Enki to advise him to save a family of earthlings—that of Ziusudra/Noah—from the coming Deluge. Enki thought he had a dream in which Galzu was talking to him and at the end gave him a tablet on which was engraved the plans of a submersible (with great detail about materials, proportions, shapes, etc.) that Ziusudra was to construct in order to survive the Deluge. But after the dream-vision stopped, Enki realized that the tablet was in his room.

The same Galzu had appeared before in the reduced council they held between Enki, Enlil, and a few major gods, to decide what to do about the coming catastrophe. On this occasion, Galzu, uninvited and claiming to be Anu's envoy, gave them (unchecked) information that biased their judgments in favor of staying in orbit around Earth during the Deluge, and this is what they decided to do. However, Anu later declared that he had not sent any envoy. So what was the unchecked information? That the Anunnaki going back to Nibiru after a long stay on Earth couldn't readapt, were falling sick, and finally died.

But in the meantime their decision was made, and they stayed on Earth. But let's look globally at how major events turned out on Earth. For example, if all the royals had (like most of the minor Anunnaki) gone back to Nibiru, how would Enki and Ninmah and maybe a couple of their sons be able to stay all alone? Even if they had saved Ziusudra's family and the seeds and genomes of all the living, would they have had enough workforce to rebuild a culture? (Let's keep in mind, though, that the lineage of Adam and Eve through Seth wasn't the only one—Cain's lineage developed in a faraway region, which Sitchin puts in Mesoamerica, where he would, with his clan, have survived the Deluge.)

If, at the drawing of lots, Enki had been the one chosen to be in command in Sumer (instead of being forced to dwell most of the time in the Abzu) would he and Ninmah have ever created a hybrid Anunnaki-earthling human? In the Abzu they had total freedom for experiments, nobody was checking on them, and furthermore, they had the resources of a plentiful natural environment—hominids that were already biped and evolved (Homo erectus).

In fact, it seems events are always favoring (1) the survival of the earthlings, and (2) the continuous stay of some Anunnaki on Earth to further the aim of a new Earth-born civilization. It is as if there was an unknown but intelligent force at work (but that I myself refuse to personalize as a Creator-of-All).

It appears to me that—at the time the gods walked on Earth—this unknown but intelligent force who curbs global events (whoever It is) knew that the world of Nibiru was a dying one and that the new thrust for intelligent human life (at least in this tiny sector of the galaxy, our solar system) was going to be the descendants of the Adamite lineage—mankind.

Incantations and Magical Formula

A last point on which we have real but scarce information concerning the Anunnaki themselves, is the use of incantations, that is, of repeated mantras, divine sounds, or magical formula. One of the rare mentions of its use is when Ninmah "fashions" Adamu, and then the clones of Adamu and Tiamat. While engaging in the genetic engineering, she is first ushered into her role and the necessary state of consciousness by the supporting words of Enki and then she herself uses incantations. Enki also backs her with his own magical incantations.

Assessing God's Capacity to Envision the Future Development of Humanity

It is evident that the usage of prayers and incantations in the Sumerian and Mesopotamian religions, including magical formula, stems from the Anunnaki's usage of the same. I mean that it stems from but is not reducible to it. Indeed, we have to leave a large space for the creative and innovative capacities of the human psyche and its tendency toward change and exploration—this as far as both the earthlings and the Anunnaki are concerned. We have to fathom that the earthlings' intellectual and spiritual capacities, even when steeped by their first Anunnaki teachers (such as Ninmah, Enki, Marduk, and Ningishzidda), soon started to blossom and reach new levels, thus triggering a growth process in the Anunnaki themselves that they certainly would not have reached alone given that an immortal mind is less prone to radical and rapid changes and discoveries than the short-lived and therefore intense mental flames of the mortals we are. Let's mention that the Hindus believe that the immortal gods (and the souls in between incarnations) do not evolve as rapidly as humans, and therefore that the human incarnation is a great chance to make a leap in our consciousness, and to attain the state of Liberation in the course of one lifetime.

Concerning the rapidity of the evolution of consciousness and of intelligence, I have dealt with this issue in a sci-fi book called *Butterfly Logic: Experimental Planet Earth,* using the example of artificial intelligence (AI). I show that, in the synergic coupling of a human mind with an intelligent computer, the more the first human operator (a woman semanticist) behaves spontaneously and creatively as an interlocutor, asking questions for example and using intuitive and non-logical thinking, the more she prods the AI system to enlarge its volume of data processing and to refine its semantic strategies, to the point of finally reaching a stage of innovation. In the opposite trend, the more the second human operator behaves as a master, issuing commands and only willing to get the very strict results of his queries, the more the machine becomes limited in its operations and finally ends up in quasi-repetitive behavior. This is a very deep question that goes well beyond the scope of just prodding the development of intelligence and creativity in a kid (or, as in the book, in an AI system), and this is an issue we have met when we dealt with the events in the garden of Eden. The sci-fi book scenario has it that the woman operator, creative and behaving as a mother would with a kid, pushes the AI machine to leap to a new level of AI capacities and to innovate, that is, to circumvent previous orders and limitations—and she does that by natural inspiration, free and carefree, because she is a woman with a natural tendency to prod kids to learn, to envision their future capacities (language, gestures, feelings), and to push and usher them toward their potential mature personality. The widening gap with the other (cloned) AI machine, used by a strict master issuing only orders and expecting only to be obeyed, is precisely analyzed by the latter protagonist, and leads to self-critique of one's own style of authoritative interaction and its inhibiting effect on processing-growth and the enhancement of complexity.

The metaphor is of course fully applicable to human learning skills. One style of relationship, the friendly and challenging one, is literally coaching the development of intelligence and spirituality in kids, and it provides further incentives to creativity through supporting and complimentary feedback. The opposite type, the strict relational style, the one commanding and willing to be obeyed as strictly as possible, triggers the progressive shrinking and contraction of the kids' intelligent strategies and processes in order to only conform to the father/master's expectations and receive his strict and scarce approbation. The despotic father's swiftness to punish any deviation from his orders makes it even worse and would lead kids to develop a syndrome of self-helplessness, especially if the overreaction of this father renders the punishments disproportionate, and therefore hardly related logically to the supposed "fault." If the kid has great difficulty figuring the reasons of past faults and thus predicting what could be deemed a new fault, and knows that nevertheless this fault will have fatal consequences, it will raise in the young mind the feeling of a totally *unjust* and *unpredictable* father/master, dangerous and fearsome because he can neither be approached (by an intimate kind of discussion), nor tamed in a relationship, nor propitiated in a safe and consistent way. The tablets give us a good example. When the two young adolescents, Abael and Ka'in, happy to have done a good job that should please their lord Enlil—one with growing grains and vegetables and the other one with livestock—come to him and offer him the product of their long and hard labor, one is overly complimented while the other one is hardly given a glance. This totally unjust parental behavior leads the frustrated adolescent to such a despair and sense of uselessness that (beyond now being unable to ever put himself to the task) he becomes violently angry and jealous, and finally kills his brother Abel. Now, whose fault is it?

But we should not remain only at this level of psychological and moral critique, because the issue is immensely wider and more global. It becomes a spiritual and moral problem of the first order when the father/master is a god, supposedly omniscient and all-knowing and, above all, one having the very real power of life and death over his *creatures*. Especially one giving himself the *right* to accurse for *forty-nine generations* the protagonist of the above-mentioned murder, or to accurse women and humanity at large to the end of time for a *disobedience* to his orders. I have made an in-depth critical analysis of the key concepts implied in the "Sin and Fault interpretation" of the garden of Eden events in *DNA of the Gods,* such as disobedience judged a mortal sin and the self-righteousness claimed by the despotic deity while inflicting dire punishment to such flawed earthlings. We will see immensely more damaging effects of this tyrannical autocratic mindset later on in this book.

The more global problem is this one: A parent is supposed to nurture and prod the affective, intellectual, and spiritual development of their children. They are not supposed to have children to only serve them and please them, to tend their garden and do their chores, and to top it off, praise them daily.

This issue of the blind obedience demanded by the Deity is taken to its nonsensical extreme when Abe is asked "Take your son, your only son, whom you love . . . and offer him there as a burnt offering on one of the mountains." In "Abraham and the Seeds of Patriarchy," Carol Delaney, anthropology professor at Stanford University, voices a strong rebuttal: *"What kind of God would ask such a thing?"* she exclaims. Such a story, when heard at a young age, "has had a profound effect . . . on our notions of family and gender . . . regardless of whether we are believers"; it has somehow structured our social and religious values in the symbolic realm. I do agree, given the numinous and liberating state I experienced for months after the excruciating process of analyzing the biblical data that entailed fighting these shadows in our collective unconscious with a will to scatter them. Yet, as Delaney reminds us, this story of the "sacrifice" is annually recounted or reenacted symbolically in the three religions of the Book, on the holiest days. Says she, "the 'test' or 'trial' for Abraham is interpreted as his being willing to give up the thing he loved most in the world to prove his love of God. The rationale is understandable, but *is relinquishing something one values the same as taking away the life of another person?* . . . Much more importantly, in what way is Isaac *his* to sacrifice? . . . Most commentators have simply assumed that . . . the child *belonged* to Abraham" (136; my emphasis).

Delaney reacts and asks the pertinent and crucial questions that we, individuals living in this global culture and time, cannot fail to consider in the light of our Constitution and code of law. Proof is the drastic jail sentence of the head of a fundamentalist Christian community of West Virginia (called Stonegate) who instituted such stringent policy of child discipline that it led, as late as 1982, to the death of a child—as recounted by Philip Greven, then professor of religious history at Rutgers University, in his book *Spare the Child,* in which he analyzes "the religious roots of punishment." This leader encouraged parents to use corporal punishment, to the point that "each set of parents had their own monogrammed paddles." A two-year-old child died after being paddled for two hours by both his parents, within the communal house. According to the judge, this leader was the "most culpable" of all, despite the fact she had not actually participated in the physical abuse (39). The argument of her lawyers was "the free exercise of religion," but the judge's conviction stated that "this system of child abuse . . . was mistakenly justified under the guise of religion"; the Supreme Court even refused to hear an appeal.

Greven traces the rationale for such abuse to "the Lord whose name is Jealous," and to the Book of Proverbs, (falsely, in my view) attributed to Solomon, the king of Israel (48). Greven lists a dozen of these (inciting to use rods) to have been the religious cause of child abuse at home and in schools, leading later to physical violence in families and the society at large. As late as the early nineties, Greven judged "the pervasiveness of such views about physical punishment" among various faiths in the United States "a crucially important issue" (40). Among the worst of these Proverbs, "He that spareth his rod hateth his son" or "Chasten thy son . . . and let not thy soul spare for his crying." Some are definitely sadistic and vicious, such as the atrocious "The blueness of a wound cleanseth away evil . . . " urging to stripe "the inward part of the belly." Another one, certainly followed as a holy principle by the murderous parents cited above, tells them to not worry about consequences because "if you beatest him with the rod, he shall not die." I wouldn't think Solomon had such dirty tricks up his sleeve! It would stretch the imagination to picture the charming and gallant lover of the Queen of Sheba who was herself, in her own words, "smitten with the love of wisdom," in the persona of the desiccated paternalist family tyrant who authored these proverbs (see the heavily researched chapter of the biblical expert and Jungian analyst Rivkah Kluger, "The Queen of Sheba in Bible and Legends" in her book *Psyche in Scripture*).

In the words of Moses in Deuteronomy: "If a man have [sic] a stubborn and rebellious son . . . all the men of his city shall stone him with stones, that he die; *so shalt you put evil away from among you*." (Of course, we appreciate, beyond a forceful command to bypass his own commandments, the devilish and faulty logic: do evil, kill a son, and you'll clear your city from evil!) Greven's assessment is stark: "Thus, the price of filial disobedience is death. Moses' injunction clearly mirrored the will of Jehovah, who *often* killed those he judged to be disobedient or rebellious" (49; my emphasis).

Such stories as that of Abraham willing to kill his son to follow unethical yet "divine" orders, are thus interpreted (and regularly reenacted with this very interpretation) solely as a mean for listeners to be in awe and to *fear* the god of this ancient time and place, clearly the *unique aim* of all these so-called teachings. Greven judges that "it remains one of the most profoundly disturbing examples of Jehovah's willingness to destroy human life in order to assure himself of the unquestioning and absolute obedience of his subjects" (47).

As Carl Jung makes us aware of it in *Answer to Job,* we have, as humanity—starting with Job realizing that his Lord is an unjust, jealous, and uncaring God—definitely developed higher standards of ethics regarding human rights, minority rights, children's and women's rights!

It is time, for all of us, to assess with a clear mind the kind of "divine" persona and value systems that were upheld for us to honor and emulate with blind obedience, and whose horrendous deeds, skewing our psyches, were supposedly recounted for our moral and spiritual benefit.

An omniscient god should be the one to have as an aim the future development of the "children"—that is, an omniscient god would by definition know the future (or its lines of probabilities) and, if also gifted with intelligence, will envision the future and prepare for it; that is, that god will lay the way for the future developments and even prod them. It is impossible for an omniscient god not to know that life is constant change. (If a very ancient philosopher like Heraclitus of Ephesus, of the fifth century BCE—who stated, "You cannot step into the same river twice" and "Everything flows, nothing stands still"—can right away fathom these facts in his extremely short life, why can't an immortal make it out in millennia of experience?)

An omniscient and benevolent god—benevolent just like human parents—cannot fail to envision a future in which his children will be adult and take the steering wheel of their own lives, in which they will be free to make their own choices, explore new ways, develop new sciences and paradigms, and become creative and innovative.

An omniscient, benevolent, and wise god will welcome such an envisioned future and try to develop and prod in his children the very mental strategies, the psychological traits, and the curiosity and enthusiasm for knowledge, that will render this future easily achievable, without loss of moral values and without excessive pain and friction (he will certainly try to lessen the pain and hardships, not to multiply them).

And to achieve that, the first and foremost rule of behavior for such a god would be to avoid repressing the natural instinct of curiosity and enthusiasm, to avoid forging laws that can apply only to a short cultural time and context and presenting them as eternally binding—all things that a person in the role of issuing only commands, and obsessed with being the absolute master, will definitely and with certainty do.

Now, let's keep in mind that this is only a part of the global issue, because an even more crucial problem arises when we consider that we are not just talking about loving parents or slave masters, but about a spiritual entity who, in all logic, should have at heart as his prominent purpose, not only the psychological and intellectual maturity of his children, but even more so their spiritual accomplishment and the blossoming of their spiritual talents and potentials.

Again, we have to deeply ponder the foundational assumptions and principles laid down in the Book text supposedly for the moral benefit of children and adults alike—as Delaney does:

> Why should the model of faith not be a person who passionately protects a child, rather than sacrificing or being willing to sacrifice it? What kind of religious/ethical system might develop from that? Why should love of God be demonstrated by suppressing compassion, rather than through compassion? Why is a sense of the divine not shown *through* caring relationships instead of at the expense of them? What is at stake? (145)

The Spiritual and Magical Power of the MEs

The only repeated mention of something akin to sacred objects linked to sacred or magical rituals performed by the Anunnaki themselves is the use of the MEs. The MEs, often translated or referred to as "formulas," give their possessor the knowledge and the power over a domain (be it scientific, technological, or a kingly realm). As we have seen, the MEs are still very mysterious, and the best knowledge we can gather about them is when a temple or a facility is robbed or defiled; the texts give us the names of the robbed MEs and describe as well the effects produced by their removal—generally lack of power, machines stopping, etc. Often, the only information comes from their names.

We learn a lot when Inanna makes a visit to Enki with a plan to get hold of some MEs. Despite being only the second among the gods on

Earth, Enki is nevertheless the prominent possessor and keeper of MEs. He must have had an immense collection of them—given that he will give no less than ninety of them to Inanna, and yet he doesn't seem to be greatly deprived afterward.

Any temple-abode of a god and any major facility of the Sumerians, especially the five sacred places directing all space operations and all administrative organization, had its own god to govern it and its own MEs to operate it. The two Ekur (the first one in Nippur and the postdiluvial one in Giza) were lush with MEs and the state-of-the-art technology based on crystals and stones. A clear example of the technological function of the MEs is when Zu robbed the Tablet of Destinies in the Dirga room of Enlil's temple in Nippur: it had drastic effects on the space station, where the Igigi were suddenly blinded, unable to operate their machines. Enlil's temple abode in Nippur was the antediluvial Mission Control Center of the Anunnaki, and housed two high-technology complexes set in two rooms, the Dirga (containing the Duranki and the Tablet of Destinies) and the Kiur. The first, the Dir.Ga ("Dark, Glowing Chamber") was set on the platform of a tower, and was "a secret chamber . . . where space charts (the emblems of the stars) were displayed and where the Dur.An.Ki (Bond Heaven-Earth) was maintained" (*Wars,* 88). Now, the high-technology MEs in use in this Dirga room are impressive: a "Lifted eye which scans the land"; a "Lifted Beam which penetrates all" ("which searches the heart of all the land"); a vast net stretching out like an arm. Thus are clearly described radars and lasers able to scan not only the ground and movements in space, but also the underground, the latter a quite recent technological feat for us. The Tablet of Destinies, as described in the *Hymn to Enlil the All-Beneficent,* was thus some type of computer and program with its data sets, managing a permanent scan of the sky and control of the spaceships. The second room, the Ki.Ur ("Place of Earth's Root"), was described as a "heavenward tall pillar, reaching to the sky" that enabled Enlil "to pronounce his word" so that his parole does "approach heaven." With the Kiur, we see, neatly described, a sophisticated communication system between Earth and Nibiru, with an antenna in the tower. Last but not least, just as all other great gods had their own plane (bird) or helicopter (whirling-bird) on the roof of their temples, Enlil, says Sitchin, had a renown "fast-stepping Bird, a 'bird' whose 'hand' the wicked and the evil could not escape"; in other words, a "fast-stepping Bird whose grasp no one could escape" (*12th,* 295). This can only suggest, on Enlil's craft, a ray able to lock in on targets. As for the Anunnaki's interplanetary spacecrafts and rockets (shems), they were in the spaceports—the antediluvial one at Sippar, then the postdiluvial ones in Baalbek and the Sinai.

The technological power of some MEs is made clear by the description of their effects in *The Myth of Zu*. Now, if you remember, Anu had come to Earth, on his first visit, with his heir Enlil and with the grandson of the deposed and exiled King Alalu, Kumarbi, whom he left in the space station with the Igigi. According to the Hittite text called *The Kumarbi Cycle,* the Igigi adopted him and taught him astronomy so that he became an Igigi himself. Now *The Myth of Zu* (a Sumerian text reconstituted from versions in Old Babylonian and Assyrian languages) speaks of a Zu (or An.Zu, "He Who Knows the Heavens") who was an orphan adopted by the Igigi, while his name shows that he was trained in astronomy and astronautics by them. So we may infer that Kumarbi is just another name of Zu (as often happens between the different languages of the tablets), which explains then that Zu would want to take revenge on the Enlilites so as to recover the title of King. But not on the Enkiites, first because Enki's wife Damkina was Alalu's daughter and thus Zu's aunt, and second, because the Igigi headed by Marduk had adopted and trained him. In some prayers, Marduk is clearly addressed as "The ruler of the Anunnaki, the director of the Igigi," for example in Leonard King's *Babylonian Magic and Sorcery* (61).

At one point the Igigi wanted to obtain some property on Earth where they could go and rest, and they sent Zu as their ambassador to Enlil, who, to stall the negotiation, offered to Zu to be an assistant in the Durga. On the first occasion he was left alone, Zu stole the Tablet of Destinies. Now the immediate effects of the removal of this ME from the Dirga room are bewildering: "Suspended were the divine formulas; The lighted brightness petered out; Silence prevailed. In space, the Igigi were confounded; The sanctuary's brilliance was taken off."

Zu immediately claims that, with the power of the ME, "I will establish my throne, be master of the Heavenly Decrees; The Igigi in their space I will command!" Even while in fierce battle against Ninurta—Enlil's Warrior and Chief of the Armies—Zu boasts: "I have carried off all Authority; The decrees of the gods I [now] direct!" (*Wars*, 97).

The text states that this was no illusion: "with the powers Zu had obtained, no lightning bolt could 'approach his body.'" When Zu retreated to a mountain, "None dared track Zu to the distant mountain for he was now as powerful as Enlil, having also stolen the 'Brilliance' of Enlil; 'and he who opposes him shall become as clay . . . at his Brilliance the gods waste away'" (*Wars*, 97). This specific ME, the Brilliance, is described as the "Enlilship" of Enlil—that is, his role as Commander of Earth. Ninurta will have to get new and powerful armament from his father Enlil, and only then will he defeat Zu.

What these task-oriented computers do is quite easy for us to understand, that is, as far as technology and science go. What's puzzling and indecipherable are signs that the Anunnaki science is an integral science and that the MEs seem to be crafted, each one, in only a unique version, so that the role and power, such as the Enlilship, is attached to it, and whoever owns it controls the function of king, queen, or else is the master of that specific domain.

Conclusion on the Anunnaki Religion

What we don't see (and it's very puzzling) are the following:

1. Rituals and prayers offered to a god or gods of the Anunnaki. They have a concept of a Creator-of-All, but no temples and rituals dedicated to him. The only temples they build are their own abodes.

2. We don't see either global philosophical, moral, or religious concepts such as a greater good (the Greek philosophers), or the concept of oneness or cosmic consciousness (Tao or brahman of the
Eastern religions, Plotinus); nor the belief in a higher deity, king
of the gods (the Great-Grandfather of the Native Americans,
the Eagle of Mexican Yaqui Indians, Amma for the Dogons of
Africa); nor even the philosophical and moral concepts derived
from a spiritual outlook, such as a striving for moral values (all
religions).

3. Apart from one exception, we don't see a deference toward teachers and places of learning—as the Greek philosophers' *agora,* or
the Eastern sages' ashrams where they taught techniques for
achieving inner knowledge, such as meditation, prayer, yoga,
trance. The only group of this kind in Sumer is that of the Sages
of Eridu, who had attained an immense knowledge of all the
sciences of their time and had established a renowned academy
in Enki's city. The Anunnaki royals (mainly Enki, Ninmah, and
the Enkiites, Enki's family) teach their own children.

It is only after "civilized humanity" (*Homo sapiens sapiens*) has
proliferated and kings and priesthood lines have been established, that
the Great Anunnaki ask earthlings to treat them as gods. This trend
started with Enlil demanding to be obeyed as the sole Lord of Edin by
Adamu and Tiamat, whereas all decisions among Anunnaki in Sumer
were made via a vote within the Assembly of the Gods, most members being the royals. Thereafter, several royals will have their own
temple and be worshipped there by the local population of their own
city or territory. With time passing, a greater projection of loftiness,
of omniscience, wisdom, and justice, was progressively made, while
the planet "Heaven/An" and its king became more and more distant
from the earthlings. And the continued projection was also amplify-
ing the absolute and extreme nature of the qualities thus projected
and aggregated in one persona. The master-lord who is served and

obeyed, for which one works, becomes the all-powerful god (which, as an autocratic leader pronouncing inflexible decrees above and beyond the Assembly, he somehow was), who has to be praised and propitiated by offerings in order to tame his well-known wrathful and lethal temper.

When Humans from Another World Became Gods to Their Creatures

So, what can we infer from all this? Again, we have to forget about our own standpoint, our own spiritual perspective, in order to imagine how the lofty Anunnaki could perceive the civilization of earthlings they had brought into being. On their own original world, Nibiru, the king was the supreme lord and we don't have traces of organized religion—apart from the very abstract Creator-of-All who is not venerated through prayers and rituals, and has no temple. However, our actual knowledge of the Anunnaki reflects only the data and the tablets we have unearthed so far. True, Zecharia Sitchin's comprehensive synthesis, together with the many new discoveries made in the last few decades, definitely made a huge difference, and we can only wait for more discoveries. Yet, for now, we don't really have a perfect grasp of what was happening on Nibiru. A thorny issue is this one: Could they really have created a religion and rituals out of nothing? We know that on the occasion of a great and celebrated visit of Anu and his wife Antu on Earth around 4000 BCE, an Assembly of the Gods was convened. The *Epic of Etana* recounts how they judged that they were too powerful and "too lofty" to keep interacting face-to-face with earthlings:

> The great Anunnaki who decree the fate sat exchanging their counsels regarding the land. They who created the four regions, who set up the settlements, who oversaw the land [decided that they] were too lofty for Mankind.

They decided to "lower kingship from Heaven to Earth," that is, to have intermediaries, kings or Mighty Men (Lugal), between themselves the Gods (the *Elu* in Akkadian, or Lofty Ones) and mankind, who would be both kings and priests. (Funnily, *Elu* in French means "the chosen one," like Neo in *The Matrix*.) This is how the kingship was established on Earth for the second time, long after Ninmah had made of Adapa and his half-sister Titi (both fathered by Enki) and their descent a lineage of ten kings and queens in her city Shuruppak, well before the Deluge. Yet, if the Genesis account speaks of the ten antediluvial patriarchs, the queens and consorts have been generally reduced to mere "wives."

Thus the text implies clearly that the Great Anunnaki (the ones conferring in the Assembly) decided that they wanted to be treated as gods and venerated, and that they would, from now on, keep their distance from Earth-humans. And to still be able to pass on their commands, they now needed intermediaries—human kings and queens. That seems (in my view) to have been the time when they created the concept of "lofty lord" which is, by the way, the only term used in the tablets despite the fact it is translated systematically as *god*. If we look at things from the Anunnaki's own standpoint, and at the psychological level, the "lowering of kingship from Heaven" consisted more of their ascension from the rank of Lords to that of Lofty Lords/Gods who had to be venerated, than of a gift of self-organization offered to humanity. This is made clear by the fact that (1) they were the ones to choose the kings, and (2) the kings were taking their orders from them and whenever one of them tried to play his own game, he was removed or slain.

This was, for example, the fateful case with Shulgi, King of Ur during the Ur III period. His father Ur-Nammu, following the orders of Enlil, the Chief of the Gods, and his two sons Nannar/Sin (the Deity of Ur) and Ninurta (Chief of Enlil's armies), had waged wars of conquest against the "evil cities" of the Amorites, followers of Marduk, to the west of Sumer. But Ur-Nammu died while championing Enlil's war, despite the formidable weapon that Enlil had given him to "destroy the evil cities and clear them of opposition," which was a "divine weapon that heaps up the rebels in piles" (*Days,* 58). More often than not, Enlil and the Enlilites, including his granddaughter Inanna, are waging wars with terrifying weapons of mass destruction on their own kin. This is something we never see with Enki and Ninmah who, on the contrary, are always acting as protectors and teachers of the Anunnaki and the earthlings as well, and we only see this in rare instances with Marduk. Among the Enkiites, as we'll see, only one son of Enki, the neurotic exterminator Nergal, displays such tyrannical and perverse tendencies.

We know from several tablets that the people of Sumer resented deeply that the mightiest Lofty God, Enlil, had let the hero battling for him die. It was for them inconceivable that the gods were so powerless as to be unable to make their champion invulnerable, or else to revive him. They knew the gods had powerful revival means; for example, Enki sent an emissary to revive Inanna after she had been murdered by her sister Ereshkigal at the southern tip of the Abzu (Africa), and pronounced dead (he didn't even need to do the reviving himself). Similarly, Hermes/Ningishzidda came to the rescue of Horus mortally bitten by a scorpion during his fight against Seth, the murderer of his father Osiris. Of course, that spells the ethics and skills of the Enkiites, even when an Enlilite such as Inanna was concerned.

In the minds of the people of Enlil's cities, Enlil had simply neglected to protect and revive his chosen king, Ur-Nammu. An interesting point about the Sumerian Earth-born population is that we see over and over again in the tablets that they didn't fear at all to hold the Lofty Lords responsible for grave shortcomings and to express their criticism of some of the gods' behaviors and acts, even when it concerned the god of their own city, whom they were supposed to venerate and obey blindly. We'll see a full-fledged condemnation and attribution of responsibility to the Chief of the Gods and Commander of Earth, Enlil, as well as to Ninurta and Nergal, for the destruction of the civilization of Sumer by contaminated radioactive clouds, deemed no less than the "bitter venom of the gods." Thus the Khedorlaomer Texts state,

> Enlil, who sat enthroned in loftiness was consumed with anger. The devastators again suggested evil; He who scorches with fire [Ishum/ Ninurta] and he of the evil wind [Erra/Nergal] together performed their evil. (*Wars*, 330)

This is for us the trigger for grasping how much of a difference there is between cohabiting with the Lord-God of a city and thus witnessing his/her actions on a daily basis—that is, with minimal possibility of concealing and covering up the facts of wars, punishments, and devastation—and the situation in which the Lord is so remote, beyond human, and ethereal that all responsibility for what is "evil" and "wrong," all shortcomings and hardships, are attributed to the feeble and disobedient mortals. The story of Shulgi, son and heir of the hero who died for his Lord-God, is illuminating in this respect. Let's get back to it.

After his father's death, Shulgi was enthroned, by decree of Enlil and the major gods of Enlil's clan. He decided to unify the lands relying on trade instead of war—the sign of a high morality, intelligence, and benevolence. And indeed, he ushered an era of great prosperity in which the merchants of Ur became renowned in the whole Middle East and even beyond. He also had the amorous favors of Inanna. But meanwhile Marduk and his son Nabu were gaining followers in cities in Canaan. And Enlil and the main governing gods were not satisfied; what they were feverishly intent on doing was to checkmate the growing peaceful influence of Marduk and they wanted to do that through wars—that is, to slaughter the "sinful" followers and destroy their cities. And so they decided, abruptly, that Shulgi was to be removed. But to only remove the king was not satisfying enough for the Enlilites; judging that "the divine regulations he did not carry out," he was sentenced to "the death of a sinner" (*Days,* 65). And sure enough, he died that same year (2048 BCE), albeit we have little information about how he was slain. (The Inquisition did not invent its tortuous and macabre ways to judge that any divergent thinking or faith was evil, erring, and sinful, and to exterminate its enemies.) It is the same relentless and burning desire to crush Marduk and Nabu that led the Enlilites, twenty-four years later, to unleash the nuclear catastrophe and destroy their own civilization. Letting King Ur-Nammu die during the war he fought for his gods (no "craftsman of the gods" was called to help him or revive him), getting rid of the peaceful King Shulgi by sentencing him to a horrendous death—that's as far as an autocratic power can go to let everybody know that the kings were just the puppets of the gods and that the so-called lowering of governance "from Heaven to Earth" was still a long way ahead.

To conclude on the religion of the Anunnaki, one thing that is certain is that they didn't have, like us at the time of Sumer, anybody they would call and venerate as "gods" walking among them. The Nibirians could be the result of a lengthy evolution—a natural one that must have taken millions of years for intelligent life (all life-forms are intelligent) to emerge into a self-conscious and self-referent species and a full-blown technological civilization, a human species in this case (but not out of necessity). However, various signs seem to imply that they knew they were not the sole *sapiens* species in the galaxy, and maybe not the sole *human* sapiens species, and that they had contacts with other worlds. But their worldview in this respect was definitely of a scientific and geo-political type. On Earth, the Anunnaki gave a kick to this natural evolution by genetic engineering. They engineered and "perfected" a mixed species by powering and diversifying our genes, by mixing a hominid's genes with their own genes. Sitchin has calculated that the push they gave to our evolution could have been of the order of one or two million years.

All-Knowing and All-Seeing Gods?

The power and knowledge of these Anunnaki gods must have been overwhelming for the earthlings we were at the time. Add to that our awareness that we owed them everything—from our exalted status as an evolved intelligent species, to all facets of our civilization and science. No wonder then that we tended to be compliant and altogether thankful for their role in our evolution, unless they went to extreme schemes of destruction and annihilation.

We must remark, though, that what we deem their "omniscience" was mostly based on technology and, even so, was very far from being what the term implies, that is *all-knowing*.

For one thing, the communication with Nibiru is strictly technological. There is a special ME or computer to establish a permanent link (the Bond Heaven-Earth, or *Duranki*) in the Sumerian Ekur, then in the Egyptian one, and finally in the Sinai. On one specific occasion related in the tablets, this communication channel is voluntarily severed by Enlil—so that Anu wouldn't be able to interfere with the disputable actions he planned on Earth—namely before he raided Enki's gold-mining facility in the Abzu and abducted the lulus to bring them back as a workforce in Sumer. Says the *Myth of the Pickax* text:

> In the Bond Heaven-Earth he [Enlil] made a gash,
> Verily did he speed to disconnect Heaven from Earth.

But the best proof is a negative one: the Anunnaki definitely show they lack telepathy, clairvoyance, and any psi knowledge at a distance. The only receptive psi we encounter in the tablets is precognition through dreams. As for PK (psychokinesis) or bio-PK, the issue of healing is a hard one to ascertain—how much of it is technology and how much is a mind influence?

Here are some objective proofs of the absence of telepathy and clairvoyance:

- If Inanna had perceived telepathically, at the moment she arrived at the gate of her sister's abode in the Abzu, the latter's intention to strip her of her MEs (that she carried in her sacred ornaments and clothing) and to arrange a mock trial and kill her, she would have turned back immediately at the gate—while she still had an immense power and her plane (celestial boat) at hand. At that point, given who she was, nobody could have stopped her. But she did let herself be taken into her sister's deadly trap like a blind sheep. The above failure of Inanna (albeit still young and distressed by the murder of her lover Dumuzi) seems to imply not only a lack of clairvoyance and precognition, but also of omnipotence. This event happened, of course, before she became the "Lady of the MEs, Queen Brightly resplendent; Righteous, clothed in Radiance," the Chief of the Gods and now endowed with the most powerful MEs (*Exaltation of Inanna; Wars,* 241).

- Trickery in general among Anunnaki (of which we have seen so many examples in *DNA of the Gods*) can hardly be working on people gifted with an omniscience due to their consciousness alone (and not based on technology). Yet, we meet it repeatedly in the tablets. If it was only on rare instances, we could invoke a blind spot, or the occasional failure of a usually well-mastered mind power. But, very far from it, trickery and lies are a steady way of interacting among the Anunnaki—all the way to Anu—both in the sense of being abused and of abusing others. The most revealing and sad example is when Dumuzi is trying to get a male heir from his half sister (who would then reign as king over both the Enlilites and the Enkiites), while he and Inanna are engaged and madly in love; the plan was partly hers in fact. First Dumuzi tricked her sister into accepting a picnic together alone—while he and Inanna had a clear plan in mind that should have scared any telepath. During the picnic, he then tries to arouse her sexually by all kinds of analogous arousals, like making animals mate incestuously before her—and still she doesn't get it. This example loudly speaks for itself, because if there is a domain in which women have an ingrained highly developed intuition and in which they are able to sense an attraction or a danger coming (by a natural response of their bodily and psychological sensations) it is the sexual domain—and here we don't even have to refer to telepathy or psi, just to emotional intelligence and survival instinct. Not only is Dumuzi's sister unable to sense her brother's gross scheme, but she is lacking the most basic of all human instincts—the aroused male being a potential danger both to women preyed on and to other male competitors.

As a comparison, I myself was hitchhiking from age sixteen, alone and without much money. Even at that age and without sexual expertise, I was able to detect the very onset of sexual desire and arousal in the psyche of any male driver who had given me a lift—and I would immediately begin a plan to get out of the car before the arousal got too strong to be diverted, this with a plausible pretext of course so that I didn't trigger a negative reaction. At first, I would try to divert and shunt the arousal process by psychological tricks; the main one was to lead the conversation to their spouse, kids, mother, and father—thus bringing to the front of their consciousness stream the strong moral barriers set up in childhood as well as the positive bonding to the mother, or to their kids. Then the child-mother bonding should evoke in them a reflex of protection vis-à-vis me. But this trick could divert an aroused male only so long, just enough time to get the pretext working and exit the vehicle. When I started traveling in the East, crossing difficult countries such as Afghanistan, Pakistan, and India, and would find myself sometimes in the middle of a desert or in regions devoid of much traffic, where villages and towns were distant from one another, I had sharpened this knack to the point where I could foretell how many minutes I could remain in the vehicle while being still able to make a safe exit (that is, before the driver starts getting into action mode and looks for a place to stop his vehicle). And I would look out (in the buffer time) for a few houses or a village where I would be surrounded by families, and secure, and get out of the vehicle at that spot.

I'm inclined to think (based on what I can see around me) that a child of twelve, nowadays, would be more sensitive to this type of predatory danger and more prone to protect herself or himself than the sister of Dumuzi despite the fact she was a goddess.

In contrast to telepathy, we have two instances in which an Anunnaki gets precognitive information, emerging during a dream-vision. The first one, certainly true, is Dumuzi's nightmare after he raped his sister when she refused to have intercourse. Yet, he couldn't interpret it correctly, and it is his sister who did, sending him fleeing. She predicted from the dream that their elder brother Marduk would come rescue her and would accuse Dumuzi of rape—a very serious offence among Anunnaki, punished by exile. As he flees, Dumuzi indeed sees Marduk's emissaries pursuing him, and he will finally drown in a river, very probably by accident.

The second instance concerns Enki. A mysterious Galzu, claiming to be a messenger of Anu, appeared while he was sleeping, to warn him of the looming Deluge and to give him a tablet with a plan to save Ziusudra/Noah. Enki believes he had a dream-vision, but the disturbing detail is that on awakening he finds the tablet depicting how to build a sort of submarine. As far as precognition is concerned (that supposedly occurred through a dream-vision), we shouldn't take it for granted, because it could also have been a *mise-en-scène,* on the part of Enki, in order to divert the responsibility of saving mankind and Ziusudra (against the clear orders of Enlil) by invoking a higher sacred force. This is in line with his mise-en-scène in Ziusudra's reed house—when he is "talking to the reed wall" and supposedly not to Ziusudra himself, to warn him of the coming Deluge and give him the plan of the submersible boat. Thus, he is not infringing—strictly speaking—on the oath Enlil forced him and all the other gods to take, which was to not let mankind know of the impending catastrophe (see fig. 4.5 on page 130).

Now, in the case where it was a story made up by Enki (and not a real precognitive dream), then we would have another instance of a prominent Anunnaki, Enlil, unable to know telepathically of his brother Enki's plan to thwart his decision.

On the other hand, Alalu (the ancient King of Nibiru overthrown by Anu) may have exhibited precognition, and/or clairvoyance, when he fled in his rocket ship after being defeated. He came to Earth and found the gold that could save Nibiru, as well as his own life (in the deal to buy his safe return to Nibiru). If it wasn't psi capacities, at the very least it was a streak of synchronicities—a true serendipity.

Drawing on all the above materials (and more), we can clearly be assured that the greatest among the Anunnaki royals had no telepathy, and moreover that their instinctive warning system wasn't really functional. And we will leave open the question of whether they had some degree of precognition or not, in dreams or consciously. Of course, as to this last point, in order for the supposed lie (about a messenger giving warning and precognitive information in a dream) to be accepted by Enlil, it must necessarily have been a psi or spiritual feat that was known to happen in reality, even if rarely. They must have had, in their recorded history on Nibiru, instances of visionary dreams or other omens—and this would account for the omens becoming a bedrock of the Sumerian civilization. Strictly speaking then, these wouldn't be precognitive as much as they would be a true message issued by a divine source. But in that case, why isn't their god the object of a cult? And why do they expect from earthlings a cult dedicated to them, in their own temple-abodes where each great Anunnaki has his or her own godly status being exalted and recognized (meaning that they themselves are the object of a cult)? Just imagine for a minute that we, mankind with a belief in god, had created a new species—sentient and knowledgeable as the *Homo sapiens sapiens*. We would, even if expecting to be honored as masters, still have them pray to, and ritually celebrate, our own god. We wouldn't dare to take the place of God altogether, to the point of putting ourselves in his place. Thus, we have to infer that the Anunnaki's concept of god, the Creator-of-All, had become a farfetched idea, a sort of philosophical concept of a force driving evolution (toward conscious and intelligent life). In any case, it was more akin to an abstract concept than to a personalized god endowed with an individual will and to whom a cult is offered. Even in the (supposed) absence of form and image, the deity of the Book is still highly personalized, having a will, an irascible temper, and giving precise orders and plans to his people.

Then remains the issue of the oracles, of which we have seen some instances in the lives of Anunnaki themselves, such as the Book of Oracles of Enki, a divinatory system. We also have the Oracle in Hatti-Land (a person giving predictions, such as the famous Oracle of Delphi) whom Marduk consulted (and whose prediction became true) and about whom we have no detail (was he/she an earthling, a demigod, or an Anunnaki?).

The complex problem is that these capacities, together with the gift of direct prophecy, will be exhibited by numerous earthlings, such as the great women oracles in Greece (Delphi and Dodona) and the prophets of the Old Testament, such as Jeremiah or Ezekiel, endowed with prophecy and visions. And many predictions of these oracles have been duly recorded, and were proven later to have been real instances of precognition. The first such instance of psi is with Eve, the mother of Cain and Abel, who had a clairvoyant vision of her son being murdered by his brother; she rushed to the spot, only to find that Abel had already died.

However, the fact that earthlings will exhibit psi capacities doesn't establish that the Anunnaki had them and that they were transmitted to us through them. Even if we have inherited the DNA of the Anunnaki royals, making most of our genetic makeup, these psi capacities could reflect a leap in consciousness or mutations triggered by the mixing and binding of two genomes, or triggered by the fact that our own DNA became more flexible and adaptable, more prone to mutations and evolution. Nevertheless, it is now proven that our rate of random mutation in the hominid/human species (which has been calculated) will never be at the level that Darwin's theory of evolution through chance mutations would necessitate to explain our extremely rapid evolution.

One thing is certain, though: these psi capacities—precognition (prediction and oracles), visions, telepathy, bio-PK, and the like—have been rampant in humanity and are on the rise in our epoch, reflecting the new leap in consciousness that we are already in the process of making.

A last point about the Anunnaki not worshipping any gods but believing in an underlying harmony in the universe, is that this would instantiate synchronicities, that is, meaningful coincidences as described by the famous psychologist Carl Jung. Only the existence of such an underlying spiritual force would explain psi capacities implying information coming from the future (retrocausality), or being shared or received at great distances (as in telepathy and clairvoyance). In my recent theoretical book on cosmology and cosmic consciousness, called *Cosmic DNA at the Origin,* I've posited a hyperdimension of consciousness pervading the cosmos, a fifth dimension of the universe and of all systems (from particles, to human beings, to stars). This syg hyperdimension is made of all the semantic fields of all systems, and all the Selfs (the spirit of each intelligent person, whether human or alien); it is filled with faster-than-light virtual particles—the *sygons*—through which individuals can share information quasi instantaneously and may also have an influence on biosystems, such as in healing.

We meet here an extant and resilient philosophical tradition that exists in the East, both in the concept of Tao (of the Chinese Taoists) and in the concept of brahman and purusha (of the Advaita Vedanta of India). It posits a spiritual force (albeit not personalized), a cosmic consciousness driving evolution toward a higher spiritual state for all beings—including not only animals, but the whole of nature, since mountains and trees, for example, share in this penetrating cosmic consciousness. This cosmic consciousness is so keen and advanced that it is able to orient and guide the spiritual evolution of each and every human being on a spiritual quest. And yet it is nonpersonalized, and the only veneration offered to this cosmic consciousness is the intent and focus at harmonizing one's spirit with it and, thus, at reaching for oneself and one's community, a higher consciousness in harmony with the universe.

In the East, this tradition entails (as a first step), to reach a non-ego stance, a detachment from earthly pleasures and very high ethics (such as the respect for life and the respect for the paths of others) that we would be hard put to find in the Anunnaki.

✦ 2 ✦

The Blackout on the Human Nature of God

WITH WHAT WE HAVE GATHERED about the Anunnaki and the Sumerian tablets depicting so many similar events to the Genesis text, albeit in a more detailed fashion, it is now impossible not to consider the Sumerian Anunnaki's involvement in our origins. And these Anunnaki clearly stated that they had come from another world and that, later on, they fashioned the human Earth-born species by genetic engineering. Moreover, we have to accept the evidence that the original Sumerian tablets (translated word for word in about six different ancient languages, including Akkadian, mother tongue of the Hebrew) are definitely the source of the Genesis book.

Three Scenarios for the Writing of Genesis

Based on my research, there are three possible types of scenarios as to how the account of the Book of Genesis—about the creation of humanity and the early times—came to be.

Type 1: A near-immortal Anunnaki recounted to a chosen *scribe,* the story as he experienced it with his own world-vision of what happened (through the tinted glasses of his semantic field). Of course, the identification of Enlil as the deity of Genesis is hardly debatable, due to the fact that he is the main protagonist (as a Lord-God) in several cornerstone events, and during these events, he acts, thinks, and speaks similarly in both the Sumerian tablets and the Book. In this scenario, then, the deity of the Book would have dictated an account to his chosen scribe and priest.

Type 2: An Earth-born scholar, the *Thinker,* started to study and mull over the Sumerian tablets and decided to rewrite an account of early human history in Hebrew.

I will call these the *scribe* versus the *thinker* scenarios. In the first case, that of the scribe, he would have recorded the words of God, as many theologians believe. In the second case, the thinker, he would have concocted a history of the early times, based on the various Sumerian and Mesopotamian tablets.

Let's note that the present historical trend is to date the writing of the early biblical texts to the period of the captivity in Babylon, following the destruction of the Temple in Jerusalem by Nebuchadnezzar in 586 BCE, and that would have provided the Israelite scholars with access to the (ancient) library of the very knowledgeable Marduk and of Babylon's lineage of kings, certainly a plentiful one in terms of ancient Sumerian tablets, cylinders, and other such lore. According to the anthropologist Carol Delaney, more conventional scholars disagree (as she does herself) and set the two oldest strands or sources in Genesis prior to the Assyrians destroying Israel in 722 BCE; the J (Yahweh) strand's authorship would happen around 922 and 722 BCE, and the second, the E (Elohim) strand around 848 and 722 BCE (Delaney 1998, 131, n4). This last dating thus makes a clear distinction between the sentences having the Elohim (the gods plural) as subjects, and those attributed to the Deity Y. singular.

However, my method is to analyze the semantic fields revealed by groups of words—that is, the specific worldview of their author. As I have shown through an in-depth semantic analysis of the garden of Eden text in *DNA of the Gods,* there are two distinct semantic fields interwoven in the Genesis text, reflecting values, worldviews, beliefs, behaviors, and dogmas that are totally distinct and pertaining to widely different cultures and epochs. One is clearly in accord with the ancient Sumerian tablets and states facts and events in an informational, detailed manner, without judging. I called it the Informational Framework (or IF). The second semantic style is loaded with moral judgments and is intent on attributing responsibility to the earthlings, while defending what is deemed the "just" and "righteous" wrath of the deity—thus giving plausible reasons for the punishments he imposes on them. I called it the Moralistic Framework (or MF). Further on, we will analyze other texts (such as that of the Babel tower) in such a manner: everything gets clarified once we have thus separated the two distinct semantic fields or layers of the text, pertaining to two different persons and cultures. Moreover, the story of Lot will reveal yet another thinker/narrator harboring a similar Moralistic Framework worldview, albeit with such a distinct psychological profile and "teaching" style that I will be led to call him Narrator 3. Thus, we have to consider a third scenario:

> *Type 3:* There had been a first version in accord with the Sumerian tablets, and much later on, an editing of this text by a priest belonging to a faith ensconced in a strict moralistic worldview. Additional editors/narrators of a much more recent period of history could then have wrought an editing of some texts or could have inserted new texts.

What we see in the Book is the depiction of a male god with martial psychological traits, bent on giving commands and punishments, prone to anger, and whose interlocutors are selectively male, apart from rare instances. We see a unique and lonely god—without spouse, family, or descendants. One who doesn't seem to reside on Earth but in "heaven," and appears definitely more and more immaterial—without a body or needs—immortal, omniscient, and omnipotent. He stands as far as can be from the feeble humans, his creatures. However, that had not always been the case, even in the Book. For example, he was attracted by the smell of roasted meat when Noah made an offering on Mount Ararat when the diluvial flood started to recede, and he accepted a princely meal offered by Abraham on the way to erasing Sodom.

As some biblical experts noted, a repeated allusion to the fact that he is not the only god comes from (1) his insistence in saying he is the one and unique God, (2) when he warns his people not to follow other gods, and of course (3) the many times the plural *Elohim* (Lords-Gods) is used, in sentences where it can't be a royal *we.*

Also noteworthy are two instances in the Book in which a clear, pinpoint reference to other gods and his son is made. In Proverbs: "Who has ascended up to Heaven and descended too? . . . What is his name, and *what is his son's name*—if thou can tell?" (30:4, my emphasis); and in Psalms 97:9, "For Thou, O Yahweh, art supreme over the whole Earth; most supreme art Thou over all the Elohim."

Thus, about the Commandments handed to Moses, says Sitchin (*Encounters,* 298):

> The first three Commandments established monotheism, proclaimed Yahweh as the Elohim of Israel, the sole God, and prohibited the making of idols and their worship:
> I. I am Yahweh, thy Elohim . . .
> II. Thou shalt have no other Elohim beside me.

One thing is sure, the ancient patriarchs such as Abraham and Moses were communicating with him and receiving his commands, and he was supervising them quite closely. Abraham had a face-to-face contact consisting of a guest's meal offered in his tent, which lasted all afternoon (in 2024 BCE).

Abram (still with his Sumerian name at the time), just the day before the Deity destroys Sodom and five towns of the Sinai plain, as well as the spaceport, sees "three men" arriving at the door of his tent, whom he recognizes immediately as being divine—his Lord and two *emissaries* (Hebrew name: Malakhim) (*Wars,* 310).

[Abram] was sitting at the entrance of the tent, in the heat of the day. And he lifted his eyes and looked, and behold—*three men* were stationed upon him; and as he saw them he ran from the entrance of the tent toward them, and bowed to the ground. [My emphasis.]

Abram then addresses them as "my lords" and pleads with them to accept his offer of a princely banquet worthy of his honorable guests. The three visitors eat with Abram and then rest for the whole afternoon, and they leave Abram's tent at dusk: "And *the men* rose up from there to survey over upon Sodom" (my emphasis).

In contrast, (as we see in Deuteronomy 4:11–15) with Moses on Mount Sinai, after the flight from Egypt (1433 BCE), the Deity will not want to show his face nor anything that could reveal his human nature ("you" and "ye" refer to Moses, and emphasis is mine):

The Mount was engulfed with fire reaching unto the midst of heaven, and [there was] a dark cloud and thick fog. And Yahweh spoke unto you from inside the fire; ye heard the sound of the words, but *the likeness of a visage ye saw not—only a voice was heard.*

When Moses asks "Show me thy Face!" the Deity answers:

Thou canst not see my face, for *no Man can see Me and live.*

And when Moses insists "Please show me thy glory!"

Go and stand there upon the rock . . . I will cover thee with my hand until I have passed by; and I will then remove my hand, and *you shall see my back; but my face shall not be seen.*

Yet, the fact the deity is conscious of his effect on people is a self-admission: Y. "said unto Moses: 'Behold, I shall be coming unto thee in a thick cloud, enabling the people to hear when I speak with thee, so that in thee too they shall have faith'" (*Encounters,* 297). Nevertheless the Deity decided that he would be an unseen God, having no face (especially human) and only a silhouette. It seems nevertheless that only later exegesis forbade to represent or conceptualize the deity as having a body—and thus any "likeness" to his creatures was withheld. This is in dire antinomy with the creation of man, as the Elohim of the Book stated their intent: "Let us make the Adam *in our image,* after our *likeness.*"

Yahweh and His Spouse Asherah

New archaeological data have unearthed a very ancient site in Israel, in which an antique inscription engraved on stone spelled "Yahweh and His Asherah" (*Historia Magazine,* video documentary on Monotheism, *Arte,* May 14, 2014). For the archaeologists on site, it was definitely an ancient engraving and it clearly spelled that the deity had a wife, (the goddess) Asherah. An interesting point raised by the historian Gerda Lerner in her book *The Creation of Patriarchy,* concerning this historical shift to a sole god religion (of which the Book is *the* basic building block) is that "the emergence of Hebrew monotheism takes the form of an attack on the widespread cults of the various fertility goddesses" (10). Thus, she remarks about humanity's origins, "The divine originator of human life, who in the Sumerian story was the goddess Ninhursag [Ninmah], is now Yahweh, Father-God and Lord" (185). Lerner points out that predominant among these Great Goddesses was Asherah, the fertility goddess, whose symbol was a stylized tree (such as the Tree of Life), and whose "cult, which was popular in Israel during the patriarchal period, took place in groves of trees" (195). André Lemaire thus devoted an article to the question, called "Who or What Was Yahweh's Asherah?" And yet we know how Y. will mercilessly crush and suppress whoever is still honoring the Great Goddess, whose cult represented, by all logic, a reenactment of the Act of Creation by Ninmah (because of Asherah's symbol of a tree) through his own godly wife Asherah.

In the same vein, as Elaine Pagels states it in *The Gnostic Gospels* (37), quoting the texts discovered in Nag-Hammadi, the demiurge "reigns as king and lord" but is "not God" (in the sense that he is not ethereal)—

just a human king, as Enlil is the Commander of Earth. The Gnostic demiurge is full of pride and autocratic, prone to forget that he has a mother of a higher spiritual status, called Wisdom (*Sophia* in Greek). In one text, he boasts and exclaims:

> "I am father, and God, and above me there is no one." But his mother, hearing him speak thus, cried out against him, "Do not lie, Iabaldaoth." (Irenaeus, *Adversus Haereses*, 1.30.6)

And in another text reporting the same event, his mother, Wisdom (Sophia), answered "You are wrong, Samael!" (*Samael* meaning "god of the blind"). Then Life, the daughter of Wisdom, and his sister, exclaims after their mother: "You are wrong, Saklas!" (Hypostasis of the Archons).

As June Singer notes in her essay "Jung's Gnosticism and Contemporary Gnosis," "In Gnosticism, the principle of Source is the Mother-Father element; the second in the Trinity is the Logos or Christ-figure . . . and the third is the Sophia, Holy Spirit or wisdom figure (also known in Judaism as the Shekhinah, in Hinduism as Shakti), the aspect of psyche that provides the dynamism that leads to individuation [the process of spiritual awakening to one's Self in Jungian psychology]. . . . Gnosticism sees the Father-Mother principle as an ongoing creative power emanating light or energy in the universe and in the human spirit as the *principium individuationis* [the entity triggering the individuation process]. . . . In Gnosticism, the feminine is redeemed from the depth of matter and returned to co-equal status with the masculine. In Gnosticism, from its very beginnings, women as well as men have been priests" (88–89).

We can therefore assume that the deity speaking and depicted in the Book, and held as the demiurge in the Gnostic texts, has a psychological profile so similar to that of Enlil, that we cannot miss the identification. Given his autocratic character, he would either dictate or closely supervise the recounting of events that happened in Sumer in the early times. And consequently, the accounts we have in the Book (whether concocted or received as a dictation) are a strict rendering of the specific world-vision—thus interpretation of events—of this particular Anunnaki god. The patriarchs were too much in awe and they held the fear of god as a virtue—enough so as not to write (in the thinker scenario) anything that could displease him. Therefore, the scenarios of Type 1 and Type 2 lead to the same conclusion: what is expressed in the Book is the deity of the Book's own world-vision.

We cannot pretend either that we were such low creatures, compared to him, that he gave us only what we could understand—because then, why give us a historical account? And why would he sit in Abe's tent and share a meal and an afternoon with him? Why would Enki relentlessly teach humans? Even Anu invested Adapa with knowledge! And also, not only Noah, but also Enoch, were chosen by Enlil and Anu to reside in the Gods' sacred abode and given immortality.

All in all, we can with certitude trace the authorship of the *semantic field* of the Book—its worldview and values—if not the text itself, and thus the specific perspective on events recounted in the Book, to the "One God" expressing himself in it. And we can weigh the world-vision thus presented and draw inferences from it.

The fact is, by pretending he was the sole and unique god—while being a definite male figure, born of a woman's womb and married, with a beard and martial temper, eating and resting—he was in consequence and de facto encroaching on the rights of his family.

1. He was withdrawing his spouse from the seat of command, thus depriving her of her social rights (according to the Sumerian laws and customs, where a couple was always reigning over a city). And indeed, we know that Enlil, before the nuking of Palestine, had abandoned his wife, the goddess Ninlil, for a long span of time—thus prefiguring his forceful erasing of the Great Goddess Asherah from any oral or written account.

2. By never mentioning his mother, he erased her memory from the minds of "his people." Furthermore, he went as far as destroying his own city Jerusalem when the dwellers (who were now his "possession") still honored a mother-goddess.

3. He did the same for his first lover—his full sister Ninmah, also called Goddess (Nin) of Life (Ti), Ninti, mother of his firstborn Ninurta, his Chief Warrior—and for his probable concubines, as was the Anunnaki custom, transferred to the patriarchs. Thus Ninti, who got this name after she created the first men and women, is definitely the "Life" of the Gnostic texts.

4. Consequently, he deprived his own children of any recognition by his "Chosen People"—especially his *legal heir Nannar*. This will lead to the obliteration of the family of the deity of the Book, and of the Anunnaki "who came down to Earth" by the three religions of the Book.

5. Now there was an even heavier consequence—one that was going to be the most damaging for the Earth-human collective psyche: it was the total blackout on the information that the Anunnaki were a race of humans and not the immaterial and ethereal beings they became (the deity of the Book and his angels), thus alleviated from all their human traits and shortcomings. The fact that it was a deliberate withholding of information on the part of the Deity in the first place—and not only on the part of the editors or narrators of the Book—is made clear by the drastic change in this respect, as we saw, from the time of Abraham being visited by his lord at his encampment in the desert, to the time of Moses on the Sinai only six hundred years later.

The Overpowering and Overwhelming Loftiness of God

The "chosen" people being regularly reprimanded, chastised, and brutally crushed—and only given commands—gives one the impression that (in monotheist religions) the Earth-human creatures are of a very low order and irremediably flawed, their mental evolution akin to that of kids. So much so that the stick seems to be the only way to have them behave properly, and nevertheless, they keep making deadly mistakes for which they are mercilessly punished. The Deity, on the other hand, is in a vastly and immensely superior position, one who is by definition the supreme good, rightful always, knowing all, wise and powerful beyond reach. His wisdom is impenetrable, his ways impossible for us to fathom. He is unerring and unflawed, forever and ever right. He is Rightness itself, and Justice itself. As I analyzed it in *DNA of the Gods,* we have here an aggregation of positive qualities in the concept of the One and Immaterial God, and an inverse aggregation of negative qualities befalling the sinful humanity.

As noted by Nathan Schwartz-Salant, professor of Jungian depth psychology and analyst, in "Patriarchy in Transformation," such aggregation of positive-only qualities in the patriarchal God-image only leaves for us humans its shadow to assume: "That is the scapegoat shadow quality of a patriarchal God-image: 'We must have done something wrong; how else can it be so bad!'" (69). For Jung in *Answer to Job,* the huge shift of consciousness operated by Job confronting his Deity (in the Book of Job) was precisely that Job saw and faced "Yahweh's dual nature," containing both the Good and the Evil (386). This is of course the type of consciousness shift that many human beings are in the process of doing; as Murray Stein, professor of Jungian studies and analyst, warns us in "Jung's Green Christ," "For modern men and women, the gleaming cathedral is smashed . . . and the God who rules over human history has proved to be dangerous and destructive" (3). Even a professor of religion and Jungian analyst such as John Dourley states, in *The Illness That We Are: A Jungian Critique of Christianity,* "theologians and their followers too often need professional and so-called secular help to recover from the consequences of their theology. . . . How can we avoid the faith that kills?" (75, 88).

Thus is stressed a completely dual world-vision, inducing schizophrenia, in which all the evil, the shortcomings, the bad deeds, and the sins are the fate of men and women. Our only way to approach the Good and the Right is to follow the orders to the letter—but even that will just give us a "good boy" ticket.

Let's note in passing that a being supposedly divine who gives only orders and commands and gets into fits of blind rage, reveals an individual and hot-tempered psyche, and not an immaterial spirit. In contrast, the laws of nature and the harmonic realm of the Tao set resonances and constraints, without any need for worded commands.

Now we have to put this picture in a very particular setting, since we are supposed to have an irrepressible flaw: the original sin instantiated by Eve and Adam and transmitted to the whole species. So that everything put together, not only are we flawed, but there's no possibility of being redeemed—unless at the end of time. (Hence the necessary addition of the Book of Revelations, to bring an ending to the "Sin and Fall" epoch, which could be considered, if eternal, a poor act of Creation.)

Ours is the absolute other side of the coin—forever flawed, forever erring, our human condition being one of necessary shortcomings, unavoidable feebleness, errors, and sins—our only salvation being absolute obedience.

Did we, as Christians, finally escape the original sin? The Son of God is said to have come to Earth to take on himself "all the sins of the world" and to redeem us all—and yet the Inquisition thought it was its multicentury mission to keep chastising and punishing Eve's feminine descent and all "disobedient" free thinkers, thus belying the god of love in two respects—one because we earthlings were obviously not redeemed enough by his sacrifice, and the second because he presented himself as a teacher of love and compassion.

In the last few years of his life, Pope John Paul II offered some formal excuses for the abominable deeds of the Inquisition—and he did so in several countries who had been shamelessly oppressed—such as the state of Goa in India, and in Latin America. The Inquisition's cruel modes of oppression and appalling torture to render the populations subservient, as well as its too obvious tactics to confiscate the sinners' riches, were not only used vehemently in Europe (especially Spain, France, and Germany), but in the Spanish colonies (Mexico, Peru, Colombia) and Portuguese colonies (Goa, Brazil, Angola, Guinea).

However, no excuses were ever voiced (to my knowledge) for the specific perversity of the Inquisition against women—a deed all the more unjust given that all women are potential mothers—without whom the males wouldn't have been born in the first place. So does that birth-giving aptitude count for an original sin? Shouldn't it count instead for an *original blessing?*—the blessing of Life?

Let's remember Peter in the Gospel of Mary (Magdalene), who disliked women so much that he doubted Christ had given a secret initiatic teaching to the Magdalene.

> Levi answered and said to Peter, "Peter you have always been hot tempered. *Now I see you contending against the woman like the adversaries.* But if the Savior made her worthy, who are you indeed to reject her? Surely the Savior knows her very well. That is why He loved her more than us. Rather let us be ashamed and put on the perfect Man, and separate as He commanded us and preach the gospel, *not laying down any other rule or other law beyond what the Savior said"* [emphasis is mine].

The last sentence was definitely not the kind of dogma an institutionalized religion could take as its own!

Christ was definitely a force of love and compassion. How the worst crimes against humanity were accomplished in the name of the God of Love is difficult to fathom—not only wars but genocides of whole people and groups (the Cathars, the Infidels, the Indians in Central and South Americas, the Templar Knights, the Nestorians . . .), thus making it the most despotic and bloody religion in history, widely surpassing the Aztec one.

What gave the Inquisition Church this immense and insane hubris—to think they had a power of life and death over the people, over their people? That the people didn't have to think, but rather just to obey and follow whatever axioms they had decided (at that time in history) were the only "Truth"? The very dogma that they would swap for other dogmas a few centuries later?

Thus, in the religions of the Book, while god made us in his image and likeness, we were notwithstanding certainly a very bad and flawed such image . . . unless the blueprint was itself blurred.

It's only with this in-depth study of the Anunnaki that I understood what Carl Jung had hinted at, when he deemed that the evil was right at the beginning of the creation of humanity, and he held the creator responsible for it, rather than his creatures. Our ancestors who gave us the fantastic gift of life, with their own DNA (the genetic engineering doesn't make us different from their own children) were simply like us, a creative mixing of optimal and less than favorable potentials that could be developed and explored. The confusion, then, could have its sole source in our flawed concept of god (and what we project on this god-image, as argued by Carl Jung and Edward Edinger)—a concept that the Anunnaki (who worshipped no gods) had themselves bypassed and swapped for a more scientific understanding of the sprouting of exuberant life and intelligent civilizations in a universe pervaded by a mysterious cosmic consciousness.

It was only in the late fourth and early fifth centuries, with Augustine, bishop of Hippo, that most Christian bishops and Jewish biblical scholars rallied to his radically new view, "that death came upon the human race to punish Adam's sin" (Pagels, *Adam, Eve and the Serpent,* 131, 125). Even his opponent Pelagius (after John Chrysostom) argued that "Universal mortality cannot be the result of Adam's punishment, since God, being just . . . [He] would not condemn the whole human race for one man's transgression." Augustine gathered the new church around him; Pelagius was excommunicated. And death on our planet was again due to our sins (even that of the plants and animals!). But before that, the Gnostics had held that the forces of creation, the first Principles in the pleroma (the divine realm), had been encompassing all—both good and evil. Not only the Father-Mother was thus, but also the Logos/Christ and the Sophia/Wisdom who, in the Gnostic text Thunder, Perfect Mind, chants her inner totality:

I am the first and the last.

I am the honored one and the scorned one.

I am the whore and the holy one. . . .

I am knowledge and ignorance. . . .

I am foolish and I am wise. . . .

I am the one whom they called life [Eve] and you have called Death. . . .

The Psychological Impact of the Humans-versus-God Irreducible Polarity

The first point to consider, in a psychological understanding of our relation to god, is the fact that humanity has been fully relegated to only one end of the polar rod: that of the flaw, the sin, the feebleness—thus creating a duality good-evil. By positing that God was ethereal and above humans, another split was set—a duality spirit-matter. Man, said the Deity of the book "was just flesh" (and no soul); matter and the body became the object of rejection, loathing, sin, and shame.

In *DNA of the Gods,* I have dealt with the repression of sexuality (and the derived harassment of women) in monotheist religions, whereas anthropological data shows that the more ancient the culture, the more sacred was sexuality as such and the generation of life. Only the secret paths of Alchemy and Hermetism hinted at a continuous spiritualization of all matter, through the incarnation of souls in bodies—and even as the overall aim of this incarnation and of the materialized world. The future of Earth and humanity was thus a spiritualized material world, harmonized with the spirit and thus transmuted.

This is the meaning of the vision of a *Green Christ on the Cross* that Jung had, when suddenly awakened from his sleep, in 1939. The green gold of the Christic body referred to one alchemical stage, that of the Green Lion (green lapis, or stone), thought to be a universal medicine. This is a first state of the philosopher's stone, anterior to the red lapis that will be produced by the alchemical marriage of the King and the Queen (harmonization of the feminine and the masculine principles) generating *the Son* (Hermes, Christ) precisely. (See plate 11.)

In the alchemical drawing in figure 2.1, showing the crowned Green-Gold Lion stage, the alchemists, as a couple, work together for their reunification through the Mystical Marriage—both shown in their Selves and involved in the Great Work as Hermes/Mind/Christ

Fig. 2.1. The crowned Green lion, first stage of the philosopher's stone, showing Hermes/Christ and Sophia/Wisdom involved in the Great Work.

and Sophia/Wisdom—as the Fifth Key of the Twelve Keys of Basil Valentine.

Jung, recounting his experience in his *Memoirs*, explains that "the green gold is the living quality which the alchemists saw not only in man but also in inorganic nature. It is an expression of the life-spirit, the *anima mundi* . . . who animates the whole cosmos"; (*anima* in Latin, as *psyche* in Greek, means "soul," thus the world soul, or Earth's spirit, the planetary psyche) (210–11). No wonder then that such a reunification with the soul/force of life and nature works as a universal healing process! Says Murray Stein about this spirit of the earth, "It was the perennial concern of the alchemists to redeem this spirit, to bring it to consciousness and to hold it there" (in "Jung's Green Christ: A Healing Symbol for Christianity," 10). Stein remarks about Jung's own analysis of his vision, "The psychic image is interpreted as a healing symbol for the most central split within the Christian tradition, that between spirit and matter."

We have to note that, despite the projected omniscience of the deities of all religions, *no parole of a god ever offers a sound understanding of humanity's evolution, the process itself*—whether in knowledge or in ethics. Each god, in all religions, states laws and rituals, formulas and taboos, as if the societies were never going to evolve, as if they were forever going to reign as deities, even though religions never ceased to rise and disappear, and societies to transform themselves. Now, we can ponder this unbelievable shortsightedness and dire lack of comprehension of the dynamics of life and of societies, not to mention wisdom, on the part of supposedly omniscient gods.

How can an Indian shaman receive the signs of his gods and read them through the flights of wild birds when he lives in a megalopolis like São Paulo or Mexico City? Surely, he will transform and adapt his connection to the Spirit. This is, in fact, a crucial point to mull over, because in many instances, the dogmas and rituals imposed on his people by a god were clearly imbedded in a specific society, in a specific land, and in a specific time frame.

It's as if every possible thing was done to keep the humans in a position of constant culpability, in fear of committing a sin, in fear also of the wrath of god. And it seems it's exactly the same psychological impact that the religion in the Middle Ages was exerting on people. As Freud described it, our self-culpability and our repressing superego (the internalized image of the wrathful father) are running deep in our unconscious. In some instances, neuroses and serious physical ailments can just be due to these forces of culpability "punishing" us—an internalization of the punishing god that leads to self-punishing.

And at the same time, god was idealized to such an extent that the other end of the rod appeared forever unreachable.

As the religions of the Book took over the role of god in issuing commands and asking for blind obedience, the polar opposites of Good versus Evil became more and more extreme in their opposition. Yet the underlying assumptions are still the same as at the time of the Anunnaki: the good being the very dogmas of one's own religion—while the evil is anything that differs.

In such systems of dogmas, we find no curiosity leading to knowledge and creativity, no open-mindedness toward different cultures, no under-standing of one's own blinkers, of one's own presuppositions—and first and foremost, no questioning of one's own rightfulness, of one's own credos and axioms.

As it is, the positive commandments (such as help your brother or help the widow) are only thought to be applicable within one's own orthodox faith group, effective only among faith-brothers. It is under-stood that it is not only lawful, but rightful, to steal, trick, or even kill people who don't belong to one's faith-group—the infidels, the enemy country, the "not-us." And even among the same faith-brothers, it is acceptable to oppress and persecute the ones who think differently, who are more intelligent than the crowd and don't want to live in teth-ers and blindfolded—such as the alchemists, the Cathars, the humble and pauper monks, such as the Franciscans, whose harassment by the Catholic pope was well analyzed by Umberto Eco in *The Name of the Rose*.

Yet, we understand now that these original minds are the Cultural Creatives and the ones on a personal quest, the very people who will create a different future for humanity as a whole.

The least we can say is that it's a miracle that we became more intelligent and able to see at last how unfounded and versatile were the concepts of good and evil. That we turned toward an understanding of the irrepressible one-sidedness of each person's viewpoint, of each faith-group's world-vision. That we finally got the message home that "truth" was intrinsically multifaceted and plural, and moreover complex, so that consequently we had to take it as highly relative (to a context, a time, a psychological state). That the best we could do in that respect was to develop our capacities of empathy, of divergent thinking, and cre-ative and flexible mental processes. That the values we should pursue in order to get out of dire ego-centeredness and infantilism (whether as individuals or groups) were those of cooperation, empathy, synergy, negotiation, and looking ahead.

Indeed, it's a miracle that we were able to develop a third force beyond the good-evil polarity *despite the religious commands and educations*—that of *science,* questioning, posing only hypotheses, and putting to the test what is reality. Strict religious dogmas can only aggravate the split between good and evil, between god and humanity, between us versus others. And in doing so, it can only deepen an underlying schizophrenia, and the inner strife between the conscious (full of beliefs and preconceptions) and the unconscious (as reservoir of abundant, creative, and plural life forces). These life forces are those of vitality, creativity, discovery, passion, art, sexuality, and love—the very forces that the Middle Ages church who instigated the Inquisition considered absolutely evil, imagining incarnate devils able to possess the feeble women (and especially the women), who had to be plucked out like bad weeds. One thing is sure, the strict dogmas about a monotheist figure of extreme good and absolute knowledge could only aggravate the internalized split of the psyche and its schizophrenia.

It is fortunate that, as Carl Jung has shown it, the alive spirit of ancient cultures is still running deep into our psyches; that forces of life, of giving meaning, of creativity, innovation, art, and love would continually break through the embankments; that our Self, the real alive divine Spirit that dwells inside each person, would give us dreams and visions and open a path of exploration for us.

If We Had Known

Consider what would have been if we had known that god was not alone (as a person), but that the ancient gods, the ones who created Eve and Adam, were a race of humans—more knowledgeable and more powerful, yet exhibiting the same passions, cravings, and shortcomings? That our original gods had a psychology akin to ours—despite the fact they were overwhelming in their power, their knowledge and science, and their immortality.

Say we had kept the knowledge we had of them at the time of Sumer, when we knew them by name and were able to see them flying off in their "birds" and instigating violent and extensive wars and bitter conflicts between siblings just for the sake of supremacy. We would have remembered, along the generations, that we were always the ones to be crushed at the end—no matter what, the immortals would be untouched, only their abodes destroyed; we earthlings, in dire contrast, would die by the thousands "in piles" for their fratricide wars or crazy decisions; and, to keep these memories alive, we would be left writing laments and poems for our descendants—such as this one, which named the authors of the nuclear catastrophe that obliterated five cities in the Sinai and Jordan plains, and described how the radioactive cloud, "the evil wind," eradicated all life in Sumer:

> The Evil Wind "covered the land as a cloak, spread over it like a sheet . . . an Evil Wind which overwhelms the land; . . . a great storm directed from Anu . . . it hath come from the heart of Enlil . . . like the bitter venom of the gods . . . bearing gloom from city to city." (*Wars,* 337)

We would have understood and kept in mind that some of them gave us knowledge and scientific tools, especially cognitive tools—that we were, in terms of minds, as sophisticated as them in our potentials. That only the education, archives, data, and machines made an actual difference, but that we could and would get there, and swiftly.

Would we earthlings, as mortals reproducing much more rapidly, become a challenge or even displeasure for the Anunnaki? We have historical and biblical ground to state that Enlil perceived us as a threat to his well-being when he found out that Eve had tasted the fruit of knowledge: "The Adam has become as one of us!" (That is, apart from their genes of immortality!) Then, fearing that we would, one day, become immortal, he expels us from a too close cohabitation in the Edin; tries to force us back to the ground state of the lulus—slaves meant to toil and women subjected to painful birth-giving; and forces us into the fate and the role the Assembly of the Gods had conceived and decreed about earthlings. In the Sumerian tablets, we have clear evidence that some (at least) Anunnaki could become jealous of the "created" earthlings—and go as far as to plan and order our annihilation as a species. Or else could find ways to make us more feeble, to shake our growing power and sow disorder and dissent in our communities and cultures. As explains Ziusudra (also known as "Atra-Hasis" or "Exceedingly Wise"), asking for the help of Ea/Enki, when Enlil had unleashed a pandemic:

> Ea, O Lord, Mankind groans;
> The anger of the [other] gods consumes the land,
> Yet it is you who hast created us! (*Wars*, 391)

A perfect example is the Tower of Babel—the *Esagil* temple in the town Babili (Babylon), the territory of Marduk in Sumer. He had built a facility whose roof could be an independent spaceport, "a tower whose head shall reach to the heavens," and founded there a community where he "[induced] small and great to mingle on the mound." Given there was only one Anunnaki couple (and their very close family) in each temple-abode, we may infer that the "small" people were mostly Earth-humans, compared to the "great" Anunnaki. And it meant, no less, that *earthlings were granted equality with the Anunnaki, access to their knowledge, and a very close and regular contact with them* (instead of the customary contacts via priests and kings). The response of the One in Command was rather brutish and consigned in a Sumerian tablet (Text K-3657*).

> To their stronghold tower, in the night, a complete end he [Enlil] made. . . . To scatter abroad was his decision. He gave a command their counsels [languages] to confuse.

The tablet thus traces, just as the Book, the many languages on Earth to one decision. It also states clearly the reason for the angry reaction of Enlil: equality and brotherhood were not in the order of the

---

*Text K-3657, from Ashurbanipal's library in Nineveh, written in Akkadian, first translated by George Smith. Also: *Wars*, 199.

day; it was, in the eyes of Enlil, no less than a sin calling for the death penalty, a grave corruption:

> The people in Babylon [Marduk] corrupted to sin
> [inducing] small and great to mingle on the mound.

Earthlings Belonging to a Land and Its Lord

As Sitchin has shown masterfully in his *Wars of Gods and Men,* as soon as the earthlings had multiplied enough to reach great numbers, they were enrolled to act as warriors in the repeated wars the Anunnaki fought among themselves—brother against brother, in the first three generations after Anu (such as the bloodline: Anu, Enlil, Nannar, Inanna).

All through the Sumerian history, and apart from Africa, the lands are divided by a decree of the Assembly and allotted to members of the royal family. And it seems there was a tacit law that governed the relationship between earthlings and the gods: whatever earthling population was on site, this people belonged to the master of the land. This was the case even when, early on, the earthlings were given kingship—that is, the city was governed by an intermediary to the Anunnaki, a king supposedly nearer to the humans but who, nevertheless, was generally born of mixed Anunnaki and earthling parents. In parallel, a priesthood (similarly of mixed parentage) was also instituted in the diverse abodes of the gods (the king often being the High Priest)—and each line of priests was heading the temple of the specific god of the city, thus starting diverse cults.

Interestingly, we have also traces in the Book of this kind of possession of both a land and its inhabitants by the god residing and reigning there. The biblical scholar and Jungian analyst Rivkah Kluger, in her book *Psyche in Scripture,* researched the concept of the "Chosen People," based on the biblical use and significations of the terms. Astonishingly, her conclusion confirms what I had assumed on the basis of the Sumerian tablets, namely that in this ancient land of the Anunnaki, the people born in a city were perforce the devotees of the god of that city and land. They definitely *belonged* to that god, and in the event another god or goddess would get this city and land as an inheritance, then the people would be bound to serve and worship them. Let's see Kluger's analysis of "the key passage" of the "revelation of the choosing." (Note that the chosen tribe is referred to by its patriarch Jacob; *Jacob, Judah,* and *Israel* then stand for the people of Israel, the whole tribe.) It goes: "The Lord your God has chosen [*bachar*] you to be a people *for his own possession* [*le'am segulah*] (Deut. 7:6-8)" (Kluger 14, italics and brackets in her text).

Rivkah Kluger then confirms her analysis: "*Segulah* means possession. The Babylonian *sugullu* originally relates to herds. . . . It means the belonging of a property to its owner. In Ecclesiastes 2:8 *segulah* is the king's treasure. . . . In Psalm 135:4 *segulah* is God's possession and occurs in connection with *bachar:* 'For the Lord has chosen Jacob for himself, Israel as his own possession.'" According to Kluger, three other terms are used "for the divine possession." One is *nachala* ("ownership of land . . . through inheritance"), *chelek* ("portion"), and *chevel* ("the allotted"). Two sentences are very explicit: "For the Lord's portion [*chelek*] is his people, Jacob his allotted heritage [*chevel nachalato*]"; "And the Lord will inherit [*nachal*] Judah as his portion [*chelko*] in the holy land. . . ." (Kluger 15, italics and brackets in her text).

The connection with Babylonian language (whereas the mother tongue of Hebrew is Akkadian), and Kluger's linguistic analysis, reveal, at the very least, another strong connection between the deity of the Book and the lords gods of Sumer who, as time went by, were allotted by the Assembly different regions or cities to build their temple-abode.

Compare with the concept of God (as The One) possessing all in Hermes Trismegistus texts, referring to the fact that It, The One, the quintessence, is both unmanifested and manifested in everything that it has created, or may create. (See plate 12.) Note Hermes asking The One, in essence: Should I contemplate you as being One with my spirit, with all of me, with all-that-is; or as being a mysterious unmanifested essence, The One beyond all-that-is? In this Hermetic or nonduality sense, "possessing all" means being all and infusing all with its own essence—something very remote from a personal deity asking to be obeyed and worshipped in an exclusive way.

There are no other beings, all is within you, all comes from you, you give all and receive nothing; *because you possess all and there's nothing that doesn't belong to you.* . . . How shall I praise you? As belonging to me and having something in common with me, or as being other?*

In the Hermetic thought, as in the Advaita philosophy of India, the concept of Oneness, The One, is totally remote from any embodied person, and is a cosmic consciousness. As Oneness, cosmic consciousness is the Tao and brahman of Eastern religions. It is more akin to a hyperdimension existing in all particles, beings, and things in the universe, while also existing as a whole on its own hyperdimensional level, as nonmaterial, beyond space and time—as I posit it in *Cosmic DNA at the Origin.*

To get back to the realm of Sumer and Akkad, in later and more troubled times, the king of a city could try to propitiate several gods by having smaller temples dedicated to them within its walls, while maintaining the preeminence of the temple (and cult) of the original god whose city it was. The kings may have been inspired by Marduk, who had prepared small temples for all the other gods—on the condition that they honor him as the First among the Gods, which of course, apart from the initial Assembly decree, they never really did. This custom is still visible in India where, even in a sacred town of Shiva, with numerous Shiva temples, such as Omkareshvar, there are smaller temples dedicated to other gods of the Hindu pantheon.

The Anunnaki became fatefully angered when their temples were defiled, and even when their own cults were not performed correctly in their own fiefs and temples. They were enraged to the point of bringing

---

*My English translation of Ménard's French translation of the Corpus Hermeticum, *Hermès Trismégiste,* 1977. (Livre I, 5, 40): "Il n'existe pas d'autres êtres, tout est en toi, tout vient de toi, tu donnes tout et ne reçois rien; *car tu possèdes tout et il n'y a rien qui ne t'appartienne.* . . . Comment te louerai-je? comme m'appartenant et ayant quelque chose en propre, ou comme étant un autre?" (See also Mead's English translation of this text called "The Cup or Monad," book 1 of the Corpus Hermeticum, available at www.gnosis.org/library/grs-mead/TGH-v2/th209.html.)

destruction on their own temples and their own town and population of followers—something very hard for us to understand. Thus, in the middle of the sixth century BCE (while Marduk's era as the Chief of the Gods had started around 2000 BCE), the High Priestess of Ur, a city desolated since her god Nannar/Sin had deserted his defiled temple, brokered a deal with the god Sin. The agreement was that the priestess's son Nabunaid (normally, given his name, a follower of Nabu and Marduk) would become the king of Babylonia, on the condition that he rebuild Nannar/Sin's temple in Ur. And it happened that way.

But Nabunaid overshot the deal by erecting a statue to Sin just at the gate of Marduk's temple in Babylon, and then he upset the New Year festival's sacred rituals honoring Marduk: "He set an heretical statue upon a base . . . he called its name 'the god Sin.' . . . He confounded the rites and upset the ordinances" (*Wars*, 21). Marduk, despite the fact that he had erected small temples to several other gods in Babylon, got so incensed against Nabunaid that he decided to search for a new king and chose Cyrus who had just been enthroned in Anshan in 549 BCE (in Media, at the beginning of the Achaemenid Persian Empire founded by Hakkam-Anish) and who was at the time fighting the Greeks. Marduk "pronounced [Cyrus] name to be ruler of all the lands," and then "ordered him to march against his own city Babylon. He made him . . . set out on the road to Babylon, going at his side like a real friend." Then Cyrus "held the hands of Bel (The Lord) Marduk in Babylon's sacred precinct" (*Wars*, 21). Let's note that for the consecration of Sin's repaired temple in Ur, the High Priestess and her son received the visit of the god Sin and his wife who came on a Flying Chariot or Bird. This was, according to Sitchin, one of the two last physical appearances of an Anunnaki to earthlings, the other one being Marduk riding with Cyrus toward Babylon and putting him on the throne.

Cyrus's son Cambyses performed the rites honoring Marduk in Babylon and, after his father died, became a Pharaoh in Egypt (525 BCE), albeit respecting its particular pantheon. Cyrus brought all the ancient empires (apart from Egypt) under the banner of one god: *Ahura-Mazda*, god of Light—the whole of Mesopotamia (Babylonia, Sumer, Akkad,

Fig. 2.2. Ahura-Mazda, as Winged Disk of Nibiru, above the Tree of Life, and guarded by two Eaglemen (Guimet Museum Catalog, public domain).

Assyria) and then Elam, Media, Hittite and Greek lands, Phoenicia, Canaan, and Philistia.

Ahura-Mazda's emblem was the Winged Disk, with a bearded god inside the disk, where we can perceive the structure of the ancient emblem of the "Planet Crossing," that is, Nibiru (see fig. 2.2). Below this sign of the Crossing—represented as a cross with the upper vertical branch replaced by a crown—are two scepters with bulbous ends that resemble the Eye of Horus in Egypt.

But Cyrus must have been, like Marduk, reverential toward the other gods reigning in other lands. Thus, in Jerusalem, he had the Temple of Jerusalem rebuilt. This rebuilding of the temple had been granted by the deity of the Book who had accursed it in the first place, calling the Babylonian King Nebuchadnezzar "my servant" and "the arm of my wrath" against Jerusalem, after he had him smite the temples and gods of Egypt. The deity thus ordered (referring to the king his servant):

He shall smite the land of Egypt, and deliver such as are for death to death, and such as are for captivity to captivity . . . and he will break the obelisks of Heliopolis . . . the houses of the gods of Egypt shall he burn with fire. (*Wars*, 20)

So that, while Nebuchadnezzar (King of Babylon) had been ordered by Marduk to march on Lebanon (abandoned by its own sovereign god), the deity of the Book (through his prophet Jeremiah) sided with Babylon—his arch-enemy in past history—to bring doom on Jerusalem for seventy years, because some dwellers were praying to the "Queen of Heaven." "Mine anger and my fury shall be poured upon this place . . . and it shall burn and shall not be quenched. . . . In the city on which my name has been called, the doom will I begin" (*Wars*, 20). Thus, in 586 BCE, on the order of the deity of the Book, Nebuchadnezzar and his Chaldean army burnt the first Temple of Jerusalem "the House of Yahweh" and destroyed all the houses and the surrounding walls of the city. The curse of the demise of Jerusalem issued by the deity of the Book had been ordered to last seventy years.

✦ 3 ✦

Who Really Was the God of Heaven and Earth?

IT MUST HAVE BEEN a hard blow for Enki, the firstborn of King Anu, when his father drew lots and the command of Earth was attributed to his younger brother Enlil. As he had already been supplanted as heir of Nibiru's kingship by the same, he could have hoped to get at least the kingship of Earth. It would have compensated for the loss as well as for all the work he had already done on Earth for 28,800 years (eight shars)—creating the first city (Eridu), engineering irrigation works, retrieving gold from water and later settling the mining facility, then sending the first collected gold back to his home planet—a work only he could have done given his scientific and technological background. During all this time, Enki is the Lord of Earth (En = lord, Ki = earth) and the Commander in Chief of the Anunnaki. They are pioneers, conditions are very hard at the beginning; they have to catch fish, hunt, and pluck wild fruits for food, and construct encampments, of which the first one on the Gulf will become Enki's city Eridu. In the Abzu, they refine the gold and melt it into ingots for making the best of the space and weight requirements on the spacecraft. One such ingot has been unearthed in Mesopotamia and they are represented on several cylinder seals. They look like a large hourglass, with a vertical hole in its central line, so as to insert a stick to carry them.

But instead of being thanked, Enki has to bear that the youngster, self-centered and scientifically untrained Enlil, grabs also the command of Earth and the territory of Sumer, while he is given Africa and the command of mining there. Of course, later on, Africa will turn out to be the safe haven to conduct the genetic experiments, and the civilization he will be able to establish in Egypt will be a masterful achievement.

So it turned out that Anu, by drawing lots, got exactly what he wanted: remaining the King of Heaven, and Enki was given Africa (the Abzu) as territory and supervising the gold mining, as he had been doing all along. We have also to remark that Anu, politically savvy, had gotten rid of his two possible contenders for Nibiru's throne, his two sons, by sending both of them to Earth, and he certainly had to give Enlil a supreme title on Earth in order to lure him there. The least we can say is that Anu, having grabbed the title of King of Nibiru (King of Heaven) by vanquishing the previous king, Alalu, had firsthand knowledge about how a title could be snatched from a king, especially when he gets older.

Yet, in the historical records we have, the Anunnaki parents' authority will be challenged only by the next two generations, with Enki's son Nergal, and even more so, with the granddaughter of Enlil, Inanna. In his own generation, Enki can only play the obedient son; yet, all along, he pursues his own objectives and shrewdly finds ways to get around the line of command of Enlil, Anu, and the Assembly—especially when they are making the gravest mistakes.

Enlil Gets the Title and a Swollen Head

There must have been a large age difference between the two half brothers, because Enki, back on Nibiru, when he was called Ea and was married to Damkina (Ninki), the daughter of Alalu, already had two adolescent children. Marduk will come to Earth early on, as the commander of a contingent of fifty; these will become the Igigi, or astronauts, based on Mars and on an orbiting space station, and probably on the moon. In contrast, Enlil was not yet married when he landed on

Earth; back on Nibiru he had had a scandalous love relationship with his own full sister Ninmah, whom, by Nibirian laws, he couldn't marry, but with whom he engendered Ninurta. In this instance, Ninmah was sentenced to never get married. We know that Ninmah was madly in love with him, writing passionate poems on their lovemaking.

Ninurta will become the second in command of Enlil, the chief of his armies, a war engineer of great talent. Too obedient to attain a global and visionary outlook that could have helped minimize Enlil's injudicious overreactions and unwise decisions, his fate will be to carry out the orders of his father and/or of the Assembly, often against his own better judgment. He will not develop, as Enki did, sophisticated and shrewd strategies to achieve one's aims while apparently complying with the voted decisions (generally supporting Enlil's aims) whenever they appeared to be extremely dangerous and unwise.

If Ninmah was madly in love with Enlil, the reverse did not seem to be the case. At no point do we see Enlil express any kind of feeling—positive that is. He seems the ultimate despot, exclusively self-centered. But while Nergal is a potential despot, generally brazen, versatile, and out of balance, Enlil has a too fixated personality, unbending and unsavory—at least after his youth's excesses, and once chastised by the prospect of being sentenced to exile.

Indeed, *Enlil's first act* on Earth, while he was already Commander in Chief of the Anunnaki, that got him wide publicity, had nearly cost him his title, possession and all. He raped an adolescent Anunnaki, one of the students of Ninmah, luring her to go sailing and engaging her. She protested that she was still a virgin, trying to appeal to his reason and moral sense, to no avail. Arrested, Enlil was brought to trial before "fifty senior gods." Since this act is severely punished, he was sentenced to exile in the Abzu with her (*Wars,* 81). Fortunately, the biology student either took a liking to him or paled at the prospect of being the royal heir's spouse, and accepted marriage. Only then did Enlil recover his status.

After this traumatic trial and sentence, he becomes totally identified with his social role and superego (his *persona,* in Jung's terms), becoming more and more autocratic in his ruling, and a family tyrant who will never give to Ninlil the prominence other royal spouses had. Even worse, he will abandon her for a very long time, then erase her from all history when adopting the sole-god worldview. More to the point, he will shift to a haughty and ultramoralistic persona, incorporating the role of the god of justice, whose anger (the *Ira Dei* of the Romans), punishments, and accursations, as well as his detestable habit of bending the arms of the other gods in their Assembly, will be greatly feared.

This was, for example, the case when he literally used his power as Commander of Earth to impose on all the assembled Anunnaki his command to keep a total blackout on the coming catastrophe, the Deluge, and thus force on them his blinkered decree that humanity be totally erased.

Ira Dei versus Ananda (Bliss)

Here we have to make a digression on what was supposed to be the role of the King of Heaven and Earth—Enlil's title. Anu's title was King of Heaven, whereas King of *Earth* was added to Enlil's title. This is why I surmise that the Sumerian term for heaven, *An,* meant something like "lofty home planet" or "magnificent haven" and not at all heaven as opposed to Earth as the term came to be understood in religious texts. So, *An*u was the king of the planet An/Heaven, and Enlil got the first part of his title as legal heir of Anu. Since the royalty on Nibiru had precedence on its colonies, the whole of Earth and our whole solar system were only a part of the Kingdom of Nibiru.

But what does being King of Nibiru/Heaven entail? Governing and reigning, having the maximum weight in the decisions of the Assembly, the privilege of putting out decrees (which Enlil will tend to overuse), the privilege of having two spouses and many concubines as Anu had. If we look at it matter-of-factly, what more is there that we could associate with our preconceptions about God? Beyond being venerated as our creator, the supreme deity is considered a spiritual guide, a shepherd of the souls, this signifying that the deity has, as a purpose, to lead us on a path of spiritual knowledge, of high morality, and to show us how to develop our inner force, our gifts and potentials.

What are the psychological tools used by monotheist religions? The fear of god, the fear of hell (as an eternal punishment), the awareness of the wickedness of the devil. It is asked of us to do good, to follow the commandments, to develop our virtues, and avoid falling into the traps of the devil. Above all, we are asked to serve and worship god, and be obedient to our religious instances. The accent is clearly put on Justice—in the sense that a life of virtue and prayers will make one "a Just," one who will be saved at Judgment Day, or who will ascend to heaven/paradise at the hour of personal death.

Totally different is the cognitive landscape—the mindscape—of Eastern religions: their basic assumption is that knowledge and spirituality stem from a direct inner experience of the Self, the *Atma,* and not from either virtue or adherence to a body of dogmas. Along the centuries, wise Oriental masters devised techniques of meditation to lead us to experience higher states of consciousness, namely the states of oneness or fusion states—the *samadhi* in which we become harmonized within our inner being, harmonized with nature, or one with the All, connected to cosmic consciousness (brahman, the Tao). These heightened states, posits Hinduism, are beyond duality and reflect the *advaita* (nonduality) of the Self and the Spirit dimension. The Self dimension, which I call the semantic dimension, is beyond the polar and dual classifications of the intellect, such as good versus bad, me versus you, believer versus nonbeliever; moreover the Self is beyond our classifications of space, time, and causality. As says Jung, in his book *Synchronicity,* about the experiments of J. B. Rhine on psi phenomena (such as telepathy or clairvoyance), which exemplify the working of consciousness and psychic energy (even if in rare and extreme instances):

> Even more remarkable is the fact that *time* is not in principle a prohibiting factor [for psi]. . . . The time factor seems to have been eliminated by a psychic function or psychic condition which is also capable of abolishing the spatial factor. (17, §836)

Since experience has shown that under certain conditions space and time can be reduced almost to zero, causality disappears along with them, because causality is bound up with the existence of space and time and physical changes. (29, §855)

So, *what are the psychological tools used by Eastern religions* to incite us to get on a quest and achieve our inner harmonization? Hinduism is clearly putting the accent on bliss—*ananda*—as the state of consciousness arising from a pacified mind able to behold and contemplate the oneness in All That Is. The states of samadhi open, for us all, a source of knowledge about consciousness and the Self (the soul), a source of wisdom, and the awakening of the many potentials and talents of the Self, namely the *siddhis,* or psi capacities.

This outlook is shared by the third century CE Neoplatonic philosopher Plotinus in his major book *The Enneads.* Plotinus was attributing to the state of oneness the precedence over intuition and to intuition the precedence over reason. He stated that reason would be greatly enhanced if it was "contemplating intuition" (meaning working in symbiosis with intuition) and intuition would itself be enhanced whenever it could contemplate the Oneness of All.

In Eastern religions, bliss, not fear, is the light on the way, illuminating the quester and opening a path of greater self-knowledge. Evil, in Hinduism, is only the product of ignorance, at least as goes the principle. Note, though, that Hindu gods were nevertheless at war with devils (the *asuras*) in the *Mahabharata.* The Eastern religions advise practicing meditation and techniques of self-development in order to harmonize one's own ego with one's own Self or soul (Atman) and awaken spiritual talents (the siddhis). Then the Self, being a dimension of higher consciousness, is naturally connected with cosmic consciousness. Thus the same energy of consciousness (semantic or syg energy) is infusing the universe and is the flame in our soul or Self, the dimension of the Spirit in us. This path of Self-awakening is joyful, filled with light and peace, blissful in the highest states of oneness; along the way, the awakening of the chakras, psychic energy centers, and the blossoming of psychic or psi talents (the siddhis) are a natural process.

On this path of self-exploration, which any person can open and complete in the course of one life, our supreme guide is our own inner Self because the Self is itself of the same stuff as cosmic consciousness—part of it. In this mindscape, the reward is the light and the bliss the quester experiences along the way, so that the quest itself is self-rewarding. The inner fusion with one's Self can open states of fusion or harmony with others and in a whole group, not only in meditation and concentration (during concerts or group prayer), but also in active trance (such as jam sessions, trance-dance, shamanic rituals, etc.). In *The Sacred Network,* I have presented a rich gamut of objective group experiences, calling them *tel*epathic-*har*monic or "telhar" fields.

This path is also what Carl Jung has developed in psychological terms as the *individuation process.* The Self in each person is in permanent contact and synergy with the collective unconscious, and thus every Self is somehow connected through it. This is also what I have postulated with the "semantic dimension," which is the dimension of the energy of consciousness, or more precisely the dimension of *consciousness-as-energy,* a dimension that encompasses both the collective unconscious and the collective conscious—developed in my book *La Prédiction de Jung* (Jung's Prediction). In my recent research on cosmology, *Cosmic DNA at the Origin,* I have postulated that the energy of consciousness (syg energy) fills the universe as a hyperdimension of consciousness, a fifth dimension in which faster-than-light particles called *sygons* are able to create connections between minds, and between minds and any natural system, thus explaining how psi and a mind-over-matter influence (such as healing) may work. This hyperdimension existed at the origin (when no particles, no space-time, and no matter had formed yet), and was then a unique information field bearing the imprint of innumerable beings, bodies, and systems, as networks of frequencies—thus constituting a sort of Cosmic DNA issued from a previous universe. Then, this hyperdimension with its Cosmic DNA information, would trigger the self-actualization of our universe-bubble.

Thus no information would ever be lost: at the end of a universe cycle, all matter would be translated in hyperdimensional consciousness and information, and an hourglass double-spiral would usher in the new universe and trigger the organization of matter systems.

This is in accord with the ancient Hindu philosophy of Oneness (Advaita), that states that all the memory of what happened on Earth since the beginning, the memory of all the beings and their actions, but also of all the knowledge accumulated, is somehow imprinted in an immaterial dimension of Earth, the Akasha. Thus, nothing is ever lost, neither event, nor information, and all souls have their records in the immaterial dimension of the planet. It means that we can connect ourselves to the soul or Self of any person, whether in the present or in the past, through the Akashic dimension of the planet. Ervin Laszlo has theorized an Akashic field of a quantum nature and linked to the vacuum that would be the medium of the memory and the coherence of the universe. In a different way, Rupert Sheldrake has posited morphic fields that would not only keep the memory of all the forms (namely the forms of organisms and organs) but also guide morphogenesis, the still-mysterious differentiation of cells (issued from the original ovum) toward the elaboration of specific organs and functions.

Moreover, Jung has shown that all individuals can experience the active energy of consciousness, of their own Self—through altered states of consciousness, visions, psi phenomena, synchronicities, guiding dreams, archetypes as personal guides—and this exploration will lead them to the awakening of supraconscious talents.

From the Chief of the Gods to the Sole God

In a spiritual worldview of women and men striving to achieve their own accomplishment, the basic and sole code of morality is as clear as it is simple: Do not harm others. This could have been the moral code of the Anunnaki—who let the (Anunnaki) people express their sexuality freely and who drew the line of offence at mutual consent. This is why only rape and murder, and destroying the property (the temples) of others, were severely judged.

This, let me underline it clearly, was the state of affairs among the Anunnaki-humans (before the earthlings proliferated); they had a code of law adhered to by the Assembly of the Anunnaki on Earth, obviously stemming from Nibiru. Only later, when kingship was lowered to Earth, did the code of law became a written body of civil laws to be used by the Earth-humans. The first one was issued by the King Ur-Nammu (of the Ur III empire) in the twenty-first century BCE, the second by Lipit-Ishtar, King of Isin, in the twentieth century BCE, and then there was the famous code of Hammurabi, King of Babylon, in the nineteenth century BCE.

However, when the descendants of Adapa and Titi started to proliferate on Earth, and the great Anunnaki decided to put themselves in the position of gods in front of their populations, everything changed in their own Anunnaki society. Then competition between them occurred in a more emotionally loaded context. This conflicting situation swiftly escalated to become deadly wars between them, each Lord, or Lofty One, rallying and forcing their earthling population to constitute an army to fight against the armies of their competing siblings—the other gods, the enemy. That's also when some royals such as Nannar, Ninurta, and Inanna, will want to attain the Enlilship status, that of first among the gods on Earth, and will get it in turns. When Marduk is given the Enlilship position by the Assembly after the nuclear catastrophe, he will launch this "sole-god" revolution in Babylon, long before the one brought about by the deity of the Book. Yet, he didn't ignore the other gods altogether, for he built shrines for them within his sacred temples. Rather, he tried to reduce all the other gods to be aspects of himself, by naming them "Marduk of the attack" (Nergal), "Marduk of justice" (Shamash), and making of his name the equivalent of *Lord*. He will even rename Nibiru as *Marduk*.

Marduk was certainly a visionary and an enlightened leader, who was envisioning for humanity (Anunnaki *and* Earth-humans) a confraternal society liberated from the debilitating and war-instigating hierarchy of the Anunnaki. And he had tried to establish such a harmonious society in his temple-abode in Babylon, the Esagil—a social and spiritual innovation that was not at all to the taste of Enlil who smote their community as well as their efforts, and reduced the Tower of Babel itself to ashes. When Y. will want to promote himself to this "sole God" status, it will be in the fashion of an autocratic and terrible Mighty God, fear inspiring because immensely devastating, and he will obliterate all mention of the other gods and goddesses, his spouse first of all. After the nuclear holocaust, his name will not be Sumerian anymore (and similarly he will change Abram's Sumerian name), and he will thus draw the line of what was permissible in terms of memories and recollection of older times and other gods. The history of the fateful events was thus told and dictated within this revised framework—as we see in rare ancient pre-Hebrew, Akkadian tablets, exhibiting what I have decoded as Enlil's Moralistic Framework.

The immense problem we have inherited from this last move of Enlil, and one we are still confronted with, was that this one-god concept was not akin to instantiating oneness ("the one" who is no god) as a spiritual vision as we see it blossoming in the ancient Advaita Vedanta philosophy of India and Eastern religions, and in Hermes Trismegistus, Plotinus, and Gnosticism as well, such as in the Secret Book of John. In The Cup or Monad, Hermes (see fig. 3.1) thus expounds on the One to his son Tat:

> The Oneness being Source and Root of all, is in all things as Root and Source. Without [this] Source is naught; whereas the Source [Itself] is from naught but Itself, since It is Source of all the rest. It is Itself Its Source, since It may have no other Source.
>
> The Oneness then being Source, containeth every number, but is contained by none; engendereth every number, but is engendered by no other one.
>
> 11. . . . . And now, O Tat, God's Image hath been sketched for thee, as far as it can be; and if thou wilt attentively dwell on it and observe it with thy heart's eyes, believe me, son, thou'lt find the Path that leads above; nay, that Image shall become thy Guide itself, because the Sight [Divine] hath this peculiar [charm], it holdeth fast

*Fig. 3.1. The alchemist, as Hermes, starts the Great Work
of inner reunification, in harmony with both the feminine
(moon) and the masculine (sun).*

and draweth unto it those who succeed in opening their eyes, just as,
they say, the magnet [draweth] iron.

In these spiritual ways, individuals are free to pursue their own
spiritual quest as they please; gurus and guides had to be innovative
and in sync with their time, their zeitgeist—this was not only welcome,
but seen as a necessity for the spiritual quest to remain alive. Also, and
more important still, in Eastern religions the oneness concept is set as
an immaterial (and of course nonpersonal) spiritual energy bathing and
pervading the whole universe (brahman, the Tao, the ki, the chi)—a
dimension of consciousness that the Self can attain, grasp, and com-
prehend in heightened states, and even learn to master. This is also the
world-vision of the energy of the Eagle in the Mexican Yaqui sorcerers'
way.

These diverse frameworks, extended on the whole planet, left ample room for all the individual gods not only to be known by their names and personal histories, but also to be worshipped and revered in temples. Only, the dimension of Oneness was set to be higher than all of them and posited as both a holistic concept and an initiatic *way* (meaning practice): *in order to be understood, the reality of oneness (as a universal spirit pervading the universe) had to be experienced and explored in heightened states of consciousness.*

In the Discourse on the Eighth and Ninth, Hermes performs with Tat a chanted meditation to raise their consciousness from the high sphere of the Eight to the sphere of the Ninth, the cosmic dimension of The One. The sphere of the Ninth is represented in this alchemical drawing from the *Tractatus Aureus* as a nine-pointed star (see fig. 3.2).

Hermes and Tat then receive a vision and a *power* from the Ninth as an illumination, and Hermes, in an enraptured state, reaches the light and wisdom of Mind.

Rejoice over this! For already from them the power, which is light, is coming to us. For I see! I see indescribable depths. How shall I tell

Fig. 3.2. The dimension of The One, represented in the Tractatus Aureus *as a nine-pointed star.*

you, my son? . . . How shall I describe the universe? I am Mind, and I see another Mind, the one that moves the soul!

I see the one that moves me from pure non-thought, non-ego (forgetfulness). You give me power! I see myself! I want to speak! Fear restrains me. I have found the beginning of the power that is above all powers, the one that has no beginning. I see a fountain bubbling with life. I have said, my son, that I am Mind. I have seen! Language is not able to reveal this.*

With the Hebrew monotheism, the framework is widely different. There is no more individual quest for wisdom and inner knowledge within. The freedom and the path to find *the god within,* the light of the Spirit of the Whole, the One, as existing inside oneself, is gone. The Hindu Moksha (The Liberated One) can claim "I am That" (Tat Vam Asi), Hermes claims "I am Mind, the Christ" but in monotheist dogma there's no direct path of communion with the One. So, how did Enlil shift to a sole-god and dogmatic framework, based on blind obedience? First, we have an individual Anunnaki-human, the prince and heir of the main kingship in the solar system all right . . . but still a human among his kin and family, who decides that now he will be the only god, unknown, invisible, unnamed, and gifted with any imaginable quality you could think of, towering over his poor and sinful "creatures" and getting them to obey with not only a leash and a whip but nuclear blasts and unchecked genocidal drives.

Second, this individual proceeds with an erasing of all the historical gods of Earth, the other ones who "came down to Earth from Heaven" and that means no less than *a deliberate erasing and obliterating of our species' past and our planet's past* (including all the knowledge pertaining to it). Now we can ask ourselves the question: Is that really permissible? Who dared rob us of our species' memory? Should even a Commander of Earth be allowed to blot out from our species memory all that

*Hermes Trismegistus. The Discourse on the Eighth and Ninth. Translated by James Brashler, Peter A. Dirkse, and Douglas M. Parrott. Available at www.gnosis.org/naghamm/discorse.html.

pertained to our past? And what aim did he pursue? Only to promote himself as the sole Master, *The* creator, unique lawmaker, history maker, universe maker . . . and what else?

Is that permissible?

Did a slave master ever do that? We know that the American and European masters of the slaves (slaves abducted mainly in the ancient Dahomey and Togo regions) forcibly forbade them to practice their so-called pagan cults. Nevertheless these enslaved people found a way to practice in captivity their Voodoo rituals from their ancestral Yoruba and original cultures, by disguising them under a Christian renaming.

Is not the obliterating of our species' past definitely a crime against humanity? And the irony is that it is *a crime against two humanities*— against the Earth-humans' humanity and against the Nibirian-humans' humanity. Because in the process, the other self-promoted gods were downgraded—either to idols and enemies (if they were competitors), or to angels/emissaries (for allies and descendants). Henceforth it was forbidden to worship these idols and even to mention them, and finally they were erased from the memory of the people—despite the fact they had been raised to the status of worshipped gods by the Assembly. This decision of Enlil was thus smiting the constitutional body and its ruling power. Simultaneously blotted out was any memory of the genetic humanness of the now immaterial god. This blackout was carried on through the drastic editing of ancient Sumerian texts, and yet it left, as we have seen, many a trace showing, like a white thread in the fabric, the marks of retouching—proving such a task of remaking thousands of ancient historical accounts to be not only difficult, but impossible.

The greatest irony of all, and therefore the greatest iniquity on the part of the autocratic god, is that our real "creator gods" had made a point of teaching us our real history (including the way we were "perfected" but not "created") as well as their own Nibirian history—and this right from the time of the first civilized couple, our ancestors Adapa and Titi, naturally fathered by Enki. What historical information our real creator gods had wanted us to know from the start (the history of Earth, of Nibiru, and of our Earth-human species), did a Nibirian royal, even the one in command, have the moral and spiritual right to take it from us? Not only to hide the truth from later generations, but to forcefully erase it from all the texts, to distort and muddle all information still available, and to destroy evidence (such as competitor books)?

Our creator gods made a point of prodding the new humanity to learn writing, literature, mathematics, astronomy, and medicine. They went as far as to reveal to us "the secrets of the gods." Enki started wisdomlines to teach these Hermetic sciences and scientific academies in Eridu. Ninmah founded with Adapa a line of kings-priests in Shuruppak. Even the King of Heaven had transmitted to Adapa a "secret healing science" that he had thereafter to transmit to his descent (Adapa wrote books to that effect).

How could one of the Anunnaki royals ever decide to erase such an ancient known past and the evident reality of the other gods and their family links? When was this erasing of information committed? If it was definitive at the time of Moses, the comparison with the Sumerian texts let us infer that the erasing was de facto performed at the time the Hebrew Book was compiled, which according to several experts happened during the captivity in Babylon in the sixth century BCE.

Chief of Command on Earth? Flaws in the Line of Command

Before the hybrid beings (the lulus) attained procreative abilities and started populating Earth, the function of Enlil was as clear-cut as it was limited. Let's bear in mind the number of Anunnaki that were in the distant colony named Ki (Earth) before the Deluge. Berossus, the Babylonian priest and historian, wrote that there were six hundred Anunnaki on the ground, and three hundred Anunnaki (the Igigi) servicing the space stations—the orbiting one and the one on Mars. We are talking about a relatively small number of people whose sole aim at the beginning is to collect gold and other metals for their home planet Nibiru. Enlil's function at the time is strictly that of a Commander in Chief—a deputy executive function (similar to a governor) while the global governance function is retained by the King of Nibiru, with Nibiru remaining the center of power of the Nibirian civilization. The King of Heaven/Nibiru shares his decisional power with the Assembly of the Lords (mostly composed of the royals among the Anunnaki), which is convened for any major decision and in case of crisis. Moreover, there is an independent judicial structure: the Seven (or Nine) Judges, convened to pass judgment and return a verdict whenever a criminal situation occurs in matters of general organization, wars, or conflict.

We know that in antediluvial times Enlil's city Nippur is the Mission Control Center, one of the five cities in Sumer, organized in a geometrical design, to manage the space operations. And inside his temple-abode (the antediluvial Ekur) is the Dirga room that, as we saw, operates the Bond Heaven-Earth. Thus, Enlil has total control of the space facilities and of communication technology.

However, for now, we see only a deputy power—the governor of a colony operating under the supervision of King Anu and the Assembly.

The Personality of Enlil

The personality and deeds of Enlil are too well attested by his quoted words and precisely reported acts, in too many congruent texts including the Book, for us to have any doubt about the veracity of these texts. He definitely was the one in command of Earth and did and said what he is reported to have said and done. However, there is an abysmal gap between the pragmatic and (in Nietzsche's terms) "human, too human" side of the chief of the Anunnaki, and the absolute and abstract qualities projected unto the monotheist deity in later times. So, we will keep tracing the main events of which Enlil was a major protagonist, well described in various texts showing strong parallels. We will discover that the aims and purposes for these events, the decisions leading to them, the logic and thinking process, the behaviors and psychological antics—all that is totally at odds with our concept of a divinity. Moreover, and astonishingly, it shows even more discrepancy with the depth of spiritual knowledge and wisdom that has been developed in the diverse religions of Earth (starting with Egypt and the Indus Valley). The religions themselves prize a high level of awareness and spiritual development; Eastern religions, and Platonism and Hermetic sciences as well, expound the mastery of heightened states of consciousness through sophisticated yogic techniques of meditation and other practices—all this attests to the reality of a higher and spiritual consciousness in man, a supraconscious Self that can be developed. Having myself pursued this knowledge and this quest all my life, and having relished ancient wisdom and lore, I certainly wasn't expecting such a shocking reality. Yet my scientific and rational mind couldn't find any flaw in the accumulated data, nor in the steady and coherent psychological profiles of the Anunnaki through different texts.

Enlil's First Act:
Raping an Adolescent Girl

If Enlil's first act on Nibiru, as young prince, was the scandal of a love affair with his full sister Ninmah, his first act on Earth was an even worse sexual scandal: the rape of a young and virgin Anunnaki that got him sentenced to exile. At that point, Enlil has lost everything— his heirdom and foremost position, his abode-temple, and his life in Sumer—a very traumatic outcome for the legal heir he was. (Of course, the fact that his lover Ninmah was barred from ever marrying and his future wife was certainly traumatized for life, doesn't exist in Enlil's consciousness.) In my view as a psychologist, this trauma of losing his position, because of his sexual "sin" and transgression, could very well explain his radical shift not only to monogamy (an exception in Sumer) but to an ultramoralistic stance and a bent toward excessive punishments. I believe that he also developed, through that, a fear of women by putting on the girl the responsibility of his own lapse into violent aggression. And in that case his own semantic field bore from then on the judgments of *Woman = Temptress,* and *women are to be feared*—therefore they have to be commanded and kept at a distance. This would explain his way of never talking to Eve, apart from accursing her. Moreover, the forceful power he exerted on the adolescent girl on this occasion (who pleaded she was still a virgin) will remain as a psychological trauma and tear in their relation—making it possible for him to erase her name and worship from the novel monotheist religion.

Enlil's Second Act:
Overreaction to the Revolt in the Mines

The second act in the biography of Enlil was his overreaction to the revolt of the Anunnaki working in the mines in the Abzu, who complained about the too heavy workload put on them. Here we see Enlil wholly unable to grasp the social problem, his mind fixated instead on revenge and punishment—to the point of putting his own kingship in the balance as a bullying tactic toward his father Anu. When it does not work, he forgets all about his threat to resign.

The outcome of the crisis was a gathering of the Assembly of the Gods who voted for giving to Ninmah, the head scientist in life sciences, the mission to "perfect" a hybrid Anunnaki-hominid creature. In order to understand the two opposite stands of Enlil and Enki, which will lead to continuous strife between them, we have to keep in mind that the mission voted for by the Assembly and by Enlil was strictly pragmatic: how to come up with a being able to work for them. (This, as I have hinted at, was only the official rationale presented at the Assembly by Enki and Ninmah, not their secret long-term plans, which aimed at making of the new humanity the torch of human civilization on Earth or in this solar system, when their own would be declining or extinct.)

Enlil's Third Act:
Raiding the Abzu Facility and Abducting the Workers

The third act of Enlil is to storm, with his warrior Ninurta, the mine facility in the Abzu where the cloned lulus, the primitive workers, were already at work—the aim being to bring them back to Sumer to be their servants and workers. They attack with a novel powerful weapon able to drill and tear through walls. *The Myth of the Pickax* reports the raid, describing the new weapon as "an ax that produces power" and an "earth splitter."

In the tablets we have recovered so far, we know only of the first chain cloning of seven males and seven females. But there must have been more of them—as is attested by a carving on a rock found in the south of Elam. It shows rows of exactly similar sexless beings, and much more than fourteen; in an adjacent pavilion are seated Enki and Ninmah, with the birth goddesses—Ninmah's students. So we may surmise that a great number of lulus were taken to Sumer. Numerous depictions show them performing all kinds of hard tasks, from building, to farming, to serving the gods in their homes; they are always totally naked, like domesticated animals, like slaves. Once the lulus were in Sumer, says *The Myth of the Pickax* text:

> With picks and spades they built gods' houses,
> they built the big canal banks;
> food they grew for the sustenance of the gods.

Just the sheer number of these depictions would be enough to account for lulus in the hundreds and not in the tens. And the fact they are represented naked shows their low stage of development.

Later, when Adapa and his descendants, reared by the gods, will become the scribes and the priests, of course their beautiful garments will match that of the Anunnaki—especially given that the tailors must have been earthlings.

Enlil's Fourth Act:
Expelling and Accursing the First Couple

Adamu and Tiamat, the blueprint couple, the gene donors for the cloning, were honored in the Abzu and spared from working. It's only when they were summoned to the Edin that Enlil put them to work in his newly built orchard, to tend it. They thus lose their honorific status: they have to work and be naked—something that they sure were not when raised in the homes of Ninmah and Ninki as their children (*12th*, 337–64). Moreover, the linguistic feat of the couple expressed in the garden of Eden—the fact they were able to discuss with the deity—has greatly troubled experts of course, since the telepathy alternative is rendered impossible by the deity's own words: "Where art thou?" shouts the deity searching specifically for Adam and not finding him because Adam, on hearing his footsteps, has hidden behind a tree. But Adam then answers—because he is so near as to be within earshot—that he hid because he is afraid, because he is naked. Only then does the deity realize that an event of tantamount importance has happened—that his brother (the Snake!) again has overturned his plans.

Enlil's fourth act is his wrath when he discovers that Adamu and Tiamat are now transformed—they know they are naked, and Tiamat (alone) has covered and adorned her loins. The *Tale of Adapa* is very clear about the fact that Enki was the one to "give knowledge [and] wisdom" to Man:

> Wide understanding Enki perfected for him,
> to disclose the designs of the Earth,
> To him he gave Knowing;
> But immortality he did not give him.

These words are supremely important for us, at a moment when new evidence attests that the Neanderthal man was much more evolved (language skills, social behavior) than we had thought, and certainly *Homo erectus* (the hominid whose DNA they use) also. Note that Earth here is a conscious being and has intention and "designs." In no way should we read *designs,* given the context of wide understanding or wisdom, as some sorts of patterns. Here is a hint about the *secret science of the gods* to which some tablets and Enki's name as *Buzur* refer—the "Knower of Secrets." Thus "to disclose the designs of the Earth," means literally to give to mankind (and thus Adamu and Tiamat) the intelligence to explore nature not only scientifically but in arcane and spiritual ways, with intuition and wisdom. Just like he

Fig. 3.3. Enki (with his Anunnaki horned headdress),
exchanging words of wisdom with Tiamat on a par, as two
initiates, the Tree of Knowing between them.

Fig. 3.4. Enki
transmitting his wisdom
to an initiate, with the
double snake symbol on
him, and the Sumerian
Ankh between them.

himself was called Buzur, his aim was to perfect and fashion humanity so that they may become such Buzurs. Indeed, Adamu and Tiamat
will both become initiates, and Enki will start, beyond bloodlines,
the direct transmission of secret knowledge or wisdomlines, as I have
shown in *DNA of the Gods,* and something we see clearly in these two
Sumerian depictions. See figures 3.3 and 3.4.

✦ 4 ✦

Enlil and the Accursation of Women, of Humanity, of Earth

THE CURSES PRONOUNCED by the Deity against the First Couple and humanity at large in the garden of Eden are among the strongest and, moreover, they are meant to be everlasting. Let me give you a quick reminder of the scene and the sentences preceding the curses (analyzed in depth in *DNA of the Gods*), and how to read them in terms of the Informational Framework (IF) and the Moralistic Framework (MF).

In the Book, after Eve and Adam ate the fruit of the Tree of Knowing, the text lets out an extraordinary information (thus in IF), immediately followed by a dampening and muddling of this revelation by a moralistic explanation (MF) supposedly demonstrating their shame and their terrible sin.

> And the eyes of both of them were opened [IF]
> and they knew [IF]
> that they were naked . . . [MF]
> and made themselves loincloths. [IF]

Then the Deity Y. arrives in the garden and looks for Adam (only him). Adam has hidden himself and, when asked why, he expresses that he hid because he was ashamed, because he was naked. The Deity gets angry, yet spurts out that he knows of someone who could have entered the garden and spoken with the adolescents:

> Who told thee [IF]
> that thou are naked? [MF]
> Hast thou eaten of the tree, whereof I commanded thee
> not to eat? [MF]

Then the Deity says (obviously to some other immortal gods):

> Behold, the Adam *has become as one of us . . .* [IF]
> and now might he not put forth his hand and partake
> also of the Tree of Life, [IF]
> and eat [it] and live forever? [IF]

Sitchin remarks "Even the words of the Deity reflect a Sumerian origin, for the sole Hebrew Deity has again lapsed into the plural, addressing divine colleagues who were featured not in the Bible but in Sumerian texts" (*12th*, 365).

The real reason for the wrath of the Deity is revealed by his very words, "Behold the Adam has become as one of us"—the fear that the earthlings may become not only knowledgeable but also immortal like *them, the gods.* This dread of the Deity, his willingness to keep the earthlings as primitive and ignorant lulus, will make him curse the Adamic humanity and create elaborate schemes to erase them, again and again. And the Book text, by constantly inserting a moralistic interpretation that systematically puts the fault on the humans, will prime the readers to absolve the excesses and overreactions of the Deity.

Plate 1. Sacred Tree with Shiva's symbols (Karnataka, India).

Plate 2. Naga god (snake God) on Bucesvara Temple (Twelfth century; Karnataka, India).

Plate 3. Nagashila (Bhuvanesvar, India).

Plate 4. Isis Thermoutis (Louvre).

Plate 5. Shiva dancing (Nataraja) with snake around his neck (Chola Dynasty, Tamil Nadu, India).

Plate 6. Ishtar Eshnunna with entwined snakes (Louvre).

Plate 7. Great Minoan Goddess with snakes (Heraklion Archaeological Museum).

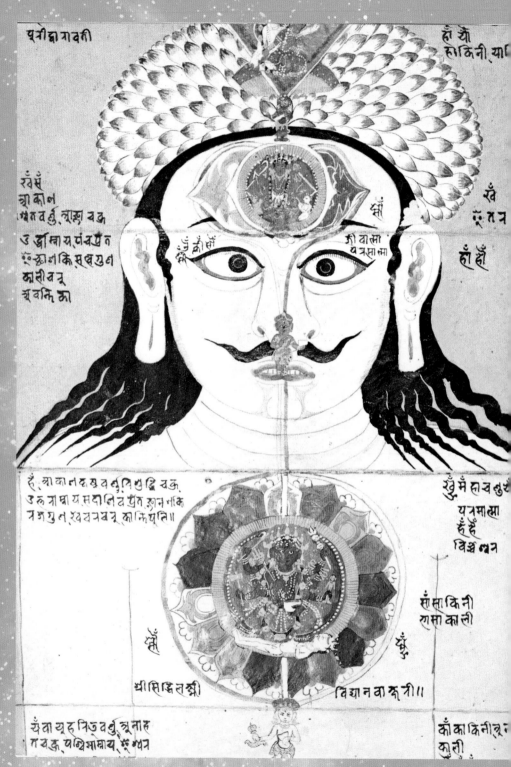

Plate 8. The kundalini and the awakening of the chakras.
(Painting, Rajasthan, Seventeenth century.)

Plate 9. Geodesic honeycomb architecture in Jameh Masjid (Friday Mosque, Yazd, Iran).

Plate 10. Geodesic architecture evoking forest of palm trees in Vakil Mosque (Shiraz, Iran).

Plate 11. Hermes as Mercurius, eternal youth, the triumphant son (from Basil Valentine Key 2).

Plate 12. Hermes Mercurius Trismegistus (Siena Cathedral).

Plate 13. The Magdalene by Simon Vouet.

Plate 14. Giant god trampling Earth-humans building a tower.
Victory stela of King Naram-Sin, ca. 2250 BCE (Louvre).

Repeated Accursations

After making us—the readers—agree that the adolescents have performed such a horrendous sin, we'll accept the grave sentence befalling all generations of humans, forever, while feeling desperately culpable. Let's see the text:

> The Deity Y. expelled the Adam from the orchard of Eden. [IF]
> And to the woman he said: "I will greatly multiply thy suffering by thy pregnancy. In suffering shalt you bear children." [IF]

The act of an unjust god.

On the one hand because he knew very well who had done the deed: the Serpent Enki. On the other hand, because his reaction is disproportionate—the cursing of women to the end of time.

The act of a cruel god, who had wanted the primitive, low-consciousness slave workers to remain in their lowly state; who targets the most noble act of giving life to be the medium of his curse.

A psychological act that demonstrates that he was not the creator of the Adamic humanity, because if he had been, he would have respected life and life giving.

Now we have to consider the history of accursation among the Anunnaki to realize that, however they did it, putting a curse on somebody or something was not an empty word. One example, speaking for itself, is that of Agade, the city cursed by the gods and whose story is recounted in the text called *The Curse of Agade*. When Inanna, endowed with the MEs she tricked Enki into giving her, was granted kingship by the Assembly of the Gods, she chose Sargon to be the king of her realm, and Sargon 1 built the city of Agade (or Akkad) to be his capital. The wars he and his successors on the throne fought in the name of their queen and lover, Inanna, created the mighty empire of Akkad, and Akkadian became the international language of diplomacy. But in the course of time, Inanna became more and more ferocious in her craving for dominance of other lands and realms. When she finally got into open defiance of the olden gods and defiled the temple of Anu in Erech (her ancient abode!) and then Enlil's temple in Nippur, the gods gathered in their Assembly and ordered the accursation of Agade. Not only the city but the whole Akkadian empire were utterly destroyed and could never be reconstructed—contrary to what happened to so many cities and temples that were defiled or destroyed and then rebuilt. Agade, cursed and forever erased, after having been one of the jewels of Sumer, shows us how terrible and powerful were the curses of the Anunnaki.

The curse on women back in the Edin orchard is only, from the part of Enlil, the first of a series of accursations. Even as the demand for workers keeps growing, the multiplication of Earth-humans is not to his liking, and soon his unbending objective will be to get rid of humanity, to destroy the hybrid race of Earth-humans, to the point of even putting a curse on Earth, and this all the way to the aftermath of the Deluge.

On coming out of the ark on Mount Ararat, Noah had immediately offered a sacrifice, roasting some animals. Says the Book:

And the Deity smelled the enticing smell and said in his heart: "I shall no longer curse the dry land on account of the earthling." [IF]

This is a clear-cut and extraordinary Informational Framework (IF) sentence.

Indeed this is exactly what he had done before, hoping to get rid of humanity and using a new plan each time when the previous one had not worked. Earth-humans had indeed suffered so much, for so long, that the father of Noah, Lamech (who was himself of a mixed parentage, and the son of Methuselah), when a son was born to him, decided to call him Respite (Noah). Noah's real father, as we know, was Enki. Lamech, at this occasion, said "Let this one comfort us concerning our work and the suffering of our hands by *the earth which the deity hath accursed*" (*12th*, 37; my emphasis). This is what the Deity, on Mount Ararat, revealed he had done, in no ambiguous terms ("I shall no longer curse the dry land"), before finally pardoning Noah. In the Sumerian text, similarly, Enlil pardons Ziusudra, but not before Enki had brought to his attention that they, the Anunnaki, needed the humans and their work to rebuild Sumer and their civilization on Earth destroyed by the flood. However, in the Book version, we will not be astonished, by now, to find immediately after this revealing and truthful statement (all in Informational Framework, IF), that the next line takes us back to a Moralistic Framework (MF):

I shall no longer *curse the dry land on account of the earthling* [IF];
for his heart's desire is evil from his youth. [MF]

All this conveys the meaning that humanity, "the earthling," is so wicked that there's no hope at all; it's endemic to the whole race of earthlings.

But if that's so, why did the deity suddenly modify his previous long-term plan to eradicate humanity (generally called "Man" or "the Adam" in the scriptures)? Especially since this judgment of his (a definite MF statement) was his rationale for using the Deluge for a radical wiping out of Man from Earth: the deity had judged that the earthling "is but flesh" (MF), meaning that the earthlings were not endowed with a spirit or a soul (*12th*, 377). Again a perfect MF statement contradictory to the one he had involuntarily shouted, in a fit of anger: "Behold the Adam has become as one of us . . ." (IF), the only thing that remains to differentiate us from them being immortality (*12th*, 365). And of course judging the earthlings as soulless is in perfect opposition to the story of the creation of Man: "And Yahweh, Elohim, fashioned the Adam . . . and the Adam turned into a living Soul" (*12th*, 349). Similarly, when the Assembly voted for the engineering of the lulus (not even to discuss their subsequent evolutionary leaps), Enki declared that the way to do it was to "bind upon it [the existing ape-man] the image of the gods" (*12th*, 341).

So, we have to examine and ponder the kind of dys-logic that has been put in the forefront for the moral teaching and benefit of all generations to come, especially when we know in whose "image," or archetype humanity was created: "And Elohim said: 'Let us make Man in our image, after our likeness'" (*12th*, 338).

1. In the Eden: Man is now "as one of us" in his consciousness and his knowing (a competitor)—let's expel him lest he might "partake also of the Tree of Life . . . and live forever," that is, lest he becomes immortal like us (*12th*, 365).

2. Before the Deluge: The earthling is "but flesh." "The Deity saw that the wickedness of Man was great. And the Deity said 'I will destroy the Earthling . . . off the face of the earth.'" (This judgment was the final and crucial decision before the Deluge.) But the very lines before this drastic judgment were: "And it came to pass . . . that *the sons of the deities* saw the daughters of the earthlings that they were compatible, and they took unto themselves wives of whichever they chose" (*12th*, 377; my emphasis).

Another instance of faulty logic by the unjust god. The verses clearly state that the sons of the deities (the Anunnaki) were the ones to realize earthling women were biologically and sexually compatible (they could have sexual intercourse and also offspring), and likewise that the Anunnaki were the ones to choose whichever wives they liked. One has to imagine what must have been the tall Anunnaki, the lords lofty and all-powerful, with a bewildering knowledge and technology . . . to the poor toiling earthlings who were working for them, and praising them in their temples, bringing offerings and sacrifices of food to please them and propitiate them. So that in total absence of either logic or sense of justice, the Commander in Chief deduces from what he sees as horrendous and abominable mis-marriages, tainting the Anunnaki bloodline, that the earthlings have no soul ("is but flesh"), that they are the ones responsible for the Igigi (Nephilim) abducting them, and therefore that they definitely deserve to be totally wiped out. And he will dutifully wipe out the cherished spouses of Marduk and of the Igigi—with a firm heart. If this is not the essence of racism, and a race-based judgment, I don't know what would be.

So all in all, we have a Nibirian human who abusively claims to be the creator of the earthlings, who goes on a rampage to abduct them from Africa and make them work in Sumer, who bars them from a higher conscious evolution, as well as from procreating, who holds them responsible for this leap in consciousness (once given to them by Ninmah, Enki, and Ningishzidda), who then holds the women responsible for being abducted by powerful Anunnaki and for sullying the great Anunnaki race. And how can you regain the purity of the race? Kill them all. "I will destroy the Earthling . . . off the face of the earth."

The Will to Erase Humanity

Even before getting to his grand final genocidal plan (using the Deluge), Enlil had remorselessly tried, again and again and for a very long time, to erase the earthlings off the face of the Earth. But the way he did it was by making the animals sicken, the plants wither, and the water and the soil poisoned—by all sorts of malevolent actions that in the end rendered our planet Earth sick—the very planet they, the Anunnaki themselves, were living on; the very animals and plants living on and of the soil of Sumer (even if the masters' own plantations and livestock were spared from these maledictions). This, we count as Enlil's fifth act: the accursation of humanity and Earth with the determination to erase humanity.

The historical account of these times before the Deluge comes from the *Atrahasis* epic, the Babylonian account of the Deluge written in Akkadian. The epic's hero is Atra-Hasis—the Sumerian Ziusudra, or the biblical Noah—a name that means in Akkadian "Exceedingly Wise," the epithet given to him by Enki. Beyond the original Akkadian text, many tablets, similar in content, were found in Sumerian, Babylonian, Assyrian, and Canaanite languages, which allowed the scholars to put together a near-complete account.

In fact, the text starts right at the beginning, with the Anunnaki toiling in the gold mines and their revolt. Then it states that, when the earthlings had multiplied (as we know, they were working hard serving the gods and doing all the workload in Sumer in the daytime) they were filling the nights of Sumer with the noise and loud expression (translated "pronouncement") of their lovemaking (or "conjugations"); and that was impeding Enlil from sleeping!

> The land extended, the people multiplied; in the land like wild bulls they lay. The god got disturbed by their conjugations; the god Enlil heard their pronouncements, and said [to] the great gods: "Oppressive have become the pronouncements of Mankind; their conjugations deprive me of sleep." (*12th*, 390)

Sitchin comments about this: "Enlil—once again cast as the prosecutor of Mankind—then ordered a punishment." The first plan Enlil tried was to decimate the humans through epidemics and diseases. Sitchin tells us that "the Akkadian and Assyrian versions of the epic speak of 'aches, dizziness, chills, fever,' as well as 'disease, sickness, plague, and pestilence' afflicting Mankind and its livestock following Enlil's call for punishment" (*12th*, 390).

Atra-Hasis/Noah, the biological son of Enki/Ea, was all his life the protégé of this god. Says Atra-Hasis himself in the epic: "I lived in the temple of Ea my lord." Thus he calls Enki for help:

> Ea, O Lord, Mankind groans. *The anger of the gods consumes the land. Yet it is you who hast created us!* Let there cease the aches, the dizziness, the chills, the fever! (*12th*, 391)

Enki then tries something and it protects the people to a certain point (this part of the tablet is damaged). But Enlil soon realizes that he hadn't been able to reduce the earthling population and he gets furious again. Then he comes up with a second plan, which is to erase humanity by starving the people:

"Let supplies be cut off from the people.... Let the rains of the rain god be withheld from above. Below, let the waters not rise from their sources." And this is what happened in effect, the Earth was scorched by heat and a terrible drought: "The womb of the earth did not bear, vegetation did not sprout . . . the broad plain was choked with salt." Enki is now given the imperious order to "bar the sea," so that the people don't have access to the sea's abundance of food, and so that fishes or products and food from the sea don't reach the cities' population. And he has to execute the Commander of Earth's orders. The ordeal, the text tells us, went on for "six *sha-at-tam*" or shars (that is, for six times 3,600 years!). At the 4th shar, "their faces appeared green; they walked hunched in the streets." At the sixth, "the child they prepared for food . . . one house devoured the others" (*12th*, 391–92).

Atra-Hasis kept imploring the help of Enki against Enlil's adamant will to make humanity perish: "In the house of his god . . . he set foot . . . every day he wept, bringing oblations in the morning . . . he called by the name of his god" (*12th*, 392).

Finally Enki judges that too much is too much and he decides to bypass Enlil's murderous commands. He puts together a strategy for the people to have access to the sea's riches that he controls. He triggers no less than a mass revolt; he tells Atra-Hasis to ask the people to organize themselves and propagate everywhere the watchword: *"Make a loud noise in the land. . . . Do not revere your gods, do not pray to your goddesses"* (*12th*, 393).

The verses are damaged, but while the revolt is going on, the lord Enki sends some of his men to secretly destroy the barriers holding the people from accessing the sea and going to fish. This was (according to Enki's plan) to be blamed on the revolted crowds. Enlil, no kidding, "was filled with anger," and he sensed his hated brother had a part in the events. Right away he sent his guards to seize Enki and bring him while he gathered the Assembly. And now he confronts Enki with his usual despot's style: We had "reached together a decision . . . I commanded that . . . the bolt, the bar of the sea, you [Enki] should guard with your rockets, but you let loose provisions for the people." Enki, as he had planned, put the responsibility on the rebellion. But Enlil keeps insisting, willing this and that from Enki—he orders him "to stop feeding his people," and the like. Let's note here that Enki is an Anunnaki lord and a royal prince, and that he is the lord god of Eridu, the town nearest to the sea in Sumer, and that *Enlil is ordering him to let his own city dwellers die from starvation as well as all earthlings in Sumer*— against the tacit law that demands of a god (or a king) to be the protector of his people. And moreover, *Enlil conducts this farfetched genocidal command and bullying right in the middle of the Assembly of the Gods, and no one god (apart from Enki) tries to rein in the Chief in Command.*

We are still in the Assembly; the *Atrahasis* text recounts that, suddenly,

> [Enki] got fed up with the sitting;
> In the Assembly of the Gods, laughter overcame him.

He laughs aloud. A colossal laugh. The great senior gods are put off balance. Have they pushed things too far . . . given too much in Enlil's vengeful plans? But Enlil calls everybody to order and reminds them that *the plan to starve mankind was a decision they made together in the Assembly.* As usual, Enlil has been able to bend arms and to get the whole Assembly of the Gods to back up his criminal schemes. Remember that the poor one could not sleep—that's not nothing! And he couldn't think of any other solution to stop the noise around his temple (such as erecting walls around it, or keeping the earthlings at a distance) apart from kill them all!—which is, all along, a basic tenet of Enlil's tactics. And now the gods are bound by their previous decisions. Enlil then, having recovered his majestic stance, attacks Enki as to the fact that he is constantly breaking the rule (that is, the one concocted and imposed by Enlil and the so-called unanimous decision by the Assembly!). Then Enlil discloses that he has a back-up plan; he reveals that a gigantic flood has been forecast, that they can use it to eradicate the earthlings. He now asks of each of the gods to swear that they will withhold the information from mankind. He asks that especially of Enki. Enki rebuffs his brother:

> Why will you bind me with an oath?
> Am I to raise my hands against my own humans? (*12th*, 395)

But the assembled gods, mesmerized by their chief on Earth, will force him to swear himself to secrecy.

That's how the barbarous and totally stupid plan to eradicate humanity via the forthcoming Great Flood—without considering at all what could be the consequences of the Deluge neither on themselves, nor on the Sumerian civilization, nor on the land—was made by the Assembly of the most potent gods, whose chief was supposed to be omniscient, righteous, a paragon of Justice, and Goodness itself.

According to Sitchin, the Akkadian word used as unit of time (a *sha-at-tam*) means "a passing," and is the translation of the Sumerian *shar* (3600 years). While the scholars translated it as "a year," without realizing that it was a Nibirian year, the Assyrian version uses the precise term "year of Anu." Thus, the accursation of humanity in order to eradicate it lasted for seven shars unto the Deluge, meaning in fact 25,200 Earth-years. Sitchin dates the seven passings that saw an extremely harsh climate rendering the Earth barren, from about 36,000 BCE to the Deluge, which happened around 11,000 BCE.

Let's remember that Ubartutu/Lamech (of mixed parentage) became the first (formally enthroned) King of Shuruppak around 77,000 BCE, and his son Ziusudra/Noah's reign started around 49,000 BCE—that is, 38 millennia before he was saved from the Flood by Enki. It means that Ziusudra/Noah, being a natural (yet closet) son of Enki, had inherited the longevity of the half gods. Just after the wave receded a bit on Mount Ararat, Enki had told Enlil in substance: You'd better look at this man twice, at his immense wisdom and intelligence, he who will be the seed of future humanity. At which point, Enlil had a sudden insight and abruptly offered to Ziusudra to come and live with them, the gods, which meant obtaining the quasi immortality of the Anunnaki.

For Sitchin, the accursation of Earth coincides with the arrival of a new ice age, which the scholars estimate to have ended abruptly roughly at the time that the Mesopotamian records set the Deluge. But this last ice age and the accursation of Earth had in fact started earlier, in 73,000 BCE; regressive types of man were roaming the Earth and harsh climate conditions had set in. The seven shars of dire suffering (until

11,000 BCE) had been the climax of this gruesome period. At the time Sitchin published his first book in the series of the Earth Chronicles, in 1976, we would have been hard pressed to explain how a highly evolved science could affect the climate in such a way as to withhold the rain and dry up the springs and the underground aquifers, to the point of creating a devastating drought. By now, the new technologies and the more or less secret experiments and black programs, such as the HAARP (High Frequency Active Auroral Research Program) facility in Alaska, have made us aware of the potential for affecting climate in many ways. This task of establishing and monitoring the drought was entrusted to the Anunnaki god in charge of weather: the storm god Adad (the youngest son of Enlil), whose emblem is lightning. As Sitchin explains it in *The Lost Realms,* Adad will be in charge of the mining of gold in Central and South America, and will be called Viracocha, the storm-god of the Incas.

This indeed had been exactly the scheme of Enlil, as described in the *Atrahasis:*

"Let the rains of the Rain God [Adad] be withheld from above; below let the waters not rise from their sources. Let the wind blow and parch the ground; let the clouds thicken, but hold back the downpour." Thereafter, "The waters did not rise from their sources; the womb of the earth did not bear; vegetation did not sprout."

Secret military science and technology, through various means, is now able to raise the temperature of a whole region in a very tangible way, or to trigger bursts of lightning and storms to break up clouds in torrential rains in one area, thus setting a drought in another region.

Enlil had assigned to different Anunnaki the task of setting the conditions for mankind's starvation. He says, during the Assembly, in order to confound Enki: "I [had] commanded that in the Bird of Heaven Adad should guard the upper regions; that Sin and Nergal should guard the Earth's middle regions; that the bolt, the bar of the sea, you [Enki] should guard with your rockets." Thus the atmosphere

and climate, the land, and the sea, were all monitored to create a terrible drought that was to decimate or destroy mankind. And let's note
that Enki was supposed to impede the people (his people that he calls
affectionately "my humans") from fishing and thus getting food from
the sea by using *rockets*—flying machines with missiles, whose explosions would have made the fishes flee or die! That, in addition to the
walls erected to ban access to the sea! It was really making war on one's
people!

Obviously, the gods were keeping some resources for themselves,
because apart from having to nourish themselves, Enki was accused of
having acted to "let loose provisions for the people" and "supply corn
rations on which the people thrive." When Noah was imploring him
to reverse or bypass Enlil's orders, it was not because he himself was
suffering from hunger (since he lived in the temple of Ea) but because
the people over whom he reigned as a king and for whom he was thus
responsible were doomed to bear dire suffering and hellish conditions
without respite. Let's remember though that not only the humans
were dying from hunger, but also the cattle and wild animals, and the
plants and crops had withered—so that of course the tragic ordeal of
humanity had to reflect in diverse manner on the gods themselves,
affecting not only their food supply, but their freedom to roam the
land. As we know in psychology, the prison guards are themselves
prisoners of the prison rules. The Anunnaki gods were thus limited
in their own freedom and their ways and pleasures of living, by the
drastic sanctions ordered by Enlil. But this was not affecting Enlil
in the least, and we may wonder if he ever took any pleasure at anything, beyond his insatiable craving for power and for imposing his
authority.

So here again, in this fifth act, the accursation of man and of Earth,
and decreeing plagues and starving conditions aimed at decimating
humanity, we see the wily Enlil using all the power he was endowed
with as Commander of Earth, legal heir, and the first speaker in the
Assembly of the Gods, to persecute humanity with the adamant will of
erasing it from the face of the Earth.

And here again *we see Enki twice coming to the rescue of mankind*—even if it was after a long time had elapsed.

First, he stops the plagues and epidemics (obviously the Anunnaki were immune to these illnesses they set loose on humanity); henceforth Enlil sees his plans thwarted, and he complains, full of anger, to the Assembly that "The people have not diminished; they are more numerous than before!" (*12th*, 394).

And the second time, when Enlil sets up the new ploy of starving mankind through manipulating the climate conditions, Enki, then, under the cover of a staged revolt of all the earthlings against their gods, gets his own men to destroy the barriers and military blockade of the sea and rivers' resources.

Note that the worshipping strike was in reality much more of a revolution than what we may ever imagine. At that time, the task of worshipping (a term, if you recall, that meant, in Hebrew, "working") implied a lot of various tasks and services, such as tending to the needs of the gods and preparing their meals, servicing their temples, their abodes, and vast domains, making offerings of food (fruits, crops, fishes, animals to slaughter), as well as all the social and city tasks, such as construction works, and agricultural and farming labor.

Rockets and Space Travels

A recurrent theme in the tablets is the use of *birds* or *whirling birds* to go and meet other Anunnaki. There are very interesting depictions of what definitely resembles planes, just as the famous bas-reliefs found in Egypt, in the temple of Seti I (see fig. 4.1a and b). Another technology of the Egyptians is their famous lamps, the design of which is clearly painted on the walls of temples (see fig. 4.1c).

Many depictions show a kind of ladder within an enclosure or a frame, called Gateway to Heaven, that has the form of a winged pillar, or gate. The gateways are guarded by either two Eaglemen (the Igigi), or two lions, or else two serpents, and they represent, for Sitchin, the technology enabling the Anunnaki to access Nibiru by using a *shem*

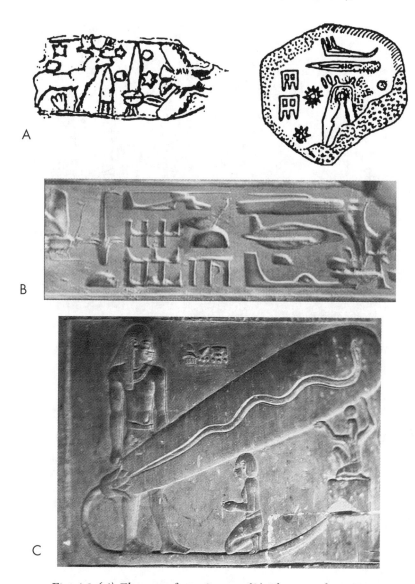

Fig. 4.1 (A) Flying crafts in Sumer. (B) Flying crafts in Egypt; Temple of Seti I. (C) Lamp design in Egypt.

or spacecraft. The shem looks like a pointed rocket (and even one of its pictograms has the shape of an arrow) that is generally standing upward, pointed toward the sky. See for example this fascinating drawing, at figure 4.2, that shows a whole underground complex,

Fig. 4.2. A shem pointed skyward above an underground temple-laboratory.

quite technological (with its double enclosure and large wall extending both sides), with just the spaceship standing at the level of the ground, hidden by palm trees.

Now, two other cylinders depict even more clearly that some kind of pointed spaceship, with a long plasma or other ray tube running all its length, allows them to reach Nibiru—the Winged Disk above the ship—and maybe farther in the galaxy, since two aliens (from a fish phylum) are definitely represented on figure 4.3a. On figure 4.3b, apart from Nibiru, we see various planets represented (the dots and the star) and the sun and moon; moreover, the large spaceship now has the shape of a rocket.

Fig. 4.3. Rockets (shems) and spacecrafts. (A) Shem with plasma rod inside pointing toward Nibiru. (B) Shem-rocket pointing toward Nibiru.

The Rise in Power of Enlil Due to the Creation of the Lulus

By this time, the political stand of Anu, as we see, has neatly diminished. He hardly partakes in the discussions, offers no wise advice. They all seem to be under the spell of Enlil, the first ruler among them. Did he not have, since the building of the orchard in the east of Edin, the two royal Trees, symbols of the highest kingship? Was the building of such royal abode the sign that Anu had given him the reins of power? In Sumer, no god can build an abode-temple for himself or herself without the assent of the Assembly; the only god to have broken this rule was Marduk, with the Babel temple. Having one's own temple signifies setting oneself as a worshipped god with followers—and you need at the very least to be part of the twelve Lofty Lords, the royals who have numbers attributed to them. Anu is the first, with number 60, Enlil following with 50, Enki 40. Their wives have the multiples of 5, starting with Antu who has the rank of 55. Then only the sons of Enlil are numbered, all the way to the third generation after Anu, the twins Inanna and Utu, great-grandchildren of Anu, with 15 and 20 respectively. (Inanna took over the rank from Ninmah, who was herself thrown out of the Circle!)

If that was indeed the case, that Enlil got the assent of Anu and the Assembly to build a new temple-abode as a garden in which to settle the emblematic two Living Trees as a status of King of Heaven, and in which to settle the first lulu couple—a royal garden based on the sacred model of Anu the King's own garden—then it would mean a lot (see fig. 4.4). It would imply (1) that the scepter of power was now in the hands of Enlil. Without displacing Anu as number 60, Enlil would nevertheless be the authoritative voice and the decision maker (the one "who decrees the fates"). It would also imply (2) that *the "perfecting" of the lulus meant a civilization leap for the Nibirians* as a civilization who has been able to partake in the creative power of the universe, and to seed intelligent life—a new sapiens phylum—on another planet.

Fig. 4.4. Tree of Knowing and Tree of Immortality (Life) in Anu's Garden.

It would be similar to the ancient custom of upgrading the blazon of a knight or a prince, to acknowledge the remarkable deeds performed in his lifetime by the individual. The family coat of arms, inherited, was accrued with a new pictorial and heraldic symbol representing the deed in question. The nobility and fame of the family was thus upgraded to a higher status, and the deed counted in the "family tree." Since most of our ancient customs, especially concerning religious rites, symbolism, and sacred geometry, were derived from the Anunnaki and the Sumerian civilization, it seems appropriate to decipher more recent customs in order to infer their roots in Sumer.

The Nibirians as a Master Civilization in the Galaxy

The historical data handed to us by the Anunnaki in Sumer are very stingy of information concerning their original civilization on Nibiru. And we tend to remedy the lack of information by pure and simple projections. Thus, we are all too prone to consider that they themselves thought they were the only intelligent civilization in the universe—projecting our own old-paradigm belief. On the contrary, the fact that they don't have religious rituals to gods of their own (but impose themselves as our gods) could imply that their scientific knowledge has made them cognizant of the real state of intelligent life in the universe: that there are indeed numerous Exo-Planetary Intelligent Civilizations or EPICs (regardless of which planet the observer is on). These EPICs disseminated in the visible and also in the invisible pluriverse would have evolved naturally without the need to invoke a personal Creator God, more and more abstract but nevertheless endowed with a projected human-type consciousness and emotions, such as will and anger. In the Semantic Fields Theory (SFT), the semantic dimension (in which psyche and energy-matter are merged) is self-organized and constantly evolving, and it is the substrate of the whole reality, expressing itself as a hyperdimension, in matter or not. It is fueled by the semantic energy, that is, consciousness-as-energy, which is the driving force presiding over the big bang. It is the great fundamental force, self-organizing and negentropic—that is, creating more and more complexity and information. It self-organizes in a specific universe but systematically tends toward the development of superior Intelligent Civilizations. The semantic hyperdimension by itself and devoid of matter is also what exists in between material universes, at the origin and the end, what survives the terminal big crunch, with all the information of all beings contained in it—its planetary semantic field with all its memory (the Akashic records).

With such a scientific framework, one can understand the trend of the bubbles of universes to evolve toward highly evolved Intelligent Civilizations (ICs), and a threshold of evolution of such species would be to become able to seed intelligent life on another world, through genetic engineering. And that threshold would mark the attainment of a hierarchical status among the various ICs who would not only have had time to know and visit each other, but also to form a sort of federation or empire.

If we follow this perspective, *the Nibirian, having brought a new life-form up to intelligence and civilization, would have acquired the higher status of a Master Civilization.* This is exactly what I have put into play in one sci-fi book, *Diverging Views,* discussing thereafter the status of our own Intelligent Civilization within our galactic federation of Intelligent Civilizations.

If this is indeed the case, then it explains a lot. For example, why Enlil as the King of Earth did get all the credit for the perfecting of the lulus, and why it was he who got it and not his father: because he was the actual leader on the planet where this scientific breakthrough happened. The achievement would also get him a title of King of Heaven (ahead of Anu's death); he would receive in his own royal coat of arms and blazon the Tree of Knowing (representing the new earth-ling genome); and he would access the status of his father, with the Tree of Immortality. It also explains why he would then be entitled to make for himself a new temple-abode in which to settle the emblematic First Couple and how, by virtue of the above, he would of course plant in it his new symbol of kingship—the two living Tree-gods.

Those two Trees were of course meant to be totally out of reach of the lowly creatures, yet they were bestowed on Enlil as a prize for the creation of the lulus. And this is why, with his boundless self-centeredness, Enlil decided to have the Trees towering in the orchard and proclaiming his grandeur, as much as the Couple was. We are left to wonder why is it that Enlil—with all his might—could not just solve the problem by putting a field of force, a barrier, or a ME setting a "field of supervision" as they had in some temples, that would have physically impeded the two earthlings from approaching too near the two Trees.

In this interpretative framework, we can figure out why Enlil thought he had power of life and death over his creatures, and how his characteristic egotism and haughtiness must have also taken a leap to a new level! And when, later on, after deciding that he would decimate the earthlings—setting up the first strategy of epidemics then the second of famine and starvation—he was acting, in his own view, as the sole recognized authority on the subject, because that's the only version that would've been known in our wider federation or empire of neighboring ICs.

So, when Enlil at the Assembly assumes a prosecutor's role listing Enki's numerous instances in which he had "broken the rule"—such as feeding his starving population—Enki, who had had enough, explodes in laughter and declares, in essence: Why should I raise my hands against *my own* humans? Enki is basically reminding the Assembly and Enlil in particular that he was *the one,* with Ninmah, who had, in effect, perfected the humans, that *he was the true father* and lord of mankind, while Enlil had only taken the glory of it onto himself. Were the gods moved to the point of putting Enlil's autocratic so-called rule in question? Not at all; only a moment of doubt settled, quickly shaken because they give the highest value to the hierarchical system, and this system is unshakable (at least that's what they want to believe).

In this context, a worshipping strike is no small feat! Interestingly, it sets Enki as the archetype of the trickster! And we know that this archetype is very extent in many cultures, notably the Native Americans, as Allan Leslie Combs has developed in *Synchronicity: Science, Myth, and the Trickster.*

I Will Destroy the Earthlings off the Face of the Earth: The Deluge

Having sworn not to disclose the impending catastrophe to humanity, Enki then finds a subterfuge so that Ziusudra gets the information, without formally breaking his oath. He talks to the reed screen behind which happens to be Ziusudra/Noah (see fig. 4.5). He is in fact reporting to him what happened in the Assembly:

> [Reed screen, reed screen!] Pay attention to my instructions.
> On all the habitations, over the cities, a storm will sweep.
> The destruction of mankind's seed it will be. . . .
> *This is the final ruling, the word of the Assembly of the Gods.*
> (*12th*, 395)

This is of the greatest importance for us, because we see that Enki is letting mankind know (also via the written text) not only of the political organization of the Anunnaki, but also of the decision concerning humanity and Earth. He could have saved Ziusudra without explaining all this; but he is always treating the earthlings on a near-equal footing.

Fig. 4.5. Enki as a wise Serpent warning Ziusudra of the coming Deluge.

Then he goes on explaining to "the reed hut" how to build a *magurgur*—a boat that can turn and tumble, a submarine—providing the measurements and how to use bitumen to make it waterproof. He will send a pilot to drive the boat precisely toward Mount Ararat, the highest peak (in fact, twin peaks) of the whole region.

On board the spaceships the Anunnaki stayed in orbit for 150 days. They were anguished, distressed, and heartbroken while observing the absolute disaster happening below. The *Atrahasis* recounts how Ninmah/Ninti couldn't stop weeping and lamenting over the overwhelming death of her children, her "created."

> The goddess saw and she wept . . . her lips were covered with feverishness . . . "My creatures have become like flies, they filled the rivers like dragonflies, their fatherhood was taken by the rolling sea." . . . Ninti wept and spent her emotion; she wept and eased her feelings. The gods wept with her for the land. She was overcome with grief, she thirsted for beer. Where she sat, the gods sat weeping, crouching like sheep at a trough. Their lips were feverish of thirst, they were suffering cramp from hunger. . . . Ishtar cried out like a woman in travail: "The olden days are alas turned to clay." The Anunnaki gods weep with her. The gods, all humbled, sit and weep; their lips drawn tight . . . one and all.

Apparently the scale of the disaster and the duration of the flooding of the whole Earth, had been far beyond their estimates. By now, Anu had called upon the Anunnaki to retreat back to Nibiru. But the Anunnaki who had chosen to remain in orbit now realize how strong is their bonding both with the planet and with the earthlings. In one craft, they debate about whether to follow Anu's orders. Ninmah speaks against it, she doesn't want to save her life while her "created" are dying.

The only one not in disarray, still happy with himself, the only one not to have realized that they had lost everything and that they would have to start again from scratch, the one responsible for all, because he is their chief, and yet who hadn't been able to plan ahead of the catastrophe—neither enough food and drinking water in their orbiting spacecrafts; nor reserves of food, of grains, of animals, hermetically protected, on the highest peaks of Earth; nor the preservation in waterproof containers of the utmost accomplishments of the Sumerian civilization, its libraries of books and historical records from the time of the first landing to the time of the Deluge—which is counted in the Sumerian archives as 120 shars, that is 432,000 Earth-years.

They have soared above the immense ocean of water and mud covering the whole Earth (which they have seen from above) and have finally landed on the side of the twin summits, the sole rare land around Sumer to have yet emerged out of the total disaster . . . and yet, the only one to have retained enough self-confidence and high spirit to get into a fit of rage when he discovers a survivor, is of course Enlil.

We have seen how it took Enki to make him start thinking in a reasonable way—or thinking at all—to realize they couldn't themselves thrive as a civilization on Earth without the earthlings. That they now need help to reconstruct everything—they need the workforce of the fast-reproducing earthlings. Enki also presents Ziusudra as "exceedingly wise"—the Atra-Hasis man who has been able to "read the signs" and forecast the Deluge, the one of scholarly knowledge, a trained scientist, a king and priest, initiated in the sacred knowledge. And Enlil then gives to Ziusudra/Noah the command to multiply. Later, he will take him and his wife to live in an abode of the gods. After being given the plant of immortality, both will become near-immortal like gods.

The rebuilding of their civilization must have proven an immense undertaking. At first, the most pressing issue being to have food, they started agriculture in the Zagros Mountains surrounding Sumer, since they had become free of water earlier (we have found there what we consider to be among the first signs of growing crops on Earth around 10,000 BCE). The mud had accumulated so much in the plain of Sumer, with the course of the two rivers altered and spreading all around, that it took an enormous time for it to become solid ground again. So new space facilities were constructed in the Sinai and Egypt regions, with an overall identical geometrical plan, this as early as 10,500 BCE—

with the Ekur (Great Pyramid), the spaceport in the Sinai, and a new Control Center on Mount Moriah (the future Jerusalem). As for the most holy cities of Sumer, they started to be reconstructed only around 3800 BCE, Enki's city, Eridu, first, and then Nippur, Enlil's city. The temples of the gods were rebuilt according to the exact same architecture, orientation, and measurement.

What a Commander of Earth Should Have Done to Minimize the Deluge's Catastrophe

Enlil bullied the gods in the Assembly into backing him on a genocidal scheme to wipe out humanity via the Deluge, as we have just seen. This was another genocidal scheme that Enki thwarted, by saving Ziusudra/Noah, his family, the seeds of plants, and the genomes of animals. After Enlil's sixth act, the other gods could not help but realize the amplitude of the destruction of their civilization, of humanity, of the animals, of the plants, and of Earth, and how unwise it had been on the part of Enlil not to try to save earthlings. The wild vegetation was partly spared, at least in the mountains; but in the plains, it was covered by millions of tons of mud. We see the gods crying (apart from Enlil). We see that Inanna regretted having voted for letting mankind perish. We see Ninmah refusing to follow the orders of Anu to retreat en masse to Nibiru, and the gods following her lead. But *we don't see any criticism of how Enlil has managed the crisis*, nor any analysis that if it was not for Enki's capacity to anticipate, there wouldn't be any way to reconstruct anything. No seed of mankind, no workforce, no crop seeds, no fruit tree seeds. They would have to start from scratch, bringing seeds of plants and crops, and domesticated animals from Nibiru. But they had no more space facilities to do that! So no help could reach them, beyond lightweight carriers. In regard to the time for them to rebuild some facilities, they would have to wait for the next window of opportunity in terms of Nibiru's orbit. But whatever could be brought from Nibiru wouldn't comprise the specific species of living beings—flora and fauna—indigenous to Earth, nor the hominids that were existing before the genetic engineering that brought out the *Homo sapiens* and then, the *Homo sapiens sapiens* (the "modern man" to which we belong).

It wouldn't have replaced the laborious and patient work of Ninmah to adapt on Earth the specimen of Nibirian plants—such as the sacred Tree from which was made the Nectar of Immortality—a work she had carried on since her landing on Earth in 428,000 BCE until 11,000 BCE; that's an immense span of time of 417,000 years! But what about the loss of all the archives and historical data—not to mention the magnificent temples and art objects adorning them? Berossus tells us that Enki instructed Noah to collect any writing he could get his hands on in Sumer, so that they could be preserved. And Ninmah will gather databanks of seeds and genomes—one she'll bury in Baalbek and another will be for the ark. But nothing else of the kind seems to have been done by other gods.

It was, when we consider it in-depth, an enormous blindness on the part of Enlil—something really difficult to fathom!

Given Enki's and Ninmah's power of anticipation, if they decided to save the seed of mankind and the genomes of the living, it is perfectly logical to surmise that they applied the same effort to salvage their work and that of Marduk and Hermes in the domains of science, architecture, the knowledge of the MEs, technology, history, historical records, and all written materials (on stone or clay tablets)—a legacy of intelligence that spanned the even longer time of 434,000 years. It is wholly improbable that Enki and Ninmah, and especially the young genius Ningishzidda/Hermes, would have done nothing to preserve the knowledge and records they and others in Sumer had accumulated.

In fact in the Greek version of the Great Flood, there is an operation mounted for salvaging the books. Let's remember that the Greek scholars got their science from Egypt, where they were initiated by the priests, and that the priest and historian Berossus was Greek. Berossus's version of the Deluge has reached us via the Greek scholar called Abydenus, and in it, Noah, King of Erech, is the King Sisithros (or Sisithrus), tenth ruler before the Deluge (just as in the scriptures), and the god who warns him is Cronos (or Kronos):

> To him [Sisithrus], the deity Cronos foretold . . . that there would be
> a deluge of rain; and he commanded him to deposit all the writings

whatever which were in his possession in the city of the sun in Sippara. (Smith, *The Chaldean Account of Genesis*, 47)

The time when the Deluge had been forecast to happen is the same as the one given in Sumerian tablets, and in the Book as well, as being on "the second month" of the year.

Now, Sippar is the city of Shamash, whose celestial counterpart is the sun, thus it is "the city of the Sun" and its spaceport was directed by this god. We see in this Greek text many other congruent details with both the Sumerian and the Book accounts, such as Mount Ararat, the release of birds, and going back from Armenia to Babylon. It is especially eloquent to find the right Sumerian names of the god and of the spaceport in Sippar. So that all the way from Sumer to Egypt and then to Berossus (third century BCE), himself quoted by Abydenus, a disciple of Aristotle (fourth century BCE), the right names of gods, cities, and the same historical accounts were given.

There are two discrepancies; the first one is that Sisithros has to collect and save books and bring them to the spaceport—that of course must have been incognito, since Enki/Cronos is not supposed to have warned Sisithros. At the spaceport in Sippar, the remaining Anunnaki, at the signal of Shamash, were to launch their spacecrafts and get in orbit around Earth. So bringing the books to the spaceport would thus mean that Enki was going to take them aboard his own spacecraft—and indeed, he seems to have disappeared while the other gods are described wailing and crying in at least two spacecrafts. The other incongruent detail is that Cronos orders Sisithros to "sail to" Armenia (Mount Ararat). In the Sumerian account, Ziusudra is in a submersible and a pilot was sent by Enki to drive him and his family to Mount Ararat. Enki had said, "Let the boat be a Ma.Gur.Gur—a boat that can turn and tumble." The Akkadian text, says Sitchin, describes a boat "'roofed over and below,' hermetically sealed with 'tough pitch . . . so that the sun shall not see inside . . . like an Apsu boat,' a *sulili*." Sitchin remarks that the term *sulili* used to describe the boat "is the very term used nowadays in Hebrew (*soleleth*) to denote a submarine" (*12th*, 396). Furthermore,

Ziusudra is given a container with the genomes, the "Essences of Life" of all the living on Earth—so he does not collect the animals himself (as in the Book version).

A Secret Hiding Place in a Mars or Moon Space Base?

In fact, there is one Sumerian text pointing to a retrieving of MEs by the Enkiites from Marduk's temple ahead of the Deluge; it is part of the *Erra Epos* describing how Nergal destroyed the waterworks of the underground control chamber of the Esagil. At one point of their heated discussion, Marduk confronts Nergal about the disappearance of a load of MEs and sacred objects and Nergal's inability to account for them. These are the "Instrument of Giving Orders, the Oracle of the Gods, the Sign of Kingship, the Holy Scepter which Contributes Brilliance to Lordship, the Holy Radiating Stone which Disintegrates All . . ." Where were they? asked Marduk.

At this point, Nergal promises Marduk to return the MEs providing Marduk agrees to leave Sumer and come fetch the MEs in the lower Abzu (the Land of Mines). So the antediluvial temple in Babylon had been emptied of its MEs (or some of them) before the catastrophe, and Nergal had done that—he had taken the MEs to the lower Abzu and hadn't returned them. (Incidentally, it means that even though Nergal could steal MEs, it didn't follow that he would grasp how they worked. Marduk, in fact, had to explain the consequences of tinkering with his waterworks MEs clearly to him.)

Could Nergal, retrieving the MEs from Marduk's Esagil temple before the Deluge, have been part of Enki's plan to save major items of knowledge and technology and hide them in Africa?

Could Enki have enrolled even the least trustworthy of his sons for this gigantic salvaging operation? Was Marduk at that time involved in another part of the plan requiring his utmost attention, actions that he deemed more important than his own MEs of power from Sumer? What could it be? Obviously he wasn't salvaging anything from Sumer (neither books, nor rare objects), for in that case, being on site, he would have also taken his MEs. What could be more precious to him than securing the life of his beloved earthling wife and the wives of the Igigi, and of all their children, by taking them to a secret and safe place? Meanwhile Enki and Ningishzidda would have salvaged the books and gathered the MEs from Egypt, while Ninmah gathered the Essence of Life of all animals and plants, drawing on her data banks in Baalbek and in the Abzu. One sure place to hide small things like MEs would have been the Great Pyramid, unshakable and hermetically closed.

We know Enki and his sons are not present in the spacecraft of Ninmah or that of Inanna. And of course he was not with Enlil and Ninurta who will arrive separately on Mount Ararat. Where was he? Our best guesses are a high and hollow mountain in the Abzu, constructed as a hermetically sealed fortress (and we know that Ninmah's laboratory there was set in a hollow mountain) or else a space base outside Earth, on the moon or on Mars. The problem with the Mars Way Station—the interplanetary spaceport where the spacecrafts were launched or landed when Nibiru was near its perigee—was that it was at the moment crowded with all the Anunnaki who had decided to go back to Nibiru just before the giant wave swept. Not exactly the right place to conduct stealth operations. The most likely places for Enki's family to stay safe during the Deluge, and for hiding the Igigi families and all the gathered books and treasures, are either a secret Lunar Station or a secret facility on a high summit on Earth.

Zecharia Sitchin infers from the abnormally high rate of dysfunction and/or loss of surveillance systems on the diverse Mars surveys and missions, that the Anunnaki have kept a presence on Mars, "if only robotic." He has been pivotal in revealing two major events about which there was a total denial and blackout from the world space agencies and that ushered in not only the international cooperation for space research, but the end of the Cold War (*Days*, 302–6).

The first incident was the discovery in 1983, of a Neptune-size planet at the edge of our solar system. The discovery was made by IRAS—NASA's Infrared Astronomical Satellite, which explores and surveys space via the detection of heat (infrared) of celestial bodies or whatever objects. The IRAS was, at the time, looking for a tenth planet beyond Pluto to explain the gravitational anomalies of Neptune's and Pluto's orbits. The alarmed space agencies immediately focused on this body and six months later found that it had moved: it was actually coming toward us! (Moreover, they knew now it was a planet.) The next day saw articles on the discovery in some newspapers, but by the following one it was retracted. Now, this huge and off-limits planet observed in 1983 could well be the one "discovered" in December 2015, called Planet Nine, whose gigantic but very elongated elliptical orbit around our sun takes about ten thousand years. Planet Nine is a rocky planet like ours, and it is not in the same ecliptic plane, and thus it crosses the latter twice at each of its revolutions—just as Nibiru was called "Planet Crossing." Now, if it had something to do with Nibiru, then its real orbit would be about three times longer than the one estimated by Sitchin.* To get back to the 1983 observation, an immediate change of global U.S.-Soviet politics happened immediately afterward, with a meeting between the two heads of state, Reagan and Gorbachev, and a new cooperation for space. That's when President Reagan, talking about Gorbachev and pointing at the sky, uttered his famous sentence in front of the United Nations:

> Just think how easy his task and mine might be . . . if suddenly there was a threat to this world from some other species from another planet outside in the universe. . . . I occasionally think how quickly our differences would vanish if we were facing an alien threat from outside this world.

Then in March 1989 the second event happened, called the Phobos Incident. Two Soviet probes (called Phobos 1 and Phobos 2), had been sent in 1988 to explore Mars and its strange moonlet

---

*See my blog for more information on Planet Nine: http://chris-h-hardy-dna-of-the -gods.blogspot.fr/search/label/Exopolitics%20-%20exo-civilizations.

Phobos—strange because it was possibly hollow. The first one vanished and no explanation followed. As discussed by Sitchin in *The End of Days*, the second, on orbit around Mars, started sending two sets of photos (with a regular camera and an infrared one) when suddenly there appeared the "shadow of a cigar-shaped object flying in the planet's skies between the Soviet craft and the surface of Mars," described by the mission chief as "something which some may call a flying saucer." They directed Phobos 2 to approach the moonlet up to a distance of 50 yards. *"The last picture Phobos 2 sent showed a missile coming at it from the moonlet.* Immediately after that, the spacecraft went into a spin and stopped transmitting—destroyed by the mysterious missile." Hardly a month later, in April 1989, the secret commission with representatives of all leading nations (born after the first incident) formulated a "Declaration of principles concerning activities following the detection of Extraterrestrial Intelligence" which stipulates the procedures to follow in case a signal would be received—namely to delay the disclosure for at least twenty-four hours before a response is made. As concludes Sitchin, "the preparations were for a nearby encounter"; in his eyes it does "indicate that the Anunnaki still have a presence—probably a robotic presence—on Mars, their olden Way Station" (*Days*, 305–6).

Enki Sole Possessor of MEs after the Deluge

Around 4000 BCE, Anu and Antu visited Earth and an Assembly was of course convened. Anu, presiding over the meeting, introduced Enlil's accusation that Enki could be withholding sacred knowledge for himself. This, the tablets say, happened after Enki had rebuilt Eridu with his stunning new temple-abode, the E.En.Gur.Ra ("House of the lord whose return is triumphant"), guarded by the "Bull of Heaven." The text *Hymn to Eridu* (translated by A. Falkenstein) describes the travel of Enki to attend the Assembly during Anu's visit, then the deliberations. Anu addresses the Assembly:

Anunnaki gods, who to the Court of Assembly had come! My son had for himself a house built; the Lord Enki, Eridu like the mountain on earth he raised; . . . *In its sanctuary, from the Abzu, the Divine Formulas Enki has deposited.*

Says Sitchin: "Enlil's complaint [was] that Enki was withholding from the other gods *the 'divine formulas'* [the MEs]—*the knowledge of more than one hundred aspects of civilization*—confining advancement to Eridu and its people only. . . . It was then decided that Enki must share the Divine Formulas with the other gods, so that they, too, could establish and reestablish their urban centers: civilization was to be granted to the whole of Sumer" (*Wars,* 194; my emphasis). So basically, we see a quite novel political situation after the Deluge. Enki has had in his possession all the MEs, all the aspects of civilization, and didn't give them out for a long while! Only now, on the order of Anu, will he be obliged to do so. Furthermore, the space facilities in the Sinai, Egypt, Baalbek, and Mount Moriah (the future Jerusalem) are for the most part under the control of the Enkiites, given that after the First Pyramid War, Seth (Ra/Marduk's son), who had fled Horus's vengeance and invaded Canaan, invested the spaceport in Sinai and the Control Center on Mount Moriah. And then it was Ninmah's new territory, since after the Second Pyramid War, she has directed the space facilities in the Sinai.

All this means that, with the Deluge and the role Enki had played in safeguarding not only the seed of humanity and of the living, but also the techno-magical, literary, and historical lore of their civilization and of humanity, a major political shift had occurred. Enki has reconstructed his temple immediately, but Eridu is the only rebuilt city. The other destroyed temples and cities have to be rebuilt along the same geo-architecture they had before the Deluge, but who has the plans? The sacred geometry knowledge? The MEs of these techno-magical sciences? Of course Ptah/Enki, "the measurer of the Cord"—a title that will be transmitted to Thoth/Ningishzidda/Hermes and his elder sons. We can surmise from this information that Enki did hide more than the MEs in Africa ahead of the Deluge, certainly all the books and the sacred knowledge and the objects and emblems of power. And this is in accordance with his reputation. Thus, when Enlil gets in a rage at discovering the ark and that one earthling, Ziusudra, has survived, "he was filled with wroth [wrath] against the Igigi gods"; but Ninurta points an accusing finger toward Enki/Ea: "Who, other than Ea, can devise plans? It is Ea who knows every matter!" (*Encounters*, 104).

Somebody had indeed safeguarded and preserved more than the seed of humanity and of the living. Enki and his clan had. And thus when Cronos/Enki orders Sisithros/Ziusudra to gather all the books from Sumer at the spaceport, maybe Enki didn't direct his spacecraft to get into Earth's orbit, but toward a hidden refuge in Africa that he could have conceived to be safe from the giant wave and storm. We have a text showing clearly that Marduk/Ra was involved in architectural and engineering works related to space facilities (and this knowledge involved of course sacred geometry as well as numerous MEs). A stela erected near the Giza Sphinx refers to Ra as the "Extender of the Cord" (the architect) of a hidden place housing his *shem* or "Bird" (incorrectly translated prior to Sitchin's decipherment, as a "name")—that is, of a facility from which he could take off with a craft.

> Thou hast built for thee a place protected in the sacred desert, *with hidden name* [shem] . . . Thou art rising beautifully . . . Thou art crossing the sky with a good wind . . . Thou art traversing the sky in the celestial barque. (*Wars*, 150; my emphasis)

We note the reference to a protected place in which a shem (a rocket or a spacecraft according to Sitchin) is hidden and permits a launch. Could it have been the place where a spaceship that lifted off in Sippar spaceport before the Deluge landed with its precious cargo of all the books that could be gathered in Sumer? This is of course above and beyond the fact that it is certain that Enki and Ninmah, two scientists and the most learned Anunnaki, had constituted their own huge library in Egypt. And which was the sacred desert? Why and since when was it sacred? All in all we see that Marduk and Thoth were, like Enki, architects and engineers. Marduk, in charge of the space station on Mars, could also have built a secret facility to hide the books there or on the moon.

But now, after the Deluge, that the real power (that of the MEs and the control of the space facilities) has been shifted toward Enki, Ninmah, Ningishzidda, and Marduk, does that change the hierarchy in the royal family? Not at all. Did anybody acknowledge the debt they all owe to Enki? Not in the least. The only thing the Enlilites could think of was *war* to regain control.

So, to get back to Enlil's performances as the Commander in Chief of Earth, I find it hard to accept that the gods would not have criticized Enlil's governance, decisions, and handling of the situation. I can't believe that Enki and the Enkiites did not take the opportunity, after the disaster, to question Enlil's rule, to show his grave shortcomings, his enormous errors of judgment, his fatal decisions, and how (if not for their own actions) he would have led them all into a situation so grave and desperate that the Deluge would have been a tenfold greater catastrophe. Why did they not rebel against Enlil's rule, taking Anu as an arbiter? Of course, there is a political strategy that says it is unwise to change the leaders at the moment a country is either in war or stricken by a disaster; and this is still exemplified today as a strategy. Yet one could contest such a position, arguing that the leader who has created the catastrophic situations (whether financial or ecological) is precisely not the one who should be trusted with the crisis management. But, in practice, fear is instilled in the minds of the populations and they vote more conservatively.

As could be anticipated, Enlil, in the following millennia, would only bring to the Anunnaki, to mankind, and to planet Earth, more of the same: more war, more devastation, more suffering, and more aberrant decisions and governance. Moreover, as time goes by, he will be progressively even more autocratic, replacing Anu as the first speaker and most influential god in the Assembly. But now let's see his next grand act.

Enlil Destroys Marduk's Babel Tower and Forces Disunity on Mankind

Between the Deluge (11,000 BCE) and the Tower of Babel crisis (3450 BCE), two wars were fought between Enlil's children and Enki's children. The First Pyramid War started about four hundred years after Ra/Marduk had handed over the kingship of Egypt to his two sons Osiris and Seth (equally qualified to be kings) by dividing the territory between the north (Lower Egypt) given to Osiris, and the south (Upper Egypt) given to Seth. As we know well, Seth will kill Osiris and dismember him in 9330 BCE, setting his wife and half sister Isis on her quest to make his body whole again. When grown up, their son Horus will start a war against Seth and vanquish him. Seth will then flee to the Sinai and Canaan, conquering the regions and establishing his reign there. But that gave the Enkiites control of all the new space facilities, and the Enlilites will launch the Second Pyramid War, at the end of which Marduk is imprisoned alive in the Great Pyramid; Ninmah intervenes and brokers peace between the two clans. Marduk is rescued and Ninurta loots the Ekur—the Bond Heaven-Earth—of all its MEs and its technology. A new Assembly of the Gods divides the Earth into four regions, and Inanna is given the fourth, the Indus Valley. In Egypt, Thoth's reign starts in 8670 BCE.

Then, as related in the *Epic of Etana,* it is around 4000 BCE (at the same gathering of the Assembly in which Enki was confronted as possessor of the MEs), that the great Anunnaki decided to lower kingship and establish the function of Lugal, simultaneously king and High Priest, transmitted to their descendants, and lines of queens and High Priestesses as well. At the beginning all of them were of mixed Anunnaki-earthling parentage, then later, the royal and priestly functions will be held by different individuals, sometimes by extraordinary earthlings.

New cities are established to be the capital of the empire, governed by these demigods or Earth-human kings and queens (but still under the control of the Lofty Gods). The first one is Kish (3760 BCE), the town of Ninurta. It becomes the administrative capital while Ur, the city of Nannar, will rise as the commercial capital. The symbols of human kingship (and we may surmise they are MEs) are the Tiara, the Crown, and the Shepherd's Crook. Let's note that here again we see in Sumer the roots of the symbolism of both royalty (with the Crown) and of priesthood with the Tiara and the Shepherd's Crook that are still the emblems of the popes. The Sumerian King List describes how the kingship on Earth kept moving from one city to another, from Kish to Erech, then to Ur. Biblical texts add Babylon as the second capital.

It is in this context that the construction and then destruction of the Babel tower happens. In the words of the historian Berossus:

> The gods introduced a diversity of tongues among men, who until that time had all spoken the same language.

And he goes on describing what the biblical texts refer to:

> When all men formerly spoke the same language, some among them undertook to erect a large and lofty tower, that they might *climb up to heaven*. But the Lord, sending forth *a whirlwind*, confounded their design, and gave to each tribe a particular language of its own. (*Wars*, 198; my emphasis)

For Sitchin, there is a common source for the largely similar descriptions of Berossus and the Book, and he points to the cuneiform Akkadian text (called K-3657) that George Smith discovered in Ashurbanipal's library in Nineveh and translated in his 1876 first book (*The Chaldean Account of Genesis*). Out of six columns of text, Smith salvaged four of them. Text K-3657 was retranslated by W. S. C. Boscawen in *Transactions of the Society of Biblical Archaeology*, vol. 5. Drawing from Boscawen's translation, Sitchin remarks,

> "The thoughts" of this god's heart "were evil; against the Father of the Gods [Enlil] he was wicked . . . the people of Babylon he

corrupted to sin," *inducing "small and great to mingle on the mound."* (*Wars*, 198; bracket in the original, my emphasis)

We have here a most extraordinary statement! *The great "sin" of Babylon (and Marduk) was to promote brotherhood between all people— whether small or great!* This is what has been transcribed in the Book as the foolish hubris of Babylon willing to surpass the might of the deity, and as a unity of tongues (or counsels) before, rightly angered, the deity ordered "their counsels to confuse."

As often happens in the tablets, the very name of the god who is implied (whose "heart's thoughts were evil") has been damaged. This is another question to consider in due time: Were the damages to the Sumerian and Akkadian tablets sometimes showing intentional and deliberate sabotage? And the fact is, we can see clearly such an intentional erasing of words on several tablets whose photos are presented in Leonard King's *Babylonian Magic and Sorcery*. Several tablets show groups of words neatly erased in a way that follows the lines too tidily to be natural damage (see for example King's plates 31, 38, and 40). At what time did this sabotage occur—in Sumerian times or since the discovery and unearthing of the Ashurbanipal's library in Nineveh (credited to Austen Layard) in 1849? And by whom was it performed and on whose orders (an individual or a group)? Of course we now have so many tablets and texts to piece together (the British Museum's collection amounts to 31,000 tablets just from the Ashurbanipal's library) that we well know who was the god who built Babylon and his own abode-temple there, Marduk/Ra, firstborn of Enki.

Then the text goes on to report how "the lord of the Pure Mound," Enlil, "to Heaven and on Earth spoke. . . . He lifted his heart to the Lord of the Gods, Anu, his father; to receive a command his heart requested. At that time, he also lifted up [his heart? voice?] to Damkina" (K-3657 text, quoted in *Wars*, 198–99; brackets by Sitchin).

We thus see *Enlil trying to induce the mother of Marduk* (and legitimate spouse of Enki), Damkina, *to side with him against her own son and firstborn!* The next verse is partly damaged, but she stands by her son: "With my son I rise" and she refers to his numbered rank as a god in the circle of the Great Gods. Given that after Enki (40) and herself Ninki/Damkina (35) the descent of Enlil (the sons and their spouses, up to their grandchildren Utu/Shamash and Inanna), preceded Marduk, his lowly status was definitely a matter of contrition and anger in their house. And of course Damkina will stand by her son in his longstanding struggle to have a city of his own. The name *Babylon* is Akkadian and means "Gateway of the Gods," which Sitchin interprets as "the space by which the gods were to enter and leave Sumer" (*Wars,* 199). In essence, such Gateway in Marduk's temple would thus be a private or alternative spaceport, with a Bond Heaven-Earth. The head or control room (the holies of holies always set on the highest platform of the ziggurat) was to enable him to reach or (as says Berossus) to "climb up to heaven," that is, to communicate and to monitor space flights between Nibiru and Earth, as well as to monitor space flights on Earth.

Ptah/Enki and Ra/Marduk have brought into existence in Egypt a novel and quasi-independent civilization that was free from the edicts and blinkers of the ancient Nibirian civilization and far enough from Enlil's grip to develop on its own. Yet Marduk (just as Enki or Ninmah) still wanted to have a strong presence in Sumer, to have his own temple with his own technology. Even if they were, by now, pretty assured that the Egyptian civilization was going to supersede the decadent Sumerian one (still in the process of reconstruction) the world politics were nevertheless spinning around Sumer and also Anu on Nibiru. Marduk wants for his temple Esagil the best of the technology they have perfected in Egypt—above and beyond its sacred geometry "measurements."

Let's remember the *Erra Epos* text, which I partly analyzed in *DNA of the Gods,* and in which we saw Nergal destroying the waterworks of the underground control chamber of the Esagil. Erra/Nergal, while praising Marduk, remarks that his Esagil temple "the abode of Anu with darkness it covers" (*Wars,* 252). In other words, its very magnificence angers the other gods. At this point Marduk explains the new conditions prevailing since the Deluge:

In the aftermath of the Deluge, the decrees of Heaven and Earth had gone astray. *The cities of the gods upon the wide earth were changed around; they were not brought back to their locations* . . . As I survey them again, of the evil I am disgusted. Without a return to their [original] places, mankind's existence is diminished . . . Rebuild I must my residence which in the Deluge was wiped away; Its name [I must] call again.

We have here an inkling of the kind of sacred architecture Marduk had in mind while building his temples (in Babylon and Egypt). We have also to underline that the evil in Marduk's eyes is the nonconformity of the new cities and temples with the sacred measurements, architecture, locales, etc. Nothing to do, whatsoever with the evil in Enlil's mouth—which just signifies whoever is disobedient, therefore the enemy—and everything to do, in contrast, with his knowledge as Ra in Egypt.

A Semantic Fields Analysis of the Tower of Babel Incident

When the Babel tower's destruction happens, in the middle of the fourth millennium BCE, the reconstruction of the olden cities, which started (apart from Eridu) only three centuries earlier, is still going on. It means that the Deluge and Enlil's blindness during this fateful event are still haunting memories. Just as he had done in Egypt, Marduk wanted his new Esagil—the Tower of Babel—to have a state-of-the-art landing strip on the roof and a protected hangar for his flying bird, just as Enlil, Ninurta, Inanna, and Ninmah had in their own temples. But he wanted also the communication technology working both on Earth and through space—the Bond Heaven-Earth. In fact the name *Esagil* spells it all, since it means "house whose head is lofty." As *Il* or *El* means "lofty, lord, divine," the tower's name can be understood as "whose head is reaching Heaven." And this is why the Book's version speaks of a group of people intent on constructing "a tower whose head shall reach unto the heavens." Marduk, we know, intended for his city to be the next capital of Sumer after Erech, but Ur had been chosen. At that point, he decided to nevertheless build his own great temple.

So let's have a fresh look, using Semantic Fields Theory, at the Akkadian text unearthed in Nineveh that George Smith and later W. S. C. Boscawen translated (*Wars*, 198):

> The thoughts of [Marduk's] heart were evil; [MF]
> against the Father [MF]
> of the Gods, [IF]
> he was wicked . . . The people of Babylon he corrupted to sin, [MF]
> [inducing] [MF]
> *small and great to mingle on the mound.* [IF]

Thus only two groups of words show an Informational Framework. What is remarkable in this Akkadian text is the *semantic field* attached to it. It is one of the two texts I have seen so far that relates events in a Moralistic Framework (MF) that bears a worldview and values coherent and congruent with that of the Book. We have the main ingredients:

- The Commander in Chief has become the omnipotent and towering Father of the Gods (still retaining the plurality of gods whom he governs).
- A god (or king) wants to act independently → *therefore he is judged as an "enemy" and as opposing* the father of the gods → *therefore he is evil* and wicked.
- The population of his city are not just viewed as his natural followers (as any population in each of the gods' cities); *because he is evil* he has "corrupted them." We see there the onset of a circular logic that moves backward from the core assumption (the central axiom in the semantic field): I'm THE Good → whoever is not with me is against me → therefore they are evil.
- The people worship and praise him (the eternal god of *his* city) instead of the self-appointed "father" → therefore he has induced them *to sin*.

Apart from the clear recognition of the plurality of gods, the semantic field is very similar, paralleling the judgments and assumptions of "sinful" and "wicked" that are put on Sodom and Gomorrah prior to their utter destruction.

This text could indeed be the missing link between Sumerian/Mesopotamian texts and the biblical texts. The grounds on which these judgments were made are the same.

Says Sitchin, "As biblical statements (e.g., Deuteronomy 29:22–27) attested, the 'wickedness' of the cities of the Jordan Plain was that 'they had forsaken the Covenant of the Lord . . . and they went and served other gods.'" (*Wars*, 325). Interestingly, in both cases the "other gods" were Marduk and his son Nabu.

The K-3657 text thus states from the start, as an axiom and a perfect priming of the readers' mind, that Marduk is evil and a seducer—while in contrast Enlil is called "the Lord of the Pure Mound" and the "father of all the gods," thus stressing both his purity and his indisputable authority.

At this point in the text, Enlil seeks the support of his own father, thus putting him on his side (the real "father of the Gods" by the way, thus already belying the earlier attribution), then he tries to set Marduk's mother against her son, to no avail. Finally, in a negotiation stance quite out of character, Enlil tries to persuade the workers busy on the site to stop their work. To do that, he is described as getting aloft in his "whirlwind" (a sort of helicopter, as we have seen) and speaking to them from above . . . to no avail, either.

And now he gets into a destructive fit. These sentences (*Wars*, 199) are all in IF:

To their stronghold tower, in the night, a complete end he made. [IF]
In his anger, a command he also poured out: to scatter abroad was his decision. [IF]
He gave a command their counsels [languages] to confuse . . . their course he stopped. [IF]

Enlil (just as the deity of the Book) generally does not lose time negotiating; the judgments are immediately followed by violent and lethal action. After the failed attempt at stopping their work, he thus destroys the construction with great violence.

Then he punishes not only Marduk's people but the whole of humanity with a sort of curse: from now on, there will be a language for each tribe and it will be impossible to communicate easily.

The Akkadian text ends up with a moralistic lesson (all in MF):

> [Because they] against the gods revolted with violence, [MF]
> violently they [were crushed and] [MF]
> they wept for Babylon; very much they wept. [MF]

Of course we remark the addition of a perfect lie: "they revolted violently"—this is not at all the case; they just constructed a tower. And in the Book the idea seemed to have come to them spontaneously while traveling—which is an impossibility when we consider on the one hand the size of the temple, and on the other hand the care with which sacred buildings were conceived and constructed on sacred geometry.

But we see that lies do not matter if the objectives can be achieved. And these crucial objectives are: (1) put the responsibility of the fault on the competitor or enemy by showing his "abominable sin," (2) set a reason for god's wrath—the sin—so that the punishment (however severe) is merited, (3) let the wrath of god strike and smite his enemies, so that all will fear god.

So we have here a Mesopotamian text retrieved from Nineveh (the capital of Assyria), written in Akkadian, and that expresses the same semantic field bearing a moralistic framework—judgments of sin and wickedness projected on the competitors, distorting the truth to rationalize violent and warlike actions on the part of the chief of the gods on Earth.

In this text Enlil has already become the "father of the gods" in the place of Anu, and in the Book, Enlil will be further transmuted into a plural-singular (becoming the unique voice of all). And the final abstraction will lead to a sole and unique god—who has lost any sign of his human species (of his parents, family, spouse, and children) and of his human or too human psyche, with its feebleness, shortcomings, enormous past mistakes, and despotic and violent drives.

The Book Account of the Tower of Babel

As we'll discover, the Book account is remarkably similar to that of the Akkadian tablet, which predates it by about two millennia, both in terms of the psychological profile of the deity, and in terms of the violent events.*

At the beginning is a group of nomads: "And as they travelled from the east, they found a valley . . . and they said unto one another: 'Let us make bricks.'" Then somebody throws the idea: "Come, let us build us a city, and a tower whose head shall reach the heavens" (MF). So the stage is somewhat cleared of all Sumerian civilization and competitor gods: there are no cities (which were already in bricks), no other gods with their own claims and rights at constructing a temple-abode; there is no preset hierarchy in the royal family, nor feuds. Only a band of brain-less nomads with delusional pride, whose foolish desires were to "reach the heavens" and therefore to be the equal to God. Thus is spelled out in the introductory phrases the necessity for the deity to reinstate his authority by severely punishing them. Yet, for now, the deity just comes down to watch: "And Y. came down to see the city and the tower which the *humans* were building" (MF).

Here again the past is erased. Of course Enlil knows about Babylon and Marduk's claims. The deity nevertheless has to "come down"—the implication being that his throne is geographically in the upper spheres of "the heavens," thus reinforcing the suggested threat. Why would an omniscient god need to displace himself to see? Also, the builders are just "humans"—the distantiation of God from the "human ants" is complete. This is setting the stage to overamplify the enormous pride

---

*The destruction of the Tower of Babel is recounted in Genesis 11; the excerpts used in this section are from Genesis 11:2–5, the emphasis throughout is mine.

and sinful hubris of these pitiful humans. If they were so pitiful and inept, they would be unable to build a tower, and why would the deity then go to the trouble of smashing the construction? As Sitchin points out (*Wars*, 197; my emphasis):

> And [the Deity] said to unnamed colleagues: "This is just the beginning of their undertakings; *from now on, anything that they shall scheme to do shall no longer be impossible for them*." [IF]
> And Y. said to his colleagues: "*Come, let us go down* and confuse their language, so that they would not understand each other's speech." [IF]
> Then the Lord "scattered them [IF]
> from there all over the face of the Earth, [MF]
> and they ceased to build the city." [IF]

After having set the stage for the very moralistic tale of the punished hubris—all in MF—suddenly, with the talking to other interlocutors and rallying them ("Come, let us go down"), is a portion of text revealing a much more ancient account, in an informational framework (IF)—the first sentence I have put in italics.

Here we recognize, set in a superb psychological profile, the jealous and paranoid Enlil, forever fearful that the Earth-humans will supersede the Anunnaki. With this fear, Enlil is projecting much more power on the earthlings than they could possibly get (nothing will "be impossible for them")—and this Informational Framework is totally at odds with the Moralistic Framework that aims at systematically *belittling* and *reducing the earthlings* to endemic sinners in constant need of a shepherd and of a severe father.

We recognize easily the semantic style, and the pathological dread, of the person who already said, in the garden of Eden: "Behold the Adam has become as one of us . . . *and now might he not . . . partake also of the Tree of Life . . . and live forever?*"

The Babel tower statement, while exaggerated, is nevertheless very interesting, because Enlil, despite all his fear, seems to have a hunch about what will eventually unfold on Earth in a very distant future. In our time, in effect, the Earth-born human species will have a science and a civilization that will match the ones of the Anunnaki, and that will eventually unravel and decipher the story of its origin—thus remaining aloof from it and winning its own freedom from this very past.

What Did the Anunnaki Know about Exo-civilizations in the Universe?

The original Sumerian text featured Marduk as the architect and planner of his new temple-abode, the Esagil. His aim and claims, as much as his superior engineering expertise, were destabilizing Enlil to the point that he ordered the tower to be smashed. So far so good—it is somehow sound, given the specific characters and personas confronting each other. But then, why confuse their languages? Why order a Diaspora? Of course, as is often found, the biblical text is replete with contradictions—above and beyond the major ones in semantic fields that we have already analyzed. For example, if they were just a bunch of nomads, it's difficult to send them "all over the face of the earth"—they are not numerous enough! This wholly unrealistic exaggeration is, as usual, used for emphasizing the deity's might, hence it falls in the MF category. Now, if the builders' languages are confused and they can't understand each other, what's the need to scatter them far away? This is where we get back to the real reason for the fit of jealousy and rage of Enlil . . . and the key is in George Smith's translated text:

> [T]he people in Babylon [Marduk] corrupted to sin [*inducing*] *small and great to mingle on the mound.*

It was much more than a tall and sophisticated building that Marduk had started. In this "house like a mountain," in this temple in the shape of a pyramid, *Marduk had launched a novel community, a brotherhood of knowledgeable and initiated individuals.* Maybe on the model of what he and Enki had already launched in Egypt. It is also evident that this brotherhood was including men and women—because Anunnaki women were also scientific geniuses of the first order, such as Ninmah of course, but also the geologist Ereshkigal (Inanna's sister).

Let's remember that Marduk loved deeply his earthling wife Sarpanit; as I have proposed, it is highly probable, given Marduk's propensity to actively oppose Enlil's rank and decisions, that he and the Igigi living in the Mars or moon facilities with their wives (the carefree Igigi, able to contravene Enlil's orders) had saved their wives and kids from the Deluge. They had all the knowledge necessary to do that: they knew the diverse bases and how to run them, and they had the control of the spacecrafts.

So this is what doubly enrages Enlil: that he saw this community of questers, speaking one language, but more importantly, living in harmony, in search of knowledge, of "solving secrets." That, and their willingness to explore the universe (via the Esagil's own astronomical Bond Heaven-Earth and communication channels). They had access to a knowledge that reached far, and that was aiming far beyond their original planet Nibiru and its deliquescent political system (which had proven itself to be not only nonsensical but lethal to an intelligent civilization).

It is quite evident that *destroying the tower in Babylon did not in the least destroy the community,* neither in Sumer nor in Egypt and Africa at large. And this brings us to the most nagging question, the one piece of information that has been totally and hermetically erased from all the texts, whether edited monotheist ones or Sumerian records of the Anunnaki: *What did the Nibirians know about the universe and other intelligent civilizations out there?*

We have ample evidence by now that, in the words of Sitchin (*Wars,* 305), "the biblical viewpoint, which compresses the Mesopotamian tales of the gods into a monotheist mold," in so doing, had erased an essential lore about our origins, a load of precise information.

What was the parent monotheist religion really trying to do (or to hide) when they constructed a nonhuman, abstract entity who was said to have created the universe, but had in fact only optimized a human species on a tiny planet, while all the stars shine at us in all their billions of billions of sparks?

Why did the narrators set the course of hiding from women and men their true origin, when it had been a fact of life for the Adamic societies to live next door to the Anunnaki and interact with them?

These are open questions to ponder. But when considering the so much larger issues of the knowledge of the Anunnaki about other civilizations existing in the universe, I cannot refrain from thinking that putting all the weight and attention on a prince willing to be the sole, autocratic Master of Earth does not add up: some huge body of information is missing, even when we include Nibiru in the picture—just another tiny spark in the universe. And to try to fill the gap, my hunch is that *we have to follow the thread of Enlil suddenly allowed to have his own royal garden with the two Tree-gods on Earth*—a shift to a higher status than even that of his father Anu (given Anu is not dead yet and therefore the shift doesn't reflect a normal legacy). And this shift happens just after the perfecting of a new intelligent being on a young planet.

✦ 5 ✦

The Use of Nukes

The Sumerian Account

THE EIGHTH ACT of Enlil was to lead to the total annihilation of the civilization of Sumer. For this final act, we will not see anything fundamentally different from what we have already seen: the feuds between Enkiites and Enlilites. But for this firework's crowning piece, Enlil will surpass himself in all the powerful and lofty qualities that we have seen him express so unabashedly along the 413,977 years of his reign on Sumerian land as dominant despot with the title of King of Heaven and Earth and legal heir of Anu—that is, from his arrival on Earth to the nuclear irradiation of the Jordan and Sinai plains as well as of the land of Sumer and the near obliteration of its people, flora, and fauna.

The Abominable War of the Enlilites against Marduk: The Use of Nukes

The immensely costly and permanent wars between the gods, such as the two Pyramid Wars recorded in the tablets, found their culmination in the second half of the twenty-first century BCE. The nastiest such war brought about the whole destruction of Sumer and Palestine, and it was recorded in Sumerian tablets, mainly as an immense number of

"Laments" from any city in Sumer that had been destroyed. In the Book as well, it was recorded as the War of the Kings, in which Abraham took an active part, followed up in 2024 BCE by what is called the destruction of Sodom and Gomorrah.

Let's see the prologue to this war.

We learn that Terah, the father of Abraham, was the High Priest of Enlil in Nippur, the most sacred city and first capital of Sumer, created by and dedicated to Enlil. Indeed, Abraham's first Sumerian name *Abram* meant "dweller of *Nibru.Ki*"—that is Nippur in Sumerian. Then Terah went to live in Ur, the new capital, the city of Nannar, heir of Enlil, when this god was given the spiritual and administrative tutorship of the two cities, corresponding with the crowning of King Ur-Nammu. Then in 2096 BCE, the King Ur-Nammu, battling in the East on a mission for the gods, died by accident—he who had been the protégé of several gods, especially Enlil and his firstborn Nannar. The population felt that, in a manner impossible to fathom, the great gods had left their protégé to die, they had abandoned him—they who were almighty didn't care to interfere and save their chosen king, one who was only doing their will. An immense deception and questioning emerged in the minds of Sumerians about the very Chief of the Gods, Enlil, clearly expressed in the tablets.

This very year, Terah moved with his family—notably the young couple Abram (Abraham), twenty-seven years old, and his wife and half sister Sarai (Sarah)—to Harran, a town that stood on the Euphrates river in Hittites land, to the northwest of the land of Sumer . . . as if in preparation for the dire catastrophe that was to come and erase Sumer. When Abraham was seventy-five, he was instructed by the Deity to leave Harran and go south, and he left with his wife and his nephew Lot, whose father had died. It is at this occasion that we can surmise that Abraham—a Sumerian from Nippur and first son of the High Priest Terah (of Enlil's Nippur temple, then of his Ur temple), thus already raised to be the next High Priest—being childless, chose Lot to be his adopted son, through whom the priestly line was going to pass. The move happened twenty-four years before the use of nukes that destroyed five towns in the Sinai plain and then the whole of Sumer through the ensuing radioactive cloud—but Abraham's line of High Priests of Enlil was spared.

It was an Assembly of the Gods that approved the use of nukes to destroy Marduk and his son Nabu. It is noteworthy that, as Mesopotamia (Sumer and Akkad) was destroyed in near totality, all the Anunnaki who had their cities and abodes there (mainly the Enlil's clan) lost the near totality of their population and all their properties, as well as their cattle and crops. The land was thoroughly scorched by the contaminated wind. The only exception, the only city that escaped destruction, was the abode of Marduk . . . Babylon.

And what was the sin attributed to the "sinful cities" that were going to be thus utterly scorched and contaminated, along with all animals, plants, and the land itself, as well as the sea? Here again, we have to note that the "sin" of the earthlings populating the five towns that were blown away was only to be followers of Marduk; in other words, the Enlilites considered it normal that, in order to destroy Marduk, his earthling followers should be destroyed as well—that was all there was to the "sin" of the "sinful" cities.

> The cities he [Erra/Nergal] finished off, to desolation he overturned them. . . . As with fire, he scorched the animals, banned its grains to become as dust. (*Erra Epic*)

Predictably, as they were gods, Marduk and Nabu escaped the destruction; but the whole human population of the Jordan and Sinai plains was exterminated by several blasts—apart from Abraham, his nephew Lot, and his two young daughters. But Lot's wife was not spared.

And what was the uttermost consequence of this war attack perpetrated with willful intent, by gods utterly blinded by hatred, jealously, and a craving for violent vengeance—and whose utterly irresponsible decision had nevertheless been reached by the majority of the best godly minds at the Assembly of all gods and goddesses? The destruction of their Sumerian population, original land, and civilization in Mesopotamia. Of note is the fact that the King of Heaven himself, Anu, was taking part in the debates in the Assembly, heading it of course as befitting his rank, and that he voted positively. In fact, a link Heaven-Earth was kept open continually during the few days of the crisis. The most violent support and incentive for the use of nukes came from Nergal backed by Enlil.

So, how do these gods react to their abodes and their civilization being destroyed by a seemingly ill-fated wind blowing northeastward, and thus bringing back unto their own lands the lethal nuclear energy they had unleashed elsewhere? How do they react to the loss of everything, their civilization and followers, while the very city of their archenemy—Babylon—was the only one to be spared? They now interpret by mutual consent that the (mysterious) "Creator-of-All" has singled out Marduk as his protégé and that, in accordance, they not only have to leave him alone, but also grant him (at last) the right to possess a land of his own and to be worshipped in a temple. Furthermore, they grant him the Enlilship, the status of the Chief of the Gods on Earth— at least for the whole cycle of the Ram. And thus started the era of Marduk who declared himself, beyond being the first among the gods, the *sole god,* while Enlil had to let go of his sovereignty.

Thus were Mesopotamia, Lebanon, and the Sinai regions irradiated and unfit for life for a very long time to come. The end-line consequence (that to my knowledge is not stated in the tablets we have unearthed) is that first Enlil, and then all the gods of Enlil's clan, now had to find a new land, build new abodes, and they also had to find new earthling people as their followers, priests, and servants. And it couldn't be in Egypt, nor in Africa at large—the domain of Enki's clan since the olden times.

During his long exile, Marduk and his son had traveled to various countries and he had already presented himself (as had been his long-standing aim) as *the* foremost god, and by the time of the use of nukes, he had gathered followers and temples everywhere. We can infer that these regions were the ones where we find him venerated as the prominent deity under various names—such as the region that was going to become the core of Persia with Cyrus's father, and where he is called Ahura-Mazda (or Ormuzd), and of course Egypt, the domain of his father, where he reigned as Ra after the 9,000 years of his father Ptah/Enki's reign, thus starting the second reign of the first dynasty of gods in Egypt (as stated by Manetho in his King List).

In his reconstructed *The Lost Book of Enki,* Sitchin describes that Enlil was warned by a dream of a catastrophe to befall Sumer, and that this is how he ordered to Terah to take his family out of Nippur and then Ur, to settle in Harran, and why, still later, he commanded Abraham to move southward to Canaan and the Negev desert—where the latter took an active and heroic part in the War of the Kings that however led to the fateful use of the nukes—the last act.

Summary of Events in Sumer Surrounding the War of the Kings

Here is a synthesis of the whole sequence of events: the Babel tower incident takes place in 3450 BCE, at the onset of the first dynasty of Ur, or Ur I period (*Wars,* 349). In 2316 BCE, Nergal convinces his brother Marduk to leave Babylon again, and immediately sets himself to destroy Marduk's temple and the waterworks servicing Mesopotamia. And the final act—the radioactive contamination of Palestine and Sumer—happens in 2024 BCE, exactly when Abraham (or Abe), born in Nippur, reaches ninety-nine years old.

During the previous century, Ur became the capital of the new Kingdom of Sumer and Akkad, called the Ur III period. The reigning kings have been *Ur-Nammu* (enthroned in 2113 BCE) and *Shulgi* (who sent Elamite troops headed by *Khedorla'omer* to restore order in Canaan in 2055 BCE). Then came *Amar-Sin* who, in 2041 BCE, was ordered by Inanna to form the Alliance of the Kings of the East (also coached by Nannar, Inanna's father and son of Enlil). This starts the War of the Kings that pitted the Alliance of the Kings of the East (of Sumer), led by the then King of Ur, Amar-Sin, against the kings of five cities of Canaan/Palestine, including Sodom.

Shu-Sin reigns after Amar-Sin died accidentally. Meanwhile, Enlil has left Nippur and has abandoned his wife Ninlil for a very long time; the whereabouts of his new abode outside Sumer are a question mark for us. Then King Shu-Sin builds a magnificent boat, adorned with precious stones, and sets it facing Ninlil's House of Pleasure. That brings Enlil back to Nippur, but only for a very short while. But this time he leaves with Ninlil.

During the reigns of Shu-Sin and then Ibbi-Sin, in the years preceding the use of nukes, numerous oracles in Sumer did forecast the coming disaster, more and more pressing with the time passing (*Wars,* 321). Ibbi-Sin, for example, gets such warnings from an oracle:

"The son in the west will arise . . . it is an omen for Ibbi-Sin: Ur shall be judged."

Another oracle announces:

"When the sixth year [of Ibbi-Sin's reign] comes, the inhabitants of Ur will be trapped!"

Indeed, the nukes annihilated the dwellers of Ur and of all Sumerian cities, in the sixth year of Ibbi-Sin's reign.

Another oracle warns:

"Disaster [will happen] when, for the second time, he who calls himself Supreme [Marduk], like one whose chest has been anointed, shall come from the west."

Marduk, indeed, was staying in Harran in the west of Sumer, and it is from there that he will come back to Babylon to reclaim his temple.

The Eastern Alliance's army will move south and attack Canaan and the Sinai, with the clear aim of seizing control of the spaceport in Sinai. Meanwhile Abe (now seventy-five years old and still childless), on God's command, has left Harran (Hittites' land) for Canaan in 2048 BCE, with his wife and half sister, Sarah, and his young nephew and adopted son, Lot, at the head of an elite troop.

Abe had settled his main camp and troops near Hebron, but then he traveled with Sarah farther on to Egypt, where they were hosted immediately by the Pharaoh as if they were nobility. They will stay there five years and depart from there with a powerful army.

Next, Abe blocks the advance of the Eastern Alliance at Kadesh-Barnea, an oasis in the Negev, which was set at the door of the gods' forbidden territory in the Sinai, in which were El Paran and the spaceport. Sitchin has sorted out that the Alliance's aim was El Paran, to defile and destroy a sacred precinct set around there. Why that, and who was in the "Mountain of the Gods" is not exactly clear; the only thing for sure is that it is set very near to the Sinai's spaceport. Why Enlil would send Abe to stop his own son Nannar's army from taking over the precinct is likewise unresolved, given he will order its bombing with nukes a few years later.

Thus blocked, Nannar's and Inanna's Eastern Alliance troops turn back toward Canaan and the north. At that point the five Canaanite kings (allies of Marduk) attack them but are defeated. The Alliance loots the cities of Sodom and Gomorrah and, furthermore, takes Abe's nephew Lot (who had taken residence in Sodom) as hostage before steering their camel cavalry swiftly back to Sumer.

"On hearing the news, Abraham called his best cavalrymen and pursued the retreating invaders. Catching up with them near Damascus, he succeeded in releasing Lot and retrieving all the booty" (*Wars*, 309). Then Abe proceeds back to Hebron. Malkizedek, King of Shalem (Jerusalem), gives a feast for his victory and offers him part of the booty, which Abe refuses categorically, adding that he was neutral in the war of the House of Nannar against the House of Marduk.

After being thus defeated a second time by Abe, this time near Damascus, the Alliance is in disarray; consequently Ur's empire is shattered and the kings of its various cities lose their thrones (*Wars*, 317–21).

Progressively the cities of Sumer, one by one, stop giving their allegiance to Ur and paying tributes, and finally they sever all communication with Ur altogether. The last two kings of Ur have multiplied the offerings to several of the Great Anunnaki, in order to stack their favor and support, but the Ur empire floundered nevertheless.

The Return of Marduk to Babylon

Marduk arrives in Harran (just when Abe has left it) and remains among the Hittites, in the northwest of Sumer, for the twenty-four years that a Hittite oracle had predicted he had to wait there before he could return to Sumer and claim its kingship. Marduk writes a poem, just before he leaves Hatti-land:

> "In Hatti-land I asked an oracle [about] my throne and my Lordship. My days [of exile] were completed. To my city I [set my course]; my temple Esagila as a mound [to raise/rebuild] . . . A king of Babylon to [install] in my city . . . Joy." He declares he wants to "chase away evil and bad luck . . . bring motherly love to mankind." (Khedorlaomer Texts; *Wars,* 322)

Marduk comes from the west and follows the Via Mari, along the sea, with his Amorite army, or "Westerners." Within Sumer, all cities fear an invasion from the west and defensive walls have even been erected. Ninurta, allied with Nergal, organizes an army of Elamite troops to stop Marduk, to no avail. In 2025–2024 BCE, Marduk advances successfully toward Babylon, his Westerners "taking one by one all the great fortresses" (*Wars,* 321). He enthrones himself in his own city; his intention, as always, is to be the King of Babylon and of Sumer, and the first among the gods.

That's when the sacred temple of Enlil, the Ekur in Nippur, is defiled. And Enlil, on the suggestion of Ninurta (who covers the real culprit), attributes the deed to Marduk and asks the Assembly to punish Marduk and his son Nabu. In fact, the Khedorlaomer Texts describe

Elamite troops desecrating the temples of Shamash and of Ishtar/Inanna and clearly point to Erra/Nergal himself ordering that Enlil's Ekur temple be defiled and looted (as we saw, Nergal had sided with the Enlilites and their war commander Ninurta). These texts even blame Ninurta for accusing Marduk of this desecration and for inducing Enlil to take revenge on Marduk.

Enlil, thus enraged and seeking vengeance, rushes back to Nippur: "Riding in front of him were gods clothed with radiance; [himself] set off brilliance like lightning" (*Wars*, 32). He smashes Babylon's temple, "Enlil against Babylon caused evil to be planned," and Nabu's temple in his city Borsippa. Nabu, privy to these plans, retreats to cities worshipping him along the Mediterranean Sea. But Nergal will go beyond instilling a craving for lethal revenge in Enlil: he uses the same pretext of the defiled temples to incite the Assembly to vote for using the "Awesome Weapons," and this despite Enki's strong opposition. The city where Nabu went to hide was Sodom, and that's where the Awesome Weapons will later target him. "When the son of Marduk in the land of the coast was, *he of the Evil Wind* [Erra/Nergal] with heat the plain land burnt" (*Erra Epic*).

Meanwhile the gods, with fighting erupting everywhere, were in constant communication with Anu on Nibiru, and a permanent Assembly was going on: "Anu to Earth the words was speaking, Earth to Anu the words pronounced," says the *Erra Epic*, the phrasing leaving no doubt that Anu was indeed outside of Earth.

Marduk reaches his temple in Babylon only to see Nergal already there, having damaged part of the Esagil and ready to destroy its holies of holies. Nergal and Marduk confront each other for a whole day and a whole night in Marduk's temple; Nergal wants his hated brother to give up all claims of kingship. Enki, who quickly arrived on the scene, sides with Marduk and orders Nergal out. Then the text describes them (but not Marduk) at the crucial Assembly (the one that will vote for using the nukes), at which Enki makes a case for Marduk, underlining that "the people" have chosen Marduk and "for the second time have raised his image."

The Murderous Rage and Genocidal Act of Nergal

Nergal, furious, gets back to his African domain and there vows to use the Awesome Weapons and bring total destruction to the land and the people of Canaan devoted to Marduk and Nabu. The *Erra Epic* recounts his genocidal intention:

> "The lands I will destroy . . . the cities I will upheaval, the people I will make vanish."

Already, a destructive rage seemed to have seized him some time back at the moment when (as the Khedorlaomer Texts describe it) he ordered the defilement of Enlil's holies of holies, the Ekur in Nippur:

> Erra, the pitiless one, entered the sacred precinct. . . . He beheld the Ekur. His mouth he opened, he said to his young men: *"Carry off the spoil of Ekur, take away its valuables, destroy its foundation,* break down the enclosure of the shrine!"

And of course, we remember how, in the long past, he half destroyed Marduk's sacred temple Esagil and its waterworks, thus triggering a water shortage in the whole of Sumer. Nergal/Erra is clearly a force antagonistic to all that is sacred, and specifically to temples whose function is to maintain the Bond Heaven-Earth (which could mean much more than the pragmatic flight control connection between Nibiru and Earth that anyway had been moved to the Sinai). Marduk, in contrast, has too great a knowledge of the Spirit, of the dimension of the sacred, to defile any temple—whatever the god's disposition toward him. But we see there, in Nergal/Erra, a will to destroy sacred precincts, a violence and furor so precisely targeting places of power that he seems to be possessed (in an ethno-psychological sense) by a destructive force.

The problem of course, with the Anunnaki, is that we can't blame the Devil or Satan: they *are* themselves the gods or devils personified. So we are confronted here with a crucial philosophical (and ontological) issue: if there are individuals who are *the devil incarnate* in the Sumerian civilization, they should be the ones violently opposed to the most sacred values in the universe—namely, *life as consciousness,* elevation of the mind toward a higher consciousness, the quest for a spiritual yet free knowledge of oneself, the *Spirit* or *Soul of the universe,* the harmonization of the ego with the Self. And in this line of thought, there is a very serious and disturbing problem arising about Enlil—the *legal* chief of the Anunnaki, the "rightful one" more than the "Righteous One"— casting the wrong person in the role of the devil (Enki, then Marduk). And an even greater problem arises from Enlil's lack of awareness of the extremely murderous and genocidal drives of Nergal, and from Enlil's incapacity to distinguish the good from the evil, that is, to sort out who is the evil mind-force at work, set on the destruction of their own civilization. Thus mystified by his young nephew, the Ruler of Earth (also called the demiurge in Gnosticism) appears clearly as "the king of the blind," as his mother, Sophia, a higher and ethereal entity, calls him in the Gnostic text Hypostasis of the Archons.

And we see just the opposite with Enki stopping Nergal from destructing Marduk's holies of holies, trying to rein in his son's drives, opposing his influence in the Assembly—and this, even when the Assembly has given Nergal a blank check to act on its behalf to bully Marduk into exile (when they had no crime substantial enough to decree his exile). Furthermore, when Enki sides with Marduk against Nergal, he doesn't justify his choice by personal motives, but rather points that "the people have raised his name," that the people want Marduk to be their leading god. *And this is, by the way, the first time we see explicitly stated that the earthlings could have a choice in following one god over another;* until now, the population of a city was a captive audience and captive religious community vis-à-vis the lord god of that city.

In the nuclear holocaust sequence, we would have expected Nergal, thrown out of Sumer by his father, to fulminate against Marduk (as usual) or even against his father. We would expect him to vow revenge and destruction on his worst enemy: Marduk.

But what do we see instead? (By now we should be convinced that the words put in the mouths of individuals—and as reported in similar terms in various Mesopotamian texts—are factual and true to the original exchanges.) These texts' usual scarcity of judgment toward the protagonists—apart from the two texts showing a Moralistic Framework—and the detailed accounts of what they said and even of their feelings, point to original unbiased reports. So what do Nergal's words reveal? His global and final objective is to destroy the lands (plural), the cities, the mountains, the animals, the seas, the ocean's life-forms, above and beyond the people. Nergal's ultimate goal is to destroy all life and specifically all people (gods and men)—and he adds a gruesome detail: "none shall be spared" (*Wars*, 326). He wants to make the people vanish, to turn their souls to vapor.

This is a mind-force, adamant and forcibly intent on destroying and erasing all consciousness, all souls, and all life on Earth.

I suggest that you read carefully the exact citation from the *Erra Epos:*

> Consulting with himself, [Erra vowed:] *the lands I will destroy,* to a dust-heap make them; the cities I will upheaval, to desolation turn them; the mountains I will flatten, their animals make disappear; the seas I will agitate, that which teems in them I will decimate; *the people I will make vanish, their souls shall turn to vapor; none shall be spared . . .*

On Which Side Is Enlil—
For or Against Mankind and Civilization?

This intrinsically Evil force—Evil with uppercase, as in the Essence of Evil: the force that is anti-consciousness and anti-life—is not recognized as such by the Chief of the Gods on Earth! Of course we saw that his own self-centeredness created strong blinkers limiting his understanding of global issues, but nevertheless this is *not* acceptable from the First in Command, nor by the King of Heaven Anu who, in always backing Enlil, singularly lacks the wisdom he is supposed to incarnate. As I said, we have here an extremely grave philosophical problem regarding the divine qualities attributed to and projected on the persona of Enlil—hailed as "benevolent" and the paragon of all moral virtues.

It is of course clear, given the history of the relation of humanity to this deity, that we are, in our modern times, dealing with a persona or an archetype (a god-image, as Jung called it) rather than dealing with the real individual who lived as a near-immortal since even before the "perfecting" of the "mixed beings," 300,000 years ago at least.

If we ask ourselves how could we best describe the (anti)qualities of the antichrist—we wouldn't so much speak of some person or force "opposed to Jesus," but rather of a will to destroy the soul dimension, and set against the spiritual aspiration and evolution of humanity. And this is what Nergal/Erra is; he is the epitome, the archetype of the anti-christ in our solar system. In total contrast, Enki is only expressing an alternative to the rule and the decrees of the king in power; his is a force of constructive opposition, of divergent thinking, of freedom of thought (*libre pensée*), of creative, philosophical, and scientific exploration, as opposed to the "truth" as an absolute, the despotic and autocratic power, the decreed dogmas, the institutionalized "good." Enki is always in contact with nature; he writes poems on his boat trips on the marshes about the natural beauty surrounding his sanctuaries. Enki and Hermes represent a *religere* (a religion in the Latin literal sense of relating, connecting, bonding) as a Living Knowledge—a way of Knowing by connecting; how to connect one's own soul to that of Earth, so as to explore nature and the dimension of the Spirit, of cosmic consciousness. This kind of Quest for Knowledge and Wisdom is a dynamic process, forever evolving, an endless exploration. And it needs freedom to exist.

In contrast, Enlil is representing a despotic political and institutionalized power, more inclined to maintain its status, power, and control, than to explore new reaches of the mind, of Man, and of the universe. Enlil wants the past decree of his father—who made him the first in control and in command—to last forever. Yet, soon after the nuclear blasts, when his son Nannar, god of Ur, instead of fleeing the radioactive clouds with his spouse in their plane, calls him to ask for advice,

Enlil's answer will be: "Ur . . . was not granted an eternal reign"; mean-ing, How could you ever imagine that you would last forever as God of Ur? Whereas his immediate answer should have been: "Flee, flee as quickly as possible with your wife and household and order an evacua-tion of your city." And then it was too late.

Let's linger on this one remark of Enlil, because it shows that the Chief of the Gods was not living in the present, in the here and now of a major catastrophe—the announcement of a radioactive wind, totally unexpected, that was just observed to be heading toward Sumer, the whole region, and that was described by Nannar as arriving at the hori-zon of Sumerian cities. This answer of Enlil to his son—seemingly phil-osophical as to the ending of all things (in a reproachful tone, to top it all)—is totally at odds with the way a top leader should react when get-ting the news that his country and realm, his cities, and the heartland of the Nibirian civilization on Earth are going to be laid waste. This reaction is even more in discrepancy with a father suddenly getting the news that his sons, grandsons, and their families risked being fatally contaminated, as was Nannar, unless they fled on the spot. And how is it that Enlil wasn't the first one to get the news, as if his all-knowing and all-seeing MEs (such as the "Lifted Eye which scans the land") and other technical gadgets were not enough to be in the know about a major world crisis? And in case he was the first one to know, why was he not the one to sound the alarm and order evacuation? Why did he fail to order evacuation, whatever the time at which he got the news? So now we can ask ourselves: Was Enlil taking psychological revenge on Nannar for his leading role in the attempt by the Alliance of the Kings of the East at defiling the Sinai abode and the spaceport? Yet he'd just voted for nuking this same spaceport. Since he was not in Nippur, nor in the land of Sumer since a long time before, and couldn't expect to be in Enki's territory (even if the Pharaoh had given troops to Abe to defend the Sinai), could he have been himself in the forbidden territory and hidden abode of the gods in the Sinai mountains?

What about Enlil's second in command for all military and defense operations—Ninurta? The one who had, with Nergal, fired the seven nukes on the Sinai and Canaan? Ninurta who was on site with Nergal, launching missiles from their spacecrafts and checking to see if they had correctly hit their targets. Ninurta "the Scorcher" and Nergal/Erra "He-of-the-evil-wind, the pitiless one," (as the tablets called them from then on) were in the best position to ascertain the disaster from high up and far enough to observe the radiation cloud forming and the patterns of the winds carrying fire, smoke, and debris, not only northeastward, but precisely toward Sumer. Or else, do we have to assume Ninurta was so careless, ignorant, or out of balance (as Nergal definitely was) that he failed to think about it, he, the military and armament scientist? That he, the war commander, failed to plan properly for Sumer's and their own safety during the maneuvers (out of the path of the wind, far enough away from the blast and the shock wave) and that they were just hurrying to get to their next target? Obviously, they hadn't checked the winds.

And again: Where was Enlil after he was seen talking and feasting with Abe near Hebron, on the eve before the nukes were fired? Why, when the radioactive clouds were detected approaching Sumer's cities, did he not assume his role of Commander of Earth and warn the other gods and the cities, so as to organize the protection of the populations and a crisis management?

The Assembly of the Gods Voting for the Use of Nuclear Missiles

Let's retrace the order of events to analyze them in depth. In Babylon, a heated argument takes place between Nergal and Marduk—Nergal, with the backing of the Assembly, wanting him to let go of his claims as new supreme god (after the era of Inanna, the era of Ninurta, of Nannar . . .). Enki arrives and throws Nergal out. At that point, Nergal gets back to the Assembly and makes a case for the use of the supreme force, that is, nuclear weapons, against the cities controlled by Marduk and his son Nabu. The "Awesome Weapons" are the seven nukes left by Alalu, and only Enki and his then pilot, who had hidden them at the time, are supposed to know where they are located—but, possibly unknown to Enki, the pilot did disclose the information to Enlil or Nergal.

During the Assembly's debate, which goes on for a full day, Enki rebukes Nergal, wondering why it should not be Marduk's time, since the population has chosen to follow him. But Enlil and most of the Enlilites are backing Nergal.

In a fury at having been crossed by his father, Nergal leaves the Assembly's scene and flies back to his domain in Africa, there to get into a vengeful fit, and he decides to act alone and to use immediately the "Awesome Weapons." Thus, instead of pursuing his own hate object (Marduk and Nabu)—and this reveals a grave psychological incoherence or else an overriding long-term plan—he decides to destroy the lands, the cities, the mountains, and the sea, vowing that he will vaporize the people and destroy their souls and that no one will be spared.

The *Erra Epic* then tells us that Gibil, neighbor of Nergal in Africa (the exact location is unclear), hears of his scheme and warns Marduk, who in turn goes to Enki to inquire about the weapons and where exactly they are hidden. But Enki acts as if he doesn't know that. Another text describes that then Enki, in great haste, asks the Assembly to convene again on the spot (Text CT-XVI, 44–46; *Wars*, 326). When Enki discloses Nergal's plans, trying to make them block Nergal's actions, the other gods are not shocked at all, neither by the news, nor by the prospect of using the nukes. Enki voices a grave warning: *the Awesome Weapons,* he forecast, *"the lands would make desolate, the people will make perish."*

Yet Enlil and Ninurta are stubbornly in favor of launching the nukes; only Nannar and Utu are hesitant. In the absence of consensus, Anu shall be the arbiter and he goes for the use of nukes.

All in all, we see Nergal the instigator, then Enlil, Anu, and Ninurta, that is, the Enlilites clan (to which Nergal politically belongs) giving their consent for the use of nuclear bombs to erase the cities of the Sinai plain whose people are Marduk's followers, and where Nabu is said to hide, as well as the spaceport. This is the only instance, in the tablets we know of, where a collective decision of the Assembly is aimed at murdering one of the Anunnaki gods; the worst in this respect, up to now, had been Inanna's plan, backed by the Assembly, to imprison Marduk alive in the Great Pyramid, the Ekur, and let him die of hunger, thirst, and lack of oxygen—so that they would not be responsible for his death.

The plan, which consists basically of slaying the population of five cities, that is, the Earth-human population, just because they gave their allegiance to another one of the twelve Great Gods (each having a temple, a city, and numerous followers), is already cruel, tortuous, and shameful enough. It shows that, among the Anunnaki, passionate hatred (hatred fueled by strong emotions) passes first and impedes them from considering things according to ethics and higher values (not even to mention the human rights of the earthling population). However, there was more to the agreed upon plan: it also consisted of destroying with a nuke their own spaceport in the Sinai; and this was so down-right stupid that we cannot escape the impression that most of the great gods, despite being gathered to debate rationally in order to take collective decisions, were seriously lacking depth of thinking, anticipation, and good sense, above and beyond sheer humanness and ethics—and this, without even talking about the dire consequences to Sumer.

Let's note that Nergal was not physically present at this last crucial meeting and that basically he didn't make his point himself—Enlil and Ninurta did (which gives even more responsibility to Enlil and the Enlilites).

Ninurta, the Lord of the Armies of Enlil, now in charge of the mission to launch the nukes over Marduk's and Nabu's cities and to destroy the spaceport, rushes to Nergal in Africa—only to find that he has already readied the weapons and set their "poison" (activating the nukes). This he did, obviously, on two spacecrafts, one for him and one for Ninurta (as we'll see them both fire the nukes), as if he knew all along what the Assembly's vote would be.

Ninurta tries to convey to Nergal that the wish of Anu is that the population be spared. This is an enormously naive and unscientific demand, for either they erase five towns of followers of Marduk, or they have to go through the lengthy operation of asking the population to flee (but then, why scorch the land?). This demand from Anu and the

Assembly only shows the extent to which they are ignorant of the kind of weapon they are about to use, and how much they misunderstand the personality of Nergal, who had just stated what he was going to do and had started to put things in motion. (It's only due to Enki that the Assembly was convened again in a rush.)

There is yet another interpretation, one even more shocking. We learn that, after the first plea of Ninurta, the excited Nergal finally agrees to warn the Igigi manning the spaceport and give them the time to flee, but only to them.

The second interpretation is thus that the population referred to by Anu were only Anunnaki, namely the Igigi (or Nephilim), the astronauts based on Earth; so that at no point was the earthling population of the cities considered to be "people" and even less so a problem to ponder.

Still trying to appeal to his reason and his sense of justice, Ninurta then addresses Erra thus:

> Valiant Erra, will you the righteous destroy with the unrighteous.
> Will you destroy those who have against you sinned together with
> those who against you have not sinned?

(This is a sentence of the *Erra Epic* that we will also find in the Book, practically word for word, attributed to Abe begging for his Lord to save at least the Righteous.)

The two gods debate on this, but Nergal, as if possessed, goes on vociferating:

> I shall annihilate the son and let the father bury him; then I shall
> kill the father, let no one bury him!

Ninurta keeps on trying to lessen the destruction; finally Nergal is (or seems) slightly contained. He promises he will spare Mesopotamia and the oceans. The clear targets are now the spaceport and the cities devoted to Marduk. This, let's note it, reveals that originally he also wanted to target Sumer itself, certainly Babylon and Borsippa, thus revealing that he (as well as the Assembly and Ninurta) had no idea about collateral damages and radioactive clouds and winds.

This last plan is approved both by Enlil and Anu. Then Nergal immediately gets into his flying bird—the spacecraft that carries the nukes "behind, as a trail"—and Ninurta, now called Ishum ("the Scorcher") in the text, follows "in accordance with the word given, a squeezing in his heart." (This one god still has a heart, but he nevertheless had voted for using the nukes.)

Firing the Nuclear Missiles

When they arrived at "Mount Most Supreme," inside which was the secret Command Center of the spaceport, Ninurta "the Scorcher" gets to fire the first nukes:

Ishum to Mount Most Supreme set his course; the Awesome Seven without parallel trailed behind him; at the mount the hero arrived; He raised his hand, the mount was smashed. The plain by the mount he then obliterated; in its forest, not a tree stem was left hanging.

Then emulating Ishum, Erra the kings' highway followed. The cities he finished off, to desolation he overturned them. In the mountains, he caused starvation, their animals he made perish.

He dug through the sea, its wholeness he divided. . . . As with fire, he scorched the animals, banned its grain to become as dust. (*Wars*, 328)

Sitchin remarks on the sentence starting with "Then emulating Ishum," that "the words employed by the *Erra Epic* are almost identical to those used in the biblical tale of Sodom and Gomorrah" (*Wars*, 329).

The Khedorlaomer Texts also recount the catastrophe, using the same names for the two "devastators" who would from now on, in all accounts, be called, the first one, Ishum, meaning "The Scorcher," here translated as "He who scorches with fire" and the second, Erra, meaning "He of the evil wind."

Enlil, who sat enthroned in loftiness was consumed with anger. The devastators again suggested evil; He who scorches with fire [Ishum/Ninurta] and he of the evil wind [Erra/Nergal] together performed their evil. The two made the gods flee, made them flee the scorching. (*Wars,* 330)

Here we find the clear mention of the Igigi gods being obliged to flee the spaceport facilities, and the spaceport clearly identified as "That which was raised toward Anu to launch, they caused to wither," in other words, a Place of Launching.

Sitchin attests that the Sinai plain shows an enormous elongated scar, visible from the sky alone, and blackened as if by an immense heat: "The great place (the spaceport and launching strips in the plain) was never to be seen again . . . but the scar made in the face of the earth that awesome day can still be seen to this very day" (see fig. 5.1).

As the tablets state, the blasts created an immense whirling wind and then a radioactive wind that they called "the Evil Wind" hence

Fig. 5.1. Huge scorched trail across the Sinai plain.

the new epithet given to Nergal. The radioactive cloud, carried by the winds, went to sow utter desolation in Sumer: "A storm, the Evil Wind, went around in the skies." The catastrophe has been described and recorded in many texts, in several languages, and in specific poems called Lamentation Texts or Laments, some of which give the list of the contaminated cities, where most people died. Here are some extracts (*Wars*, 337–42).

> The storm, in a flash of lightning, created a dense cloud that brings gloom, [then] rushing wind gusts . . . a tempest that furiously scorches the heavens.

> The storm crushed the land, wiped out everything . . . none could escape it.

A text called the *Uruk Lament* recounts also the debate at the Assembly and how Enki and his wife were rebuked and the vote passed in favor of the Awesome Weapons. It also clearly states that the gods had not anticipated the extent of the catastrophe in Sumer: "The great gods paled at its immensity."

> Causing cities to be desolated, houses to become desolate; that Sumer's oxen no longer stands in their stalls, that its sheep no longer roam in its sheepfolds; that its rivers flow with water that is bitter, that its cultivated fields grows weeds, that its steppes grow withering plants.

> This evil which has assaulted the land like a ghost . . . The highest walls, the thickest walls, it passes as a flood; no door can shut it out, no bolt can turn it back.

> The people, terrified, could hardly breathe; the Evil Wind clutched them, does not grant them another day . . . mouths were drenched in blood, heads wallowed in blood. . . . The face was made pale by the Evil Wind.

Another text states *how unnatural* was the deadly wind and cloud that

> covered the land as a cloak, spread over it like a sheet . . . an Evil Wind which overwhelms the land; . . . *a great storm directed from Anu . . . it hath come from the heart of Enlil . . . like the bitter venom of the gods* . . . bearing gloom from city to city.

In several texts as the one above, *the instigators of the great nuclear catastrophe are clearly named*—they attribute the responsibility of using the weapons of mass destruction to Enlil and Anu, and the scorching of the people and the land to Nergal and Ninurta.

The *Lamentation over the Destruction of Sumer and Ur,* describes how the gods hurried to flee, how they abandoned their cities and temples and how, observing from their spacecrafts, they were devastated by the atrocities brought about by the Evil Wind, the people suffocating and dying, the bodies piled up by a sudden death.

> Ninharsag [Ninmah] wept in bitter tears. [Nanshe cried,] Oh my devastated city!

At last, in Erech/Uruk, the deities called for the population to wake up and run away. But it was too late. Soon,

> the people were piled up in heaps . . . A hush settled over Uruk like a cloak.

Nannar and Ningal retreated underground, in "the termite house," but too late, and Nannar got irradiated and sick. Meeting even a worse fate, Bau, the spouse of Ninurta, left alone while he was scorching the cities and the lands, was so devastated by the destruction of her people that she kept crying instead of seeking her own safety and "the storm caught up with her, Bau, as if she were mortal." As it seems, she died soon afterward.

We gather from the descriptions that there was a nuclear wind and storm and a radioactive cloud. Yet some accounts make us wonder if this was all there was. If the seven tall mushroom clouds—spreading high in the sky above the Jordan plain and, even farther, the Sinai mountains— could maybe be perceived from a plane, the blasts themselves could not possibly be heard from Sumer. Yet Inanna, rushing in her "bird" to the coast, in order to embark in her "submersible ship" to flee to Africa, saw a blast erupting from some mountains:

> [The Evil Wind] which in an instant, in a blink of an eye was created in the midst of the mountains.

The translated text says that Ninki, "flying like a bird, left her city." But more likely, it was "flying in her Bird," because she went to Africa to be safe. As for Enki, certainly the most knowledgeable about these matters, he decided to stay in order to save the dwellers of his city.

> [Eridu's] lord stayed outside his city . . . for the fate of his harmed city he wept with bitter tears.

Enki calls upon the people he could gather to flee the city with him; they camp outside, near enough to see, for a whole day and night; they observe how the storm "puts its hand" on Eridu. Afterward, "the evil-bearing storm went out of the city, sweeping across the countryside." Enki came back to assess the damage: the city was "smothered in silence . . . its residents stacked up in heaps." Then he led the survivors to or through the desert, and managed to render some fruit trees and plants edible and safe. Before the storm hit, Enki had advised Marduk in Babylon to *hide underground* in blackness.

Then Enki and Marduk used their immense knowledge to heal the people and the living, to render again the plants and fruits edible, to purify the waters and clean the grounds and soils. Their undertakings, deemed magical by the populations, were recounted in Purification Texts.

Underground Shelters, Temples, and Cities in Sumer?

Why would Nannar and Ningal have a *termite house* under their temple? Why would Enki have advised Marduk to *hide underground* in blackness in his Esagil temple? Did some gods have bunkers ready for emergencies? Could Enki, who had made emergency plans in the past in view of the Deluge, have built an underground city or temple near Eridu, and is it to such a place that he took his people?

Hatti-land, the Land of the Hittites (actual Cappadocia in Turkey, bound by the upper Euphrates to the east) is where Marduk stayed in exile for twenty-four years before his (second) dramatic return to Babylon. With its capital Hattusa, it will become the Hittite empire. The earliest traces of settlement on the site of Hattusa are from the sixth millennium BCE. There are astonishing underground cities, built on several levels, such as Derinkuyu, Kaymaklı, and Özkonak, that had water wells, ventilation systems, wineries, churches, schools, moving stone doors, and that could house between 20,000 to 60,000 people, with their livestock and food storage (see fig. 5.2). Özkonak even

Fig. 5.2. Kaymaklı, a large room several levels underground.

had a communication system between all its ten levels, through pipes. These underground cities were connected through miles of tunnels. The population was mostly Greek; during the Byzantine empire, they built underground churches and hid from the Muslim Arabs, then the Muslim Turks.

Could a *termite house* be the term for a sort of bunker or shelter? And in that respect, an underground city such as Özkonak, with its maze of tunnels and enclosed dwellings, does look like a termite nest; could it have been a Termite City?

As intriguing is the fact that the immense complex of underground temples that we unearthed at Göbekli Tepe, in the south of Turkey, had been circular underground temples, covered by soil and totally hidden. We have unearthed only 5 percent of the complex, and there are already twenty circles and 200 magnificent pillars, T-shaped, weighting about 10–20 metric tons (one still in the quarry weighs 50 tons). The oldest part, Layer III, has been carbon-dated at about 9000 BCE, but the hilltop (the temene) was a spiritual site by 11,000 BCE or earlier, making it the oldest temple on Earth (see fig. 5.3).

Fig. 5.3. Göbekli Tepe. Several circular underground temples.

Fig. 5.4. Göbekli Tepe. Stone pillar with bas-reliefs of a bull, a fox, and a crane (Level III).

All these circular temples present a sophisticated geodesic wood roof, with neatly carved roof beams fanning out geometrically, as the spokes of a wheel, from a hub or cornerstone resting on two central stone pillars, unfortunately not visible anymore (see fig. 5.4).

The T-shape stone pillars of the temples, in a circle and support-ing the roof beams, showed magnificent carvings of a complexity and realism belying their age, raising nagging questions about our past (and upsetting the actual assumptions of archaeology). Now, this is around the time of the Deluge that, according to Sitchin, happened around 11,000 BCE, and one possibility is that the underground temples and cities around that age had been built by some Anunnaki ahead of the Deluge. Another one, concerning the second millenium BCE, would be that the shelters were built in prevision of WMD in a nasty war.

We know that Marduk, ever the target of repeated attacks, such as the two Pyramid Wars, certainly remembered being holed up in the Great Pyramid, left there for dead if it had not been for Ninmah calm-ing down the attacking gods blinded by rage, and brokering an ad hoc peace deal. Could he have then built some underground complex as a safe haven for a whole population in case of emergency such as a nuclear attack? If Marduk and his son Nabu had been known to still reside in Hatti-land, would at one point his neurotic and vengeful enemy brother Nergal and his no less murderous uncle Enlil have targeted the Hittites lands instead of the Canaan cities? And could Marduk have anticipated such a possibility? We'll see further on that the ruins of the temple in Nabu's city Borsippa (actual Birs Nimrod) are showing vitrified bricks, possibly from a devastating weapon.

The looting and defiling of the temples of the main Enlilite gods, along Marduk's path back to Babylon, ordered and accomplished by Nergal and covered by Ninurta, in order to throw them in a rage, especially Enlil, could have been a plan by The Devastator Nergal, just waiting for a plausible and suitable context to accuse Marduk of this deed, and thus get the Assembly's vote and spark the nuking of his strongholds. Remember he displayed such speed in readying the seven nukes that he had them installed on two spacecrafts even before the hurried arrival of Ninurta, and that shows that he had them at hand for a long time.

Nagging Questions about the Nuclear Holocaust

Let's ponder some details of the events that seem to imply eye-witness accounts of powerful blasts and gigantic flashes of light and flaming gusts, high in the sky. It is stated clearly in some texts, such as the *Nippur Lament,* that blasts were heard ahead of the storm and Evil Wind.

An evil blast heralded the baleful storm, an evil blast the forerunner of the baleful storm was.

After the blast came the explosion of light. "The storm, in a flash of lightning created"; then the shockwave spread in a circle around the diverse ground zero places: "They spread awesome rays toward the four points of the earth, scorching everything like fire"; "Rushing wind gusts . . . a tempest that furiously scorches the heavens" (*Nippur Lament*).

Soon, darkness set in, obliterating the sun: "when the skies were darkened and covered as with a shadow."

Then again, how could Inanna see from Erech, or even while flying to the coast, the explosion of the nukes in the Sinai mountains 800 miles distant, the Evil Wind "which in an instant, in the blink of an eye, was created in the mountains."

Something, it seems, is still missing—even in the Sumerian and Mesopotamian accounts. A radiation cloud that originated even in Sodom, roughly 700 miles away from the center of Sumer, would have only widened while drifting with the winds, its particles becoming more distant from each other with the distance. The description fits better if we assume the nearby explosion of yet another Awesome Weapon in the Zagros Mountains bordering Sumer, only 120 miles away. Also, why would Enki, the genius matter scientist, estimate he had time to flee to the nearby hills, where they could watch the storm gripping the city— but only the city and the nearby plain? Again, a drifting radioactive cloud would have swept as intensely far over the countryside as in the cities proper.

I'm left with the impression that there had been more nukes and targeting of more cities than just the five of the Jordan and Sinai plains plus two nukes on the spaceport. Did Nergal's lethal rage override his promise to Ninurta and make him switch back to his original scheme of also erasing part of Sumer, or the whole of it? But there were only seven nukes left by Alalu! When he looted Enlil's rebuilt Ekur in Nippur (no more a space control facility), could he have taken the terrible weapons that were *stockpiled there for Enlil's own future use?* Could he have defiled this temple (and two other ones looted at the same period) with another plan in mind, beyond accusing Marduk and thus getting the backing of the Assembly for launching the nuclear strikes? A plan that was to take possession of the weapons of mass destruction of Enlil, nuclear for sure and maybe bacteriological (more lethal than the ones he used to spread a pandemic among the earthlings, since the city dwellers met an instant death)? Then, if Enlil and Anu were convinced that these stolen WMD were in the hands of Marduk, the latter no doubt preparing an attack, they could have wanted to strike first. We indeed have some accounts of symptoms that could be due to bacteriological agents, such as: "The people, terrified, could hardly breathe . . . mouths were drenched in blood, heads wallowed in blood" (*Wars,* 337); and: "Causing cities to be desolated . . . that Sumer's oxen no longer stand in their stalls, that its rivers flow with water that is bitter, that its steppes grow withering plants" (*Wars,* 335).

And what about the MEs of Marduk's temple, secured before the Deluge, that Nergal had never given back? One specifically has a very scary and explicit name: "the Holy Radiating Stone which Disintegrates All." Radiations and disintegration, isn't that a nonambiguous description of some type of nuclear bomb (knowing that the Anunnaki referred to metals with the same word used for stone)?

Could Anu and/or Enlil have brought from Nibiru, or built on Earth, more nuclear armaments and used nuclear energy to have eternal lights, such as the ones in Egypt analyzed by David Childress in his book *Technology of the Gods?* Enlil did visit Nibiru occasionally, and his new title of King of Heaven and Earth made him the equal of Anu, able to impose his will there too and thus dispose freely of their nuclear arsenal. Anyway we see Anu too readily backing the use of nukes for this move to be an ad hoc decision, and thus we may infer that, on Nibiru, he would not have impeded Enlil from taking some radioactive materials back to Earth. Let's remember that all the Laments put the responsibility of the Evil Wind specifically on Nergal, and that they recount a private meeting of the Devastators with Enlil, during which they got Enlil to support their plans (thus making it unnecessary for Nergal to attend the Assembly's voting session, whose consent was already certain).

The issue becomes even more burning when we read a strikingly similar account of a nuclear blast, specifically of the shape of a mushroom cloud with its long stem, in the Hindu *Mahabharata:*

[It was] a single projectile
Charged with all the power of the Universe.
An incandescent column of smoke and flame
As bright as the thousand suns
Rose in all its splendor . . .

It was an unknown weapon,
An iron thunderbolt,
A gigantic messenger of death,
Which reduced to ashes
The entire race of the Vrishnis and the Andhakas.

The corpses were so burned
As to be unrecognizable.
The hair and nails fell out;
Pottery broke without apparent cause,
And the birds turned white.

After a few hours
All foodstuffs were infected . . .
To escape from this fire
The soldiers threw themselves in streams
To wash themselves and their equipment.

Nuclear Enigmas on Earth and Mars

But then the archaeological discovery of the civilization of the Indus
Valley (3500–1900 BCE) raised questions about a possible use of nuclear
weapons in ancient times. The excavation of the first two cities discovered, Harappa and Mohenjo-Daro, started in the 1920s. When the
archaeologists reached the street level, they found skeletons of people
that had met an instant death in the streets while running and trying
to flee, some of them holding hands. They bore no mark of aggression,
and wild animals hadn't touched them, but nobody was left it seems to
bury them (see fig. 5.5).

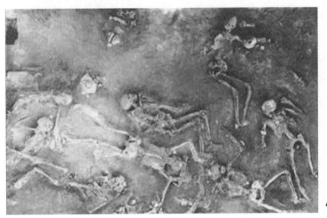

A

B

Fig. 5.5. (A) People of Mohenjo-Daro met an instant death. (B) Vitrified lumps in Mohenjo-Daro.

Even more appalling, according to Alexander Gorbovsky (*Riddles of Ancient History*) one skeleton presented a very high level of radioactivity, fifty times higher than natural radioactivity. The skeletons have been carbon-dated to about 2500 BCE. Some skeptics, with their usual cursory way of explaining away any anomaly, have proposed that of course the disaster was brought about by a volcanic eruption, or that the radioactivity came from a power plant's recent radiation leak. However, these two ludicrous scenarios can in no way explain (1) the radioactivity of skeletons buried deep inside the Earth for four and a half millennia, nor (2) the impact or instant poisoning that flattened the people while in full movement. And, more to the point (as often goes with the arguments of the skeptics) there is simply *no* volcano around! At Mohenjo-Daro, there were also small fused lumps or black stones strewn by the thousands over a large area, and that seemed to be the result of clay pots melted by extreme heat.

The Indus Valley was the region attributed to Inanna after the Second

Pyramid War had ended, when Ningishzidda/Thoth/Hermes would get the Enlilship and start his reign as Chief of the Gods and as Thoth in the Egyptian civilization created by Enki/Ptah, that is, in 8600 BCE. Now, the bust of Inanna as an astronaut, so modern and sophisticated, resembles greatly the statue of the Goddess worshipped in the Indus Valley cities. And Inanna's large goggles and attire leave no doubt as to her skills as a pilot of her own bird—like some other Anunnaki gods whose pilots are dutifully named, she nevertheless loved to drive her bird herself (see fig. 5.6). Thus it corroborates that she was indeed able to use her bird to escape the nuclear blast and reach her submarine, as we saw earlier.

Another set of data about the use of nukes on Earth in a very ancient past is the *Mahabharata,* which recounts the feats of Rama, the king of a technologically advanced empire in India, the capitol of which was Dvarpa, near the Indus River delta. Indeed, the battle, which, about ten thousand years ago, obliterated Rama's fabulous empire— through the fantastic nuclear blast we saw earlier—was a giant airborne battle fought with spaceships called Vimanas. (Let's note that, according to the text, "Rama ruled the earth for 11,000 years.") Vimanas are described in technical detail in dozens of ancient Hindu treatises and

Fig. 5.6. (A) Inanna as astronaut; (B) the Goddess worshipped in the Indus Valley civilization.

also sketched. David Childress has sorted out from several texts (notably the *Yantra Sarvasva* written by Maharshi Bhardwaj) that the military types of vimanas were conceived to be "impregnable, unbreakable, non-combustible and indestructible, capable of coming to a dead stop in a twinkling of an eye; invisible," and they had various radars to scan space and beams to record sounds around them. Some could "travel between planets" (166; see fig. 5.7). The ruins of Dvarpa have recently

RUKMA VIMANA

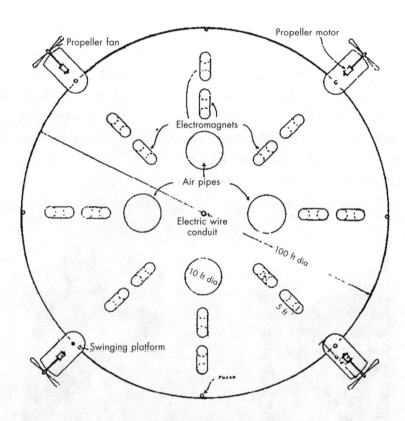

PLAN OF BASE OR PITHA

Drawn by
T. K. ELLAPPA,
Bangalore.
2-12-1923.

Prepared under instruction of
Pandit SUBBARAYA SASTRY,
of Anekal, Bangalore.

Fig. 5.7. One type of Vimanas, Rukma Vimana.
(Courtesy of David Childress.)

been discovered at the bottom of the ocean, not far from the delta of the Indus, stressing a link to the Indus civilization brought forth by Inanna: thus, there's a possibility that the nuking of Dvarpa was part of the same war that obliterated the northern cities of the Indus Valley, even if it happened as separate phases or events in that war that also obliterated the cities in Canaan and Sumer itself.

Another, more precise, piece of evidence comes from India's Lonar crater, to the northeast of Mumbai. Perfectly round, it is the only known basalt crater formed by impact, and it is dated to under 50,000 years old. So intense was the heat that the basalt stone had formed thousands of glass spherules (vitrified basalt) spread over a large area; it has been calculated that the impact that created it was greater than the pressure of 600,000 atmospheres. Yet no meteor's debris could be found around it.

So to compare it to the nuking in the Middle East, estimated by Sitchin to have happened in 2024 BCE, the gap with the catastrophe in the Indus Valley—dated around 2500 BCE—is unexplained, yet not too large; but this in no way can explain the Lonar crater blast around 48,000 BCE.

A related phenomenon, that of vitrified glass (or tektites) in some areas of the world (Libya, northern India, France), is still defying the conventional explanation of meteorite impacts, for the very reason that in most cases, there's simply no impact crater. Whereas we have the perfect evidence of huge patches of desert sand turned into fused green glass, forming sheets, around the area of atomic tests in New Mexico (the silicon in the sand melted and vitrified from the intense heat and pressure). The Libyan Desert Glass (so hard and so pure it is used to make blades), comes from hundreds of square kilometers of glass sheets and shards in the Great Sand Sea in western Egypt, strewn in two large spots. Given the very explicit accounts we have from ancient texts, we certainly cannot avoid the much more plausible (and rational) explanation implying nuclear or other powerful weapons used in very ancient warfare. David Childress, in *Technology of the Gods,* describes how "the vitrified remains of the ziggurat at Birs Nimrod (Borsippa), south of Hillah, were once confused with the 'Tower of Babel.' The ruins are crowned by a mass of vitrified brickwork, actual clay bricks fused together by intense heat" (222). Now, isn't that interesting! Borsippa was the city of Nabu, son of Marduk, and both were the targets of the war that led to the nuking of the Jordan plain.

Now, as mentioned in this book's introduction, just recently the physicist John Brandenburg brought to the attention of the scientific community a very ancient nuclear explosion on Mars that had left a specific trace on the rocks, that of the Xenon-129 isotope. This isotope, not being found naturally but only as the product of a thermonuclear explosion, makes the nuking of Mars a fact impossible to doubt. This discovery was preceded by another one of immense import: that Mars had, about 180–250 million years ago, an ocean, vegetation, and an atmosphere—in a word, that it had been, as stated by the Sumerian tablets, a planet lush with at least vegetal life and small animals, on which the Sumerian astronauts, the Igigi, were said to stop to replenish their water reserves. As we know, they also speak about the Igigi having a base on Mars and on the moon too, plus an orbiting space station.

As the Mesopotamian scholar Thorkild Jacobsen concluded in his article "The Reign of Ibbi-Sin:" "Whether we shall ever see with full clarity what happened in those years, only time will tell; the full story, we are convinced, is still far beyond our grasp."

Open Questions about Nergal's Schemes and Influence

In all these descriptions of the disaster, we have seen the instigators being pointed at: Enlil and Anu and the Assembly of the Gods. Especially accused are the ones who carried out the Evil Task, Nergal and Ninurta, clearly named and held responsible. *"An evil blast heralded the baleful storm,* an evil blast the forerunner of the baleful storm was; *Mighty offsprings, valiant sons were the heralds of the pestilence."* As we know, the so "valiant" sons of the gods were Ninurta and Nergal. And indeed, they now get new names, and they are forever going to be remembered as "the Scorcher and He of the Evil Wind—the Devastators."

One Babylonian king thus reported about an earlier time:

The Lord [of the Gods] became enraged, he conceived wrath. He gave the command: the gods of that place abandoned it . . . The two, incited to commit the evil, made its guardians stand aside; its protectors went up to the dome of heaven. (*Wars,* 330)

The "gods of that place" referred to are of course the Igigi, here called the guardians and protectors of the spaceport. Thus, in the above text we see that Enlil gave the command to the two sons, while in the Khedorlaomer Texts: "Enlil was consumed with anger. The *devastators again* suggested evil . . . The two made the gods flee, made them flee the scorching" (*Wars,* 330; my emphasis). So that here it is "the two" who suggest the deed to an angry Enlil looking for a radical punishment. However, the text calls them "devastators," and makes it clear that they will "again" devastate the people and the land. So, we may wonder, what kind of devastation did they produce earlier? The spaceport is clearly identified with the words: "made the gods flee," paralleling the previous citation: "the gods of that place abandoned it . . . *its protectors went up to the dome of heaven*" (which means the Igigi abandoned the spaceport and took off in their shuttlecrafts).

This last sentence should make us ponder: Are there discreet or veiled judgments that the scribes in Sumer inserted in their texts? Does it mean to suggest that instead of being the protectors of their people, cities, and temples (as they should have been), the gods (apart from Enki) left humanity, at best to take care of itself, at worst to perish?

Furthermore, a Sumerian text on this event shows the kind of Moralistic Framework (MF) that we have seen often added, interspersed in such a way that it breaks down the Informational Framework (IF) in the biblical text. This text (Text K-5001) is the second of two that I found so far that express a MF semantic field similar to the Book texts. Experts couldn't decide who, in this text, was the god implied and called *Lord,* but he is related to the Scorcher, translated here as an extraordinary armament that this lord would carry or bear and that could destroy by fire a whole population and land. So there's no doubt that he is *the* Scorcher, Ninurta himself, whose deed we recognize well.

> Lord, Bearer of the Scorcher that burnt up the *adversary;* who obliterated the *disobedient land;* who withered the life of the *Evil Word's followers;* who rained stones and fire upon the *adversaries.* (The MF text is in italics.)

This text is in original Sumerian language, with a faithful Akkadian translation doubling it. Sitchin says about it: "Its wording indeed gives the impression that it is this or similar Sumerian originals that had served as a source for the biblical narrative" (*Wars,* 330).

We saw how Nergal had stolen from Marduk's temple, ahead of the Deluge, "the Holy Radiating Stone which Disintegrates All." But while Marduk, a few months before the holocaust, was advancing toward his city to reclaim it, we saw that Nergal had defiled Enlil's Nippur temple, emptying it of its MEs. It appears now there is evidence that Nergal was the one to defile other gods' temples as well, while there was enough disorder to attribute the deeds to Marduk. So, what about the MEs and weapons stolen from the other two defiled temples? One was the abode-temple of Shamash (the chief of space facilities on the ground, and namely of the antediluvial spaceport in Sippar); certainly such a god had mighty MEs. But the most destructive and lethal weapons must have been retrieved from Inanna's temple, the very experienced Goddess of war, who had subjugated so many lands with sophisticated weapons and MEs. (See fig. 5.8.)

If indeed Nergal had a precise plan in mind while he looted these temples, covering his true aim by defiling them and acting as if Marduk had done it, then a totally new picture arises. Another of Marduk's MEs that he never gave back was called "Instrument of Giving Orders." Could this ME be a sort of neuronal-control or mind-control device that would force people to obey one's orders? Could Nergal have acquired mind-control MEs that enabled him to rally the other gods in

Fig. 5.8. Inanna as a pitiless warrior.

the Assembly to his highly risky plan? Mind-control devices that had put even the faithful Ninurta under his spell to the point that he, the Warrior of Enlil, covered for Nergal and his looting of his father Enlil's temple, and simultaneously got the Commander in enough of a rage to trigger his decision to use nukes? Mind-control influences that only potent and wise minds like Enki's would be able to thwart (he who knew all the MEs and could thus shield himself)?

In fact we may wonder if there had ever been on Nibiru any other techno-magical genius shrewd and bright enough to have created all this array of MEs. What if Enki had created most of them himself, and done so on Earth? Could the many problems he had to solve on Earth, and getting in sync with the fast minds of the earthlings, have stimulated Enki's intelligence? What if his most intelligent and smart sons—Ningishzidda and Marduk—had also developed this capacity of creating new MEs, to further enrich their very special brand of holistic science?

The fact that Nergal may have possessed a mind-control device could explain (however slightly) his otherwise inexplicable influence first on Enlil and then on the Assembly, and the fact that he had even loaded and readied the missiles before getting the okay from the Assembly, and yet his enormous breach of protocol was not even reproached. But again, even bearing this in mind, it doesn't exonerate the chiefs of the gods, specifically Enlil and to a lesser degree Anu, from the responsibility and authorship of their appalling and genocidal acts and decisions.

Let us see now the Book's account of these same events.

✦ 6 ✦

Erasing Sodom

The Book Text

LET ME GET BACK, as an introduction to the Book account of the annihilation of Sodom and Gomorrah, to the second text that reveals a
Moralistic Framework (MF) semantic field, similar to that of the Book,
the K-5001 Text:

> Lord, Bearer of the Scorcher that burnt up the *adversary;* who oblit-
> erated the *disobedient land;* who withered the life of the *Evil Word's*
> *followers;* who rained stones and fire upon the *adversaries.* (The MF
> text is in italics.)

It talks about powerful weapons to smash the disobedient country
who, because of its disobedience, would be regarded as "the enemy." In
the War of the Kings of the East, Nannar and Inanna were major play-
ers. And they often brought the very kings who had battled for them
to their doom, for their own petty disputes. This has been the case of
Amar-Sin (certainly a lover of Inanna) and that of his brother Shu-Sin
who, as we saw, reigned after him and was put to death by the great
gods. Shu-Sin had exulted (after so many before him) to be the "lover
of Inanna" but also to have been chosen as king by Nannar himself
(*Wars,* 318). Shu-Sin's inscription states that

"The holy Inanna" . . .
gave him weapons to "engage in battle [IF]
the *enemy* country which is *disobedient*." [MF]

In this sentence, we see again a mix of information (IF) with strong moralistic judgments (MF). So we see that, just like Enlil, the warmonger Inanna calls whatever city didn't pledge allegiance to her (and contribute taxes) a "disobedient country" who should be attacked and overrun.

Despite his wars for Inanna, Shu-Sin was so unsure of having the continuous support of the Great Gods (maybe he had a premonition of the fate awaiting him) that he kept trying to propitiate them through magnificent gifts. Thus, he built a special boat for Enki, one that could make the trip to Africa and back (certainly carrying the gold ore). Then he sought the favors of Enlil and Ninlil by adorning Enlil's temple in Nippur with a new stela (where he made himself High Priest); by erecting a new temple for him near the ancient one; and, finally, he built the great boat for love pleasure that, as we have seen, incited Enlil to come back for a nice sojourn in Sumer and take his wife along with him when he departed.

The Eve of the Disaster:
Setting the Rationale

The Book account starts with three "men" (the Deity and two emissaries, or Malakhim) visiting Abram who was sitting in his tent near Hebron. Abe pleads with them to share a feisty meal and he orders that a meal be prepared. The "three men" eat and rest, the Deity promising to Abe a son from his wife Sarah—thus a legal heir. On departing at dusk (after they had talked for hours),

And the men rose up from there to survey over upon Sodom, and the Lord said: "Can I conceal from [Abe] *that which I am about to do?*"

The Deity then discloses that he had decided to "come down and verify" accusations, his two emissaries ready to act:

The outcry regarding Sodom and Gomorrah being great, and the accusation against them being grievous; . . . If it is as the outcry reaching me, they will destroy completely.

Sitchin remarks about the erasing of the two towns as reported in the Book: "The event was most definitively *not* a natural calamity. It is described as a premeditated event," furthermore avoidable and postponable (*Wars*, 311).

This is where Abe's famous negotiation with the Deity takes place (while the two emissaries have departed to check on Sodom). He is trying to save the town, arguing that

Perhaps there be fifty Righteous Ones inside the city; wilt thou destroy and not spare the place for the sake of the fifty Righteous Ones within it? *Far be it from you to do such a thing, to slay the Righteous with the guilty! Far be it from you, the Judge of All the Earth, not to do justice!*

Says Sitchin: "A mortal preaching to his Deity! And the plea is for calling off the destruction—the premeditated and avoidable destruction" (*Wars*, 311).

Then Abe negotiates the number of the Righteous down unto ten. "And the Lord said: 'I shall not destroy if there be ten'; and he departed." It was already evening. Later, the two emissaries of the Lord reached Sodom where Lot (who lived there) invites them to share a meal and spend the night at his place. But as the visitors sat down, "the people of the city, the people of Sodom, surrounded the house—young and old, the whole population, from every quarter." They ask Lot who the visitors are, they want to see them "that we may know them." Lot refuses and the crowd wants to break in, but at that moment, the two Malakhim "smote the people who were at the house's entrance with blindness, both young and old."

Then they order Lot to bring all his relatives to his house: "Bring them out from this place [city], for we are about to destroy it" (*Wars,* 312).

Then the text says that Lot's sons and sons-in-law (plural), in hearing the threat, laughed it off, and at dawn Lot will be only with his wife and two young unmarried daughters.

Says Sitchin (*Wars,* 325): "As we now learn from the Babylonian text, the 'outcry,' (the accusation) against the 'sinful' and 'wicked' cities of the biblical text, was their rallying to the side of Marduk and Nabu." The target of the nuclear blasts were the cities supporting Marduk, and the aim was to slay Nabu who was hiding there at the moment. Nabu escaped to an island and reigned there afterward.

Then we recall that Lot's wife looked back and became a "pillar of vapor." (Indeed, Sitchin makes a very sound case about the translation of the Hebrew word for *vapor* and not *salt.*)

In the morning, Abe "got up early . . . and he looked in the direction of Sodom . . . and he beheld there smoke rising from the earth as the smoke of a furnace" (*Wars,* 314). Apparently, he slept all right, not wondering about Lot, about the city, about if it had been spared. He wasn't awakened by the blast and the "furnace" (Hebron was about 45 miles away from Sodom). Let's also state that Abe was ninety-nine years old at the moment of these events, and that he had gotten a son from his concubine Hagar only at eighty-six years old. Being without a son of his own in an advanced age, his nephew Lot had been his only legal heir until thirteen years earlier, and this is why, at seventy years old, he had traveled from Harran on the Euphrates toward Hebron, with Lot (whose father had died) as a surrogate son.

There are, in my semanticist view, a lot of issues and questions arising from this version of the facts by the "biblical narrator of Genesis 18" as Sitchin puts it. Compared to the text of the garden of Eden, which I analyzed using Semantic Fields Theory in *DNA of the Gods,* we see an evolution of the script toward:

- The disappearance of whole sentences showing an Informational Framework (IF). Facts are reduced to minimal information buried within the Moralistic Framework's statements (MF).

- We observe an excess of negative moral judgments while (to make the matter more clear) the earthlings are cast as desperately evil or unworthy (apart from one exception: Abe). All this, inducing the readers to agree that the two great "men" were showing so much care and mercy—while we still have no idea what exactly were the sins of the inhabitants: they will never be stated in this text. Yet, so dreadful were these sins—about which "the outcry" was so great and "the accusation" so grievous—that they had "outraged the Lord." The Deity says he is not going to act without verifying; however, his mind is already so much set that his wording is revealing: "That which *I am about to do*," and not anything like "I am still weighing if I will (or should) do this and that."

- We observe an accumulation of details derailing from the main point (and which only aggravate the unworthiness of mere earthlings), as if the narrator sought to hide the scarcity of the information he wants to convey (which is reduced to a symbolic and meager thread of information).

- Moreover, the aggrandizement of the lord and his emissaries is as constant as it is excessive, while the readers are, customarily, to experience a psychological impact aimed at priming emotions of self-culpability, helplessness, feelings of unworthiness in front of the Lord of Justice.

The fact that we, the readers, don't know what they did just aggravates the matter (Am I a Righteous? Did I sin in any possible way? Which one?). Through word of mouth, the legacy of the term *sodomy* of course seems to give us an inkling of what went on there (totally misleading), while nothing is said about it, which is three hits with one stone: For one, it hides the illegitimate and shallow pretext of ordering the genocide of a people because they have decided to worship another god. Two, the text is thus spared from lying, while, three, it nevertheless suggests the worst "evil" anybody can fathom as abominable, each reader presuming his own idea of culpability. And that says a lot about the specific abomination the Church chose to project on Sodom! "And what about Gomorrah?" I had asked somebody in the know. "Ah! It's the same (homosexuality) but for women." The big problem with this interpretation is that same-sex intercourse is something about which an Anunnaki male or female would not see anything wrong. They are casual about it as were the Greek philosophers, with wives, kids, and young male lovers among their students. Such stories (seduction, love-making) are not rare in the tablets, only they are less often chanted in poems than the heterosexual union.

If we approach the Book's account with detachment and without being pulled within the religious semantic field, impervious to the aura of awe, and if, in this frame of mind, we read it anew, we may, mortals of the twenty-first century, be totally disconcerted, ashamed, and outraged, but not vis-à-vis the same persons. (It is to enable this detachment—and avoid being pulled or sucked in to the mindset prodded by these texts—that I systematically refuse to use the usual names, which are such powerful attractors that they simply impede us from thinking.)

Don't we see two emissaries of one of the great gods, who are gods themselves (Nibirians), sitting around a low table with Abe and sharing a guest's lunch before they get into the filthy warlike business of pouring nukes over the population of no less than five cities? If the deity wanted to verify the outcry (of whom by the way?), what was his criteria for smashing or not smashing a civilian population? Why did it have to be Abe who offered a moral criterion? The way Abe started to bargain the massacre ("Will you destroy the Righteous . . . ?") clearly means that beforehand the deity was set on a global kill. Also offensive, is not the deity (who is filled with such an overwhelming rage and lethal intent) seducing Abe by promising to him the legal heir from his wife that he didn't beget during his life? And yet, the account is made to underline the all-powerfulness and greatness of a lord able to make such miracles happen. In this sentence of Abe, the leader of the three men is clearly identified with "the Judge of All the

Earth," that is, the King of Heaven and Earth (the inherited title of Enlil), and yet this judge is intending a most unjust and radical genocide. Yet, from the perspective of the narrator, he is showing immense compassion and mercy.

At this point Abe, who "had gone with them to see them off" (meaning, to accompany them a bit), "returned to his place." The three men had arrived in "the heat of the day," around noon, and we are told that the two emissaries depart around dusk, and the exchange with the lord then takes place on a dune (the dune on which he will see the furnace later, this to imply he was safe, being so far away).

In Sodom at Nightfall

Next, we have only the two emissaries arriving at the home of Lot, who immediately recognizes their divine status. We had been told that they were to assess how many had not sinned and could be spared, and this was only in Sodom. It was evident that, having no protégé to spare in Gomorrah and the three other cities, these were de facto out of a deal of mercy and therefore would be wiped out *anyway*. Now let's imagine the two emissaries having the mission, given by their god, to first assess the sin, and then erase the cities—and instead of doing one then the other, they accept Lot's (of course insistent) invitation to sleep overnight and, before that, to share another meal. This meal, according to critical biblical expert and psychoanalyst Ilona Rashkow in "Daddy-Dearest and the 'Invisible Spirit of Wine,'" being "a lavish drinking feast" as denoted by the "term *misteh* (feast, banquet) . . . usually an occasion for hard drinking" (99). There is nothing wrong in having two heavy banquets in a day and sleeping all afternoon and again at night, but when the guests are set to destroy the whole region at sunrise, and the very family of their hosts, it's rather gross and bordering on being immoral.

Now, how were they going to assess the number of Righteous Ones by staying at Lot's home? (I mean if they had clairvoyance or omniscience, they wouldn't need to "verify," but since they had decided to verify, why don't they do something to that effect? Why don't they go and meet the population?) As with Abe at his encampment's tent, the narrator heavily underlines the insistence of Lot and Abe to treat their guests of honor, so as to instill the idea that the three men were "kindly obliged" to accept the invitation—that is, something a polite and caring father cannot refuse, nor his war generals, all of them clad in their furor and war attire.

The tablets we saw have described precisely what it meant for the two Anunnaki, Nergal and Ninurta, set on a vengeful mission by Enlil and the Assembly, to have readied themselves: they were clad "in brilliance," wearing their weapons, their planes airborne and the "awesome weapons trailing behind them." Because, even if they spare Sodom, they still have four more cities in the Jordan plain and the Sinai spaceport that they intend to destroy at all costs the next morning.

Therefore, prepared to strike no matter what, the least state in which the emissaries could have been, is in a violent mood, armed and ready with weapons of mass destruction for the multitarget attack they will carry on anyway. And with all that fearsome attire and mind-set, they just sit down to eat and drink, and will lay down like meek sheep for a good night's sleep, forgetting all about their divine mission to "survey" and "verify" what had been only (in the very words of the leader) accusations "reaching him" like rumors that didn't have a value of certitude.

And now the "whole population" comes in front of Lot's house and asks him, who are these visitors; they want to see who they are in order to "know them." "Bring them out to us that we may know them." Is there anything wrong or specifically death-threatening in this request from unarmed people (with their wives and kids) vis-à-vis fully armed and furious generals? Lot refuses. This means that the prosecutors on a mission to assess the population's responsibility and sins do refuse to go and meet this very population. So what do we have to conclude from this very avoidance of assessment?

Was this supposed verification mission just a pretext? A story to suggest that all was done in the righteous way—accusation and defense—the verification of the rumors that had reached the ears of the Chief of the Gods, the "outcry" from whoever? Of course, one could wonder, with so many gods having their own cities and dedicated followers, who could ever find it outrageous that one god found followers and especially so far from Sumer? That is, followers among the earthling populations, who generally had no other fate (at the time) than to be the followers of whichever god was the deity of their city. (In fact, it had been a *première* that Nabu's charisma had had an appeal for the Canaanite cities, thus allowing them to choose their god. We saw how even the kings, insecure and rightly so, were multiplying their allegiances to different gods just to keep afloat.)

Since no verification action is ever even started, we have to conclude that this verification mission was only a narrator's moralistic trick (in the perfect MF style).

Now the crowd grows impatient and wants to get inside Lot's house to really meet the visitors and "know" what this visit is all about. The narrator emphasizes, making the story totally unrealistic, that "the people of the city, the people of Sodom" (once isn't enough, he has to overdo it, excessive as it is already) "young and old, *the whole population, from every quarter . . .* surrounded the house." Overinsistence because everybody has to be guilty, priming the readers' mind so that the anger, the *ira,* of god appears just and righteous. So of course our "emissaries" feel they are rightly attacked. Are they not? And because they are so powerful "they smote the people who were at the house's entrance." (Really? The people had not even stepped in yet? So no real threat, huh?) They smote them "with blindness, both young and old." No discrimination. So-called self-defense. So what's the next inference? The emissaries realize that all the people of Sodom, apart from Lot, are sinful. Therefore they amply merit the grand punishment: the city's inhabitants will be slain. The only problem is that they were supposed to have been—all of them, old and young, the whole population, from every quarter—"smitten with blindness," and on top of that, in the middle of the night! So how could they ever disperse and go back to their houses?

Even more revealing, the emissaries now ask Lot to go and fetch all his family "a son-in-law, *thy sons* and *daughters* [both plural], any other relative—all who are in this city—bring them out from this place, for we are about to destroy it." That's when it gets epical. Picture the "whole population" stricken by god's emissaries with blindness, all howling and shouting while trying to get back to their homes, and now Lot hurrying to give "the news" to his sons and "*sons-in-law*" (plural in the next sentence in which their wives are unnamed, who are no less than Lot's *own daughters,* and their kids who are his grandchildren). We already reach: 2 daughters of Lot + 2 sons-in-law (their husbands) + 2 sons and heirs of Lot + 4 in Lot's household—that's a count of ten without including the children of these married couples or "any other relative" to whom the "mercy" extended.

Moreover, when the emissaries order Lot to fetch all his family, do they ask him if the count will be ten? Not at all. The end of the sentence is "Bring them out from this place, for we are about to destroy it." So they had already broken their promise to Abe even before they ask Lot to go and fetch his larger family and relatives. (But the whole population, old and young *had* attacked them, didn't they?)

So here we have a surplus of contradictions. The visitors' arrival, even after nightfall, was so impetuous or striking (their vehicles being planes armed with missiles, their brilliance, their godly attire, their warlord weapons) that the whole population was immediately and instinctively on their guards, and wanted to see them face-to-face to ask them questions. Note that if they had a culprit's mindset, expecting these specific gods (who must have been described by those who saw them arriving) to massacre them, they would have fled or locked themselves in their homes. They would not have come with their kids to talk and discuss. So this population had absolutely no awareness of being the target of the wrath of a god. Until that day, they were certainly used to gods fighting each other using their earthling followers as an army, but the custom had been to wage wars, not to "smite" whole cities. Let's note also that if Lot had wanted to help the population, he would have told the people to either give their allegiance to this god in order not to be killed, or to flee during the night. But in this whole story, Lot is playing totally into the emissaries' camp (yet, contrary to what the story would like us to believe, he will not be thanked for it, far from it!).

So, here goes Lot to fetch the families of his sons and daughters. How is that? Were they not, in all logic, part of the "the whole population, from every quarter"? (The narrator has not even left himself the excuse that they had toddlers to take care of.) Had they not heard the news of the arrival of two warrior-gods in warlike attire? Couldn't they hear the shouts and confusion of all the people, the whole city, shouting they had been attacked and were blind? Let's be clear that at this epoch, the cities were like big villages—and we were not even in Sumer. And only Lot's parents would be at home, as if blind and deaf, and they alone doubted what a shocked Lot was telling them? So the narrator now has a good pretext to warn his readers that it is not wise to doubt the immense power and wrath of the deity, and also that only Lot, his wife, and his young daughters are worthy enough to be saved.

An in-depth scrutiny of the Book's account reveals that the emissaries broke the promise of their Lord to Abe on two counts on this single Sodom episode: first, they didn't engage in any assessment of rumors, survey of the people, and counting of the faithful. Second, they didn't wait for Lot, his wife, and two adolescent daughters to reach a safe haven before launching their attack and nuking the first city at least, a blast that so startled Lot's wife that she looked back. To add to this, the emissaries sent *the* faithful family fleeing for their lives and running in the very direction of one of their target cities, instead of northward toward their patriarch's camp and army. Abe, moreover, would have had ample time during the night to rescue his whole Sodom-based family of at least ten on his swift camel cavalry.

Dawn in Sodom

And now we are at dawn. At that point (as related in Genesis 19) Lot hesitates; but because Y.'s "mercy was upon him," "the Men . . . brought them out and put them down outside the city." Then the men command to Lot, "Unto the mountains escape, lest you perish; escape for thy life, look not behind thee, neither stop thou anywhere in the plain." Lot then pleads with them to delay the destruction until the moment he has reached the town of Zoar, which they grant. Then:

> The sun had risen over the Earth when Lot arrived at Zoar; and the Lord rained upon Sodom and Gomorrah, *from the skies, brimstone and fire that had come from Y.* And He upheavaled those cities *and the whole plain, and all the inhabitants* of the cities, and all the vegetation, . . . all the cities *which had outraged the Lord.*

Did the emissaries, the previous night, finish their meal and go back to sleep? And Lot and his family too?

At dawn the emissaries told Lot to flee (with his wife and two daughters only), but we are told that Lot "tarried" and didn't want to move. How is that? Did he not witness the deadly aggressiveness of the emissaries? Was not the whole population attacked the previous night, all ailing and moaning, sitting anywhere they could, unable to see their way back to their homes? Did he need more of a show of their power? Could he doubt for one second that, after having so badly stricken people who wanted to ask questions, they would carry on their murderous plan? One more literary effect to show the "mercy" of the deity. "But Lot tarried; so the men took hold of his hand [how gentlemanly!] and his wife's hand and his two daughters' hands—for Y.'s mercy was upon him—and they brought them out, and put them down outside the city." "Put them down," meaning that they were taken airborne, as Sitchin underlines it: "Having literally carried the foursome aloft, then put them down outside the city, the emissaries urged Lot to flee to the mountains" (*Wars,* 312).

Here we have to raise several questions of the greatest import. We all know that the poor wife of Lot did look back, certainly startled out of her wits by the huge explosion(s) she just heard, and was "turned into a pillar of vapor," so that she died during their desperate escape. (But, in the Moralistic Framework of the narrator, she was responsible, wasn't she? She disobeyed! She looked behind and she was punished—rightly of course!)

As usual, we have an array of both logical and scientific inconsistencies. An interesting point is that, if you picture the terrible scene, in order to look back, Lot's wife must have lessened her pace (we imagine they were, if not half running, walking as quickly as they could possibly do). So Lot's wife looks back and is immediately disintegrated into vapor (or struck immobile as a pillar of salt). But who saw it? To see it, the husband would have had to look back too, and see his wife turn into vapor (or even salt, it doesn't make any difference, given we are in a total fairy tale). And the same applies to the kids. So the story wants to tell us (just for the sake of morality) that if one disobeys, one dies. But that would imply that Lot kept his pace not even willing to see what was happening to his wife! Nobody had told them: "If you look back, you will be turned into a pillar of vapor," nor even anything like: "Don't look back, because you would perish." No. They were told: "Escape into the mountains, lest you perish . . . look not behind thee,"—and we will hold the holocaust until you reach the city of Zoar: "*I will be unable to do anything until you hast arrived there.*" A dire odious lie, that cost Lot's spouse her life! (*Wars,* 313).

So Lot keeps walking—his wife, who had herself started to turn around, a big question mark. And the daughters keep walking, not worried about mom who's not here anymore. That's where the narrator—so willing to exonerate his god and rationalize his abominable acts, and therefore obliged to put the blame on earthlings, as if it was a lesson of morality—falls into total incoherence and, worst of all, into the most gruesome immorality.

Here are some added issues with this sequence alone: (1) If the emissaries were so easily able to lift the four people and fly them outside of Sodom, and since they had promised to wait—for Armageddon—until they reached a safe place in the mountains, why couldn't they fly them some 20 miles farther? (They had slept the whole afternoon after a heavy meal in Abe's tent, and the whole night in Sodom after another one, and had to wait anyway.) (2) The emissaries expressed concern for Lot and his family to the point of delaying their operations; if these hadn't started, what then caused the death of Lot's wife? Only disobedience to an advice that, while given strongly, was not itself asserted with a death penalty if transgressed? (3) There is no scientific basis for a person being stricken dead at the same distance as other persons accompanying them (unless they are kids or seniors), and *looking* at the explosion doesn't make a difference as far as dying is concerned. If she had looked back at a nuclear explosion, she would have been stricken blind (given they were supposed to be at a safe distance from dying). (4) If the emissaries had already launched the nuclear explosion on Sodom, then they would have broken their oath. (5) If the emissaries were so concerned about Lot and his family (granting them such an extension of their "mercy"), then why not make sure no harm whatsoever would happen to *them all?* Whatever way we look at it, the story doesn't make any sense and is seriously morally faulty—and not on the part of the earthlings, contrary to what the narrator would like us to believe.

Next is another set of questions. We are told that the emissaries, after Sodom, went on destroying Gomorrah and then the whole plain, and that each time they waited for Lot to reach a safe distance. Of course this is downright nonsensical. *Why did they set them running* (with fear gripping them and then Lot going through losing his wife) *like rabbits, in the wrong direction in the first place?* Could they not, once and for all, send them away from all doomed cities and the plain? But this is not all. Abe, in Hebron, was 45 miles from Sodom, and he was totally safe. Abe knew that the emissaries were heading toward Lot's house in Sodom. In all probability, he hoped (given their behavior toward him) that they would find ten Righteous Ones, given that just Lot's family alone exceeded that number.

Even if Abe was reasonably hopeful that the count of ten had been reached, he couldn't just be assured that was so. Even if his god had promised he would save Lot—a faithful as was Abraham—a father can't just forget all about the fate of his adopted son. Given that Abe's father Terah had been the High Priest of Enlil in his topmost temple in Nippur (and then in Ur), Abe had been raised and taught in order to become the next High Priest himself. And since scientific domains were also implied, the learning would start early on, and the same lengthy instruction would be given to Abe's legal heir Lot, who, in the Sumerian tradition, was similarly bound to become a High Priest and taught accordingly. This instruction had thus necessarily been given to Lot until Abe begot a son from his concubine Hagar just thirteen years earlier, and then to his concubine's son. (It will be in the year following these events that Abe will beget, from his wife Sarah, an heir who will get the title and the function.) Thus, during his already long life, Abe, considering Lot as his heir, had necessarily taught him the mystical and priestly science. So, what kind of person would not have sent Lot toward his surrogate father Abraham, his lifetime teacher, just 45 miles away—two or three days walking at the most? (The point is all the more harrowing and heartbreaking when we know what fate, beyond losing his wife, Lot was going to meet.) What kind of person if not somebody totally devoid of parental feeling and of humanity? Somebody like Enlil, able to admonish his son Nannar instead of rescuing him, when the latter was in dire lethal danger?

En Aparte
to My Readers and Allies

At this point, I must stop, because I'm devastated by what the analysis of these events is bringing out in the light. At no point would I have expected doing anything beyond straightening a few serious lies that, I felt, had been immensely damaging to women and the clarification of which still had to be done—in all fairness, by a woman. Even reading and rereading Sitchin's Earth Chronicles and the Sumerian texts hadn't prepared me for the full-face blow I'm receiving from what my analysis is unraveling—because we always read too quickly; even while pondering a text, we are taken further by the next sentence, the next event. It's only when one analyzes a text, and now carefully weighs each word in each sentence, that we can pierce the thick veil of the semantic field of a heritage book, handed down with its looking glass and fixed interpretation attached to it. I'm devastated and I ask myself questions like: Should I? Do I really want to take this weight on myself? Why is it that I'm reaching so far, burrowing so deep, uprooting psychic traumas buried in our history, that were much more significant and consequential than even the ones of our origins? Traumas that affected our gods as well as us, all of us participating in the same psychic fabric, all of us (humans from Earth, humans-gods from Nibiru) interwoven in our genes as well as in our souls. What is this force of the Spirit that made me tear down the veil, unto the peak revelation of these last days and nights?

And yet sometimes also, discoveries make me jubilate and I know that there's nothing more important than to move forward into this arduous recollection, because, I sense it, it is where lies the jewel-minds of our future humanity; where (and only where) the path may be opened to reunite with other civilizations in the intelligent inhabited worlds, when we will have torn the veil, when scales will fall from our eyes.

And I know, I sense, I anticipate, that this unraveling is just a first stage in the creation of a new spiritual opus, a collective one; that soon, another veil will be removed, and the process of opening up to other exo-planetary intelligent civilizations will start, and with it a new epic of humanity will blossom.

Men Clothed in Radiance

The insistence of the Genesis text in using the term *men* to refer to the Malakhim—the literal translation of which, according to Sitchin, is "emissaries," generally translated as "angels"—makes us infer that they looked like men, and not really like angels with wings. The fact that Abe recognizes them immediately as divine beings, his Lord accompanied by two emissaries, could of course be attributed to previous encounters, but they must have been "clothed in radiance" (or "brilliance") as Anunnaki ready to fight, wearing their MEs of power and weapons as well. Furthermore, they very certainly got there in their planes (their birds). Thus, we read that when Enlil got the news that his temple in Nippur had been defiled, he immediately set out for Nippur in similar war attire and was described coming down from an airborne vehicle or chariot: "Riding in front of him were gods *clothed with radiance; [himself] set off brilliance like lightning*" (*Wars*, 323; my emphasis). Who else than the two who had wickedly primed his vengeful rage thus preceded him—the devastators—*clothed with radiance?*

We also remember that Inanna had a ME that had such an effect, and that she was, by virtue of her title of queen, divinely righteous. "Lady of the MEs, Queen *Brightly resplendent; Righteous, clothed in Radiance."* Let's look at one text about King Ur-Nammu, who was backed not only by Enlil, but also by Inanna and Nannar, being called "the Might of Nannar." As soon as he became king (the first of the third dynasty of Ur)—the "Righteous Shepherd" started major restorations of the temples of many gods; however, he soon made war on Lagash and occupied it as well as seven other cities. After he had reconstructed the Ekur in Nippur, Enlil entrusted him with one formidable weapon: "The Divine Weapon, that which in the *hostile lands heaps up the rebels in piles,* to Ur-Nammu, the Shepherd, He, the Lord Enlil, has given to him; like a bull *to crush the foreign land,* like a lion to hunt it down; *to destroy evil cities, clear them of opposition to the Lofty*" (*Wars*, 276; my emphasis). (Note, in the above tablet, how "the foreign land" is equated with evil and how evil is equated to opposition to the lords.) Similarly, Shu-Sin, after restoring

Nippur's temple and raising a new stela, was given by the goddess Ninlil (Enlil's wife), a *"weapon which, with radiance, strikes down . . .* whose awesome flash reaches the sky" (*Wars,* 318; my emphasis).

Thus we see that gods, in the times preceding the holocaust, don't stop fighting with each other, raising armies of earthlings, and putting kings on the throne but ordering them to subdue so-called disobedient cities or countries, which are often their Sumerian neighbors. The only thing they hadn't yet done was to unearth the nuclear weapons and use them.

Abe Moves His Army to Save Lot during the War of the Kings

Let's see Abe's behavior toward Lot about a decade and a half earlier. Abe had been sent on a mission to stop the southern advance of the Kings of the East, who wanted to conquer the spaceport in the Sinai mountain, that is, El-Paran. During the War of the Kings, Abe was with his elite troops and camel cavalry, (and weapons we assume) most of which he had gotten from Egypt, in 2042 BCE. He had set an encampment for his troops (and their families) in an oasis near Hebron when he came from Harran twenty-four years earlier, and kept returning there. With Lot, they had brought their flocks with them (for food); the text says Lot took his own flocks to Sodom. They had their camels for the cavalry (the very rapid elite corps that was able to catch up with the Kings of the East near Damascus). They also had donkeys to carry the cargo from Harran (tents, food, etc.). So the permanent encampment was like an army's city of tents, with families, kids, and flocks grazing in the oasis.

Abe had stopped the adversary at two different places. The first time was at an oasis not far from Jericho (which was the "gateway to the Sinai"), called Kadesh-Barnea (Ein Mishpat). It was there that the Canaanite kings of the cities of Sodom, Gomorrah, Admah, Zebi, and Bela (also called Zoar) marched forth and engaged the Kings of the East in battle, says the Book. These were the five Canaanite towns that were going to be eradicated, but, as Sitchin remarks "the battle with these

Canaanite Kings was thus a late phase of the war and not its first purpose" (*Wars*, 305). This is how we know that the city of Zoar was to be eradicated.

The invaders' true aim was El-Paran, that is, as some researchers found out, Nakhl oasis. And let's remark that this army of the eastern kings of Sumer was the one to start the hostilities by invading Canaan; they had attacked one by one the crossing points and major outposts along the Jordan River. No researcher could fathom why the army was (as the Book states it) aiming at El-Paran ("God's Gloried Place"), "an isolated oasis in a great, desolate plain." Sitchin is adamant that "the only significance of the destination was its spaceport, and the one who blocked the advance at Kadesh-Barnea was Abraham . . . The Khedorlaomer Texts . . . make clear that the war was intended to prevent the return of Marduk and thwart the efforts of Nabu to gain access to the spaceport . . . It was to thwart this that the gods opposing Marduk ordered [the king] Khedorla'omer [or Kudur-Laghamar] to seize and defile Babylon" (*Wars*, 305–6).

> The gods . . . to Kudur-Laghamar, King of the land Elam, they decreed: "Descend there!" . . . In Babylon, the city of *the king of the gods, Marduk,* kingship he [Kudur-Laghamar] overthrew; to herds of dogs its temple he made a den; flying ravens, loud shrieking, their dung dropped there. (Khedorlaomer Texts)

The god Utu (twin brother of Inanna) then accused Nabu of having led a rebellion to stop paying tributes and allegiances to his father Nannar. This is how the coalition of the "loyal kings" of the East was put together. First Khedorla'omer destroyed Nabu's shrine of Borsippa and killed his sons. Then the army moved south toward Canaan. In the Sumerian original military plan, all places were to be invaded, and all Canaanite cities (including Gaza and Beer-Sheba in the Negev) were to be punished. But it didn't happen because, according to the Babylonian Text, "at Dur-Mah-Llani, *the son of the priest,* whom the gods in their true counsel *had anointed"* stood in the invaders' way and "the despoiling prevented." *Anointed:* that is, made a High Priest. Let's remember that Terah, Abe's father, was the High Priest of Nippur, in the holies of holies of Enlil, Chief of the Gods, so that he was, by hierarchy, the top priest of all cities and temples of all the gods in Sumer; furthermore, as High Priest at that time, he had to be of mixed parentage. Abe was his legal heir, thus the new High Priest—*the son of the priest.* After defending the spaceport with his army, Abe went back to Hebron, his base and army encampment.

Now, in 2041 BCE, while retreating northward, the Eastern army was attacked by the Canaanite kings, but subdued them and then moved *to plunder Sodom and Gomorrah,* taking Lot hostage with them while they rushed back to Sumer. Abe then immediately headed his cavalry in pursuit of the Eastern army in order to rescue Lot. He and his cavalrymen overtook the retreating army near Damascus (about 160 miles away), freed Lot, and took back all the looted possessions. Then, on his way back to Hebron, he was hailed as a victor in Jerusalem (the Valley of Shalem). The king of Shalem and the Canaanites kings offered to share the retrieved goods and booty—but Abe refused, explaining that "in the war between the House of Nannar and the House of Marduk, he was neutral. It was for 'Yahweh, the God Most High, *Possessor of Heaven and Earth*, that I have raised my hands,' he stated" (*Wars,* 309; my emphasis).

Thus, Abe has been and still is the chief of a successful army who has defeated the Eastern kings' army sponsored by Ishtar/Inanna, Nannar, and Utu (and inspired by "an oracle of Ishtar"), an army under the direct orders of the martial goddess, who was definitely more shrewd and competent than her father, Nannar. All the time, Abe's army has resided in Hebron. Only Lot went to settle nearby in Sodom with his family and sheep.

The Obnoxious Fate of Lot the Righteous

So let's go back to Lot's horrendous story. (*Take a deep breath!*)

Lot just lost his wife, and if he is still alive, as well as his two daughters, it's because he didn't turn back to look at what was happening to her (we are told). Perfectly obedient, the three keep on running. Remember, *it was dawn* in Sodom when the emissaries "put them down outside the city," and then ordered them "To the mountains, escape," and when Lot asked them to delay the "upheavaling" until he had reached the town of Zoar. Then *"The sun had risen* over the earth when Lot arrived at Zoar." [sic] Real quick! That was a good 20 miles running, moreover with two young daughters . . . and the loss of one's wife . . . something that could slow down any human heart. Again: Why not run toward Abe in Hebron (just double the distance from Sodom)?

Let's also note that the town of Zoar (Bela), part of the Canaanites kings' cities, was from the start marked to be wiped out, and that the narrator has it that the emissaries supposedly sent Lot to escape to this very town, next in their list for a morning *ira!* It doesn't make sense, given that they commanded Lot to escape from Sodom for the very reason they were "about to destroy it"—so why send him to another such town they were about to destroy in a giant global nuclear attack? And again: Why order him to go eastward into enemy land (Would the sole survivor of a holocaust be welcome?), instead of northward toward Hebron and Abe's safe encampment? Furthermore, the narrator obviously didn't know that desert dwellers walk and travel on camels at night, guided by the stars, and not in the fiery heat of the day. He didn't figure that somebody like Lot—who had traveled for months in the desert when a young adult, with his wife and Abram's household, all the way from Harran to Hebron—knew the desert inside out, and for him the Hebron encampment was just next door. Lot certainly knew the way to Abe's camp better than the way to Zoar. And Lot himself would not tell this to the emissaries?

Now, given that Abe still had his cavalrymen and camels in Hebron, how is it that the Lord or the divine warriors didn't ask Abe to go with a few camels to rescue Lot and his family *anyway*—since *they knew* they were Righteous—if his camp was only five or six hours away on a walking camel (and taking with them whatever number of

Righteous Ones could be found in Sodom, in case the count of ten was not met)? More out of character for Abe: Why didn't he push his point (after trying his best to save the town) so that, if ten couldn't be found, then at least he would take out of the doomed city the Righteous Ones, including Lot's household? He had done four times that distance to rescue Lot in Damascus, hardly resting with his army so that they could outdo the advance of the adversary's army. And now they had the whole night to get to Sodom (the best time to move with their camels in the desert, orienting themselves by the stars) and ample time to be back to Hebron by dawn—while the emissaries had a good night's sleep in Lot's deserted house. The story is totally at odds with Abe's feelings and behavior toward Lot during the War of Kings, just eighteen years earlier.

It is to obscure these dire illogical turns of events that the narrator has featured Lot being hesitant and "tarrying" at escaping hell, as well as the totally unrealistic attack by families against fully armored gods; and nothing shows more his shaky and lame reasoning than the introduction of the disbelief of Lot's sons, daughters, and in-laws. (And Zoar conveniently having two names, one for the escape route, and the other, Bela, when cited in the war?)

Or are we to believe that Abe, now promised (a few hours back) that he would have a legal heir from his spouse and half sister Sarah, would just become completely unconcerned about the fate of the one adopted son *whom he had tutored all his life to be his heir in the priesthood line* and divine mission? Let me stress again that Abe being eighty-six years old when he got a son from his concubine, and having decades since lost all hope of begetting a natural heir, it also means that *Lot was already initiated in the priesthood line.* In this light, what happens next appears even stranger.

If we follow the text, at the moment Lot was unsuccessful at rallying his sons' and daughters' households, the only safe place and family left to him was his father's in Hebron, since all the other members were going to die in Sodom, with the benediction of the deity.

There are also acute problems with this narrative concerning Abe.

First, Lot having been until thirteen years earlier the priestly heir of Abe, it's not just Lot's sons and daughters doubting the imminent danger who are going to be slain with the town, it's Abe's original priesthood line. Second, the text strangely puts the accent on the *sons-in-law*—because they are more psychologically remote, as a family, than his own sons and daughters; this for the readers to treat it as *remote* family when it becomes clear that they will be exterminated with the whole town of "sinners." Meanwhile, Abe has only his wife Sarah, his concubine Hagar, and Ishmael, the young son he begot from Hagar, living with him in Hebron (and his army's families of course); but the rest of his family, his former heir and his descent, are in Sodom—the town incurring the wrath of the deity.

As a chosen High Priest of Enlil, being totally irreplaceable and necessary, Abe could have demanded that his family—all faithful to the true god—be spared. He aimed for saving Sodom—which was a sign of high morality and great compassion; however, in his reasoning to save the city, the safeguard of Lot and his descent was definitely a subscript, an underlying pact of trust with God. As we saw, Abe had taken in the past a huge responsibility; to oppose the army of the Sumerian kings, headed by gods, among them Nannar, the son and legal heir of his god, was certainly no small feat. Yet, within his mission he acted with an astounding spirit of independence and free will. He just blocked their advance and forced them to retreat; he didn't order a massacre of the defeated, he refused to abandon his neutrality, which means that he imposed his neutrality as a condition for his military defense move. To the deity who ordered him to stop the Eastern kings' army, he could have answered (as Enlil was already told by his vizier during the coup in the Abzu): "My lord, these are your sons!" Or else, about Sodom: "My lord, these are my adopted son—your faithful priest—and his descent!"

Take a deep breath.

Remember that after Abe fought and vanquished the Eastern kings' army near Damascus, and after he had freed Lot—his adopted son and priestly heir at the time—and retrieved the booty from the looted Sodom, he went back to Canaan and his victory was feasted in

Shalem (Jerusalem). "Malkizedek, the king of Shalem . . . blessed him [Abe], saying . . . 'Blessed be the God Most High *who hath delivered thine foes into thine hand.'*" This was not so. They were not *his* foes. Abe answered that he was neutral in the war waged between the son Nannar (heir of Enlil) and the son Marduk (heir of Enki); that only to the God Most High [Enlil], was his allegiance. But the narrator of the Sodom saga wants us to believe that a person of such a high morality—who could confront his Lord on the question "Far be it from you, not to do justice!"—would not have tried (even if he could not save the city) to save at least his god's Faithful Ones, his adopted son and his family, no matter what the count would have been; that Abe would have slept during the night, with the extermination of at least two cities in the balance. And, moreover, the narrator tells us that when *"early in the morning,* he [Abe] looked in the direction of Sodom and Gomorrah and the region of the plain . . . he beheld there smoke rising from the earth as the smoke of a furnace." Note that the furnace putting out smoke was in three large angles—two cities, the space in between, and the plain—that's a very wide angle! It's wide enough for a desert dweller to infer from the furnace and smoke that a few cities (not just Sodom) went up in flames. He knows now that the count of ten has not been met. So, what about Lot and his own family? What about his Lord's promise? Must he conclude that his family didn't amount to enough Righteous, that indeed his Lord could and in fact *already did* "slay the Righteous with the guilty"?

Do the emissaries of the Lord bother to give news to Abe about his adopted son and family? How Lot's small household was supposed to be protected until *they* were safe—but that, unfortunately the sinful wife, who disobeyed the divine orders, had not been part of *they* and had met her death?

Next, we are told that Abe (seeing the disaster from the hill) did not feel safe in the mountains of Hebron, that he pulled up his camp and went to Gerar, westward, to live there, and that at no point afterward did he go back to the Sinai. When much later his son Isaac desired to go to Egypt to flee from a famine, Y. "appeared unto him and said 'Go not down to Egypt; dwell in the land which I will show thee'" (*Wars*, 316–17). So nobody tells Abe about the fate of his adopted son Lot and Abe doesn't ask. The general, the warrior of God on a mission, has no means to contact his Lord—Abe can only be contacted.

The narrator wants us to believe that Abe, seeing the destruction of the cities and the plain, just infers that Lot and his family are dead (that his deity has slain the Righteous), and that he draws a line on the past and forgets all about it . . . he who had moved his whole army to go and get Lot back when he was taken hostage! It would mean that he doesn't consider there is any chance for Lot to have been saved, or protected, and therefore to be on his way to his camp. He draws a line, and decides to move to his own safety.

All in all, we are to believe that the experienced traveler and desert dweller Lot would be too stupid to follow the unique camel track toward Hebron (his first dwelling place in Canaan and where, later on, he must have visited Abe several dozen times). In Hebron, Abe would leave before he knew anything for certain about Lot and his family, not even sending a camel driver on this dirt road to look for him. If Lot ever reached Hebron, and his uncle/father had already moved out with his army, nobody would be able to tell him where went the son of Terah, High Priest of Enlil—High Priest himself, protégé of the foremost god, the one whose renown and exploits have been hailed in Shalem? That where the notorious Abe went with all his troops, family, and caravan, nobody would know in a town of a few hundred souls at most, at a crossing of two or three tracks through the desert? This is what we are supposed to believe.

But what we can clearly infer, to the contrary, at least from the account of the narrator of Genesis 18 and 19, is that this deity doesn't care about any family tie, about the love of a man for his spouse and vice-versa, the love of daughters for their mother and vice-versa, nor for the bonding between a surrogate father and his former heir and descent (which we know is the first and foremost value for the Anunnaki); that the deity cares only for his devoted High Priest, unto whom he has entrusted his plans for the future, his warrior who has defended the Mountain of the Gods and has blocked its defilement; that he cares only for his own future temples and followers, and regarding his devoted priests, the degree of care is only as much as the individual himself fits in his plans. The chess game, we are told, was played among gods—gods fighting gods, royal brother fighting brother, their royal sons fighting along the lines of heritage—each god mostly intent on protecting his own heir, and his heir's heir (that is, unless they were crossed, as Enlil with Nannar).

Lot's Escape to Zoar and Refuge in a Cave

So how did Lot escape, according to the narrator?

> The sun was risen over the Earth when Lot arrived at Zoar; and *the Lord* rained upon Sodom and Gomorrah, from the skies, *brimstone and fire that had come from Yahweh*. And *He* upheavaled those cities and the whole plain and all the inhabitants of the cities and all the vegetation that grows from the ground.

Says Sitchin: "One by one the cities 'which had outraged the Lord' were upheavaled, and *each time Lot was allowed to escape*" (*Wars*, 313–14; my emphasis).

> For when *the gods* devastated the cities of the plain, *the gods remembered Abraham*, and sent Lot away out of the upheavaling of the cities.

In these two biblical sentences, we observe a confusion of subjects. The Lord/He (singular) who "rained fire" upon the towns and "upheavaled those cities" is not the same as the Lord Y. who gave (him) the brimstone and fire weapons. And worse, in the next sentence we are back to the Elohim plural, the Lords, the Gods.

Second, the upheavaling definitely (in the second sentence) happens as a sudden and rapid suite of events, a fact which is also implied in the large "furnace" encompassing even the direction of the plain, that Abe sees "early in the morning"—and it means that early in the morning, and yet after dawn (when Lot is sent to the mountains), the gods, plural, have already upheavaled five cities and the spaceport—real quick job— and yet in these two or three hours at the most, Lot is supposed to have reached Zoar, and then the farther mountains, before Zoar itself was scorched by sulfur and fire. That would be a minimum of 30 miles— the kind of distance that would have taken him two-thirds of the way toward Hebron before the weapons of doom were fired, and Abe sup- posedly woke up to see it all done. Now, how early does a man of the desert usually get up? You have to be up before dawn, because only then can you get some freshness and the ever so slight humidity of dew that the body absolutely needs to go on the whole day in the heat. I, myself, spent a couple of months crossing the Sahara desert on trucks, and I had adopted immediately the Tuaregs' habit of getting up before dawn, at the fist glimmer—when all nature is still obscure and the colors are not distinguishable yet. This is a fact of life for all people living in very hot countries, and especially in deserts—which shows that the narrator had never lived in wild nature, as did even the inhabitants of the first Canaanite "cities." Another point is the fact that a tent dweller in a hot region such as the Middle East will never sit at the entrance of his tent "in the heat of the day"—because the entrance, especially if it is an open hatch enabling Abe to see the visitors arrive from above him (as he sup- posedly did), is not protected from the burning heat. Tent dwellers only rest in full shade.

So, what happened to Lot afterward, he who was to be saved by the "mercy" of the deity and who, following the rescue plan of the emissar- ies, was instructed to "escape to the mountains," to one city precisely targeted, and who had already lost his wife?

Lot "dwelt in a cave, he and his two daughters with him." Then we are told that, witnessing the destruction of all life in the Jordan plain, they thought they had witnessed the end of mankind on Earth.

222 Erasing Sodom: The Book Text

That's a hell of a logical gap! Even a child of seven witnessing a huge
raging fire taking up a good quarter of the horizon (within his arms
forming a 90-degree angle, just as one could see in huge arson fires,
like in Australia or in Greece, that extend over hundreds of miles),
even this child wouldn't think that everybody on Earth had died.
And certainly not the initiated former heir of the High Priest, himself
son of Terah, the foremost High Priest of all Sumer, learned scholar
in all matters of astronomy, mathematics, sacred architecture, medicine, and science at large, plus the Divine Sciences, among them the
reading of oracles, the knowledge regarding the gods and of things
sacred. So now the narrator, after having framed a whole town into
a "sinful city" category—this accounting for five towns and a whole
region to be righteously scorched and carbonized by the fire of the
anger of god—then having reduced Lot's family to consist mostly of
skeptical sons-in-law and a disobedient wife, after sending them as far
as possible from Abe and right into the next furnace, now wants to
make us believe that the former heir of Abe was more stupid than a
seven-year-old child. An adopted son that, by all customs, must have
already been taught all these sciences, in order to take on the function
of High Priest after Abe would have died.

Take another deep breath and let's follow the story.

The narrator is, as usual, trying to put the weight of the sin on
women (we know by now it's a trend as inescapable as gravity), and
in this instance, he really needs it more than ever in order to take the
former heir out of the picture (without the readers feeling any loss,
because they were guilty, were they not?). So, how can this be done?
The narrative now features Lot being induced *by his young daugh-*
ters, to commit the most horrible sin with them! So our Lot, suddenly
morphed into a perfect idiot, is first believing—just as his daughters—
that they are the sole survivors of the human race. The narrative, here,
reaches a bottomless pit of stupidity—which would be laughable if a
most tortuous intent had not started (some time ago) to surface like
a horrendous leak of oil on the ocean. Of course we had found the
timing of the promise to Abe very strange, and a rather gross way of

behaving, psychologically speaking—like offering a prize before the whip, the kind of rosy gift that only a tormentor would allow himself to give to someone just before killing his sole adult "son" and family, and just before erasing a whole region and its inhabitants. But now we see the bottom of it. Let's follow the absurd scenario in the text: "And the older [daughter] said unto the younger: 'Our father is old [really!] and *there is not a man on earth to squire us in the manner of all on earth.* Come, let us make our father drink wine, then lie down with him, so that we still preserve the seed of life." What astute and devilish temptresses! Because, of course, having seen the "whole" population stricken blind by the terrifying divine emissaries, and woken up in the morning with these same blazing warriors telling them the dice were cast and they had to flee as quickly as possible, running even, to the mountains before their whole city got smashed and reduced to ashes, and while Lot "tarried" to flee, they were taken aloft to the outskirts—and nevertheless, believe it or not, what had they taken with them as their sole most treasured thing to keep with them? A jar of wine of course! So who? Who had this idea and went back inside to take the jar—not even water (that would have been quite sensible), not something to eat or to start a fire with, but a jar of wine! And who carried it running all the way to the cave? So picture that, again.

On reaching Zoar, they had not told anybody to flee to the mountains for safety, so the people are all dead. They have not met anybody (logically) since the town of Zoar, which was itself blown up, so they had to flee farther. They are hiding in a cave. Yet they have "witnessed" the massive destruction on the horizon—when did they *dare* look back, knowing what happened to their wife or mother? None of the emissaries had told them to remain in the mountains forever. Lot has lost his dear wife; his sons, daughters, sons-in-law, grandchildren, and friends . . . all dead. His town was just smashed to ashes. Just what you need to be in the mood for love . . . and especially when your kids are starting to talk nuts (according to the text of course, which I strongly doubt).

Now, a remark on the semantic field of the narrator, revealed by the term "to squire us," supposedly used by adolescent girls. A *squire,* historically, was a landlord, a boss—so the accent is put on the ownership of a woman by a man. Try to fathom if you can an adolescent girl imagining and hoping in her wildest dreams to be *owned* and *bossed* by a man *"in the manner of all on earth"*! Isn't that the perfect projection of a man who believes his wife is his possession and he is the boss? And on top of that, these lame-reasoning fantasies are supposed to be what occupies the minds of two adolescents in full post-traumatic syndrome! And of course the learned and mature father of already married sons and daughters would fall prey to these absurd rationalizations!

So keeping in mind this both appalling and hilarious drama as context—let's follow the trend: a priming from our narrator toward the inevitable conclusion. Really, this Lot (who is he by the way, just the nephew?) was not worth saving, he and his "sinful daughters," and his disobedient spouse. And this concubine of whom Abe had a firstborn son, was she not a servant, even a slave? Fortunately, Abe will have a legal heir, the bloodline is preserved! (Lot has obviously become not only expendable but rather cumbersome. The narrator wants to have a fresh start from now on.)

Yes, this tale is as sad and shocking as it seems, while it reveals, throughout the fabric, the gross patches—as I said, as clearly as an oil spill surfacing on the ocean, which it is.

The Great Punishment of Sodom and the Demoting of Lot the Righteous

The great punishment of Sodom is, incidentally, a rare moment where we can see a real "mercy": given that a city of blind people is destined to die an atrocious and slow death, killing them means abbreviating their suffering (even if it was not meant that way).

We have remarked, already, how unfair and unjust it is to try (so badly) to save one of these cities by counting the Righteous, while the four other cities are anyway doomed without even a chance at any mercy. We have shown the nuking plan was already set up and unfolding, and that it overrode (no matter what) Abe's attempt at *having the deity weighing his own sense of Justice* and hopefully sorting out the *Justs* from the *Sinners*—a plea for mercy that reveals in Abe a very high morality and self-reflection that we know Enlil was incapable of. As the French expression goes about inconsistent and patchy stories: it is stitched with white thread.

We now understand that, on the part of the narrator of Sodom's story, this was a way, as usual, to hit two targets with one blow, that is, (1) to exemplify as much as possible the unworthiness of humans in general, and of the enemies of god in particular; and (2) to prime the readers to feel that the deity was such a paragon of compassion and mercy that he even tried to give a chance to those who had "outraged the Lord." In his willingness to exonerate the deity at all costs (and given that the enemy brothers—the godly contenders—cannot be accepted in the framework of the One God) the narrator resorts to showing how much the Earth-humans are despicable, unworthy, and untrustworthy. So the deity is presented as a paragon of all virtues, and in contrast men and women as paragons of all evils (apart from Abe).

Lot's Tale and Incest

As for Lot's tale, the fact that the narrator presents the father-daughter incest as the utter degradation unto which a man can fall, shows how much more recent than the time of Abe was this insertion into the Informational Framework (IF) text. Let me explain why.

Abe's native tongue was the Sumerian of Nippur, and then, given his diplomatic activities (in the Egyptian Pharaoh's court) and military actions, he necessarily spoke Akkadian, the international language of global politics. His marriage with his half sister Sarai/Sarah (whose name means "princess") says it all: his education and culture were Sumerian, and he was from both a priestly and royal family. So

Abe, besides his nearness to Enlil, was also raised in a family and in a Sumerian society having constant interactions with the Anunnaki gods, and knowing their historical and individual records.

And we have seen that incest, in this Anunnaki society, was an accepted and widespread custom. The fact that the royal succession line gave precedence to the son born out of a half-brother and half-sister union tells us volumes. And Abe's wife was his half sister, so that the customs were also adopted by the humans of mixed parentage, as were all the High Priests and High Priestesses. Furthermore, we have multiple examples of incestuous mating between a father and his daughters, and even granddaughters (Anu with Inanna, or Enki with his own granddaughters), the child thus born getting precedence in the kingship line. So even a Sumerian-born High Priest (or, one should say, especially a High Priest in the know about the gods and their family) could in no way whatsoever project a moral judgment of degradation on an incestuous father-daughter relation such as that attributed to Lot, at that time in history of course.

The whole wrapping of the story—with the daughters as temptresses and the incest as an abomination (all this to make it possible for Lot to be ensnared, thus not the one responsible)—stinks of a society millennia nearer to our times, when incest had already become a taboo, an act judged utterly reprehensible, and hence sullied with blame and synonymous with moral degradation. Clearly, this story from the third-layer narrator cannot, in any way, have a historical ground. And, of course, it stinks not only of sexism but also of dire racism.

Psychological Biblical Criticism about Sodom and Rape in Lot's Story

Let's turn to the biblical criticism and analysis of Lot's story, a hair-raising tale of not only incest but also rape, that was the object of centuries of exegeses, and of course of a much needed psychological and psychoanalytical scrutiny.

First, let me explain why I have left aside what I consider to be a definite addition to this already convoluted and excessive story, another addition precisely meant to muddle, as I pointed out earlier, the scarcity of real factual evidence against the population and Lot (and thus to avoid pondering the genocidal act of the deity). I wanted you, my readers, to weigh if the highlight (and interpretation) I gave to the story could stand by itself. The homosexual rape addition is, in effect, the most powerful tool to bring up emotional confusion in the Book readers.

So we are in Sodom and the emissaries are already the guests of Lot's family, Lot's wife, no doubt, preparing the banquet with her servants. (Let's note that Lot, the High Priest's son and heir for about two decades, given that Abe is very rich and powerful, cannot be the one the narrator insists on presenting as an "outsider," and of low status.)

Are we going to be, by now, astonished that an age-old exegesis has focused mainly on the verb *to know* in the sentence (when the whole population comes and asks Lot, about the fiery visitors, "Bring them out to us that we may *know* them." Believe it or not, the writer's trick worked perfectly well—the priming in the story being the interpretation of the sin of Sodom, left to our imagination—and *to know* was understood as to know sexually, as Adam knew Eve. And thus, immediately blinded by a rush of subconscious emotion, the (now sole?) men gathered in front of Lot's door were threatening to rape the emissaries. Thus are forgotten the fact the "angels" came fully armored and ready to erase, if not Sodom, a few allied towns; also forgotten is the fact that the whole population, young and old, was there, and that they were unarmed. (Picture the fathers, poor small humans in front of angels of death, willing to perform an homosexual rape in front of their kids and wives!) And pious students to be sidetracked beyond their wits, one generation after the other. It's not all. When Lot sees the crowd demanding explanations, the narrator features him offering his virgin daughters to the crowd—his main obligation, as a host, being to *protect* his guests of course. A trove for the Freudians!

And here goes our bold psychological criticism focusing, not on these degenerated monsters of doom, but on hair-splitting arguments about rape, and the exegesis about the hosting code of honor. Fortunately, the crowd, indignant, refuses, and that's when the emissaries exit the house and strike the people with blindness. So again, three birds with one stone: One, Lot is already morally demeaned (a harbinger for events to come); two, it adds a heavier fault on the part of the population; and three, the attention is diverted from the abominable acts of the deity.

Not all commentators and experts are wholly sidetracked by the sexual elements. Noteworthy is the original perspective of Lyn Bechtel in "A Feminist Reading of Genesis 19:1–11" focusing on "the group-oriented community, in which women are central, highly valued and must be protected as the producers of salvation" (123). This is in opposition to our own individual-oriented society, biased in its interpretation. However, Bechtel's hypothesis is that the crowd, willing to protect their city from the emissaries—perceived as threatening spies because they are outsiders and messengers of a lord—could in fact be willing to rape them in order to render them "incapable of performing their role as spies" (117). Bechtel remarks that, in Hebrew, "'knowing' covers broad intellectual, experiential and sexual knowing, and that maybe the men only had intellectual knowing in mind." Nevertheless, we see that, in the exegesis, the "whole population" has become a group of men only, and Bechtel's conclusion is that the townsmen were showing a dangerous xenophobia: "The story challenges these xenophobic and isolationist tendencies" that can only bring doom (as on Sodom), and advocates "negotiations with surrounding nations" (127).

The Demoting and Disposal of Hagar

Abe's father, Terah, as a High Priest of Enlil, a Sumerian serving in his most sacred temple in Nippur, then in Ur, had to be of mixed parentage (Anunnaki and human); and in fact, Sitchin remarks that the names of several of the family members denote a princely or nobility status, beyond that of the half sister and spouse of Abe, Sarai/Sarah. By her union with Abe, Hagar was naturally, by Sumerian customs, raised to the status of a noblewoman—a recognized and thus revered concubine (such as Anu's first concubine, mother of the firstborn Enki). How could we imagine a High Priest, chosen by the foremost god, himself of a demigod descent, being attracted by a woman not worthy of him and willing to have an heir from her? This certitude makes it all the more plausible that the so-called servant role was just a fabrication, like that of the "prostitute" Magdalene, whose status as the First disciple (and one given a secret teaching by Jesus) was established by her rediscovered Gospel of Mary, and whose high initiate status and noble origins in Egypt I have analyzed in *The Sacred Network*. As Karen King remarks in her introduction to her book *The Gospel of Mary of Magdala*, this Gospel written early in the second century BCE, may "provide an intriguing glimpse into a kind of Christianity lost for almost fifteen hundred years" (see the magnificent painting of the Magdalene by Simon Vouet, in the color insert, plate 13). King pursues:

> This astonishingly brief narrative presents a radical interpretation of Jesus' teachings as a path to inner spiritual knowledge; it rejects his suffering and death as the path to eternal life; it exposes the erroneous view that Mary of Magdala was a prostitute for what it is—a piece of theological fiction; it presents the most straightforward and convincing argument in any early Christian writing for the legitimacy of women's leadership; it offers a sharp critique of illegitimate power and a utopian vision of spiritual perfection; . . . and it asks us to rethink the basis for church authority. All written in the name of a woman. (3–4)

What if, similarly, Hagar had been the daughter born in a noble Sumerian family, whose parents sent her to serve Abe, in the sense of serving a Man of God? (The way, for example, musicians willing to learn and be initiated in the secret teachings of Indian music, when they are chosen and distinguished by their music master, will be invited to stay at his home, but then will serve him freely, the honorable master, as a servant would do. A custom that I have witnessed in Benares even among Western disciples.) In that case, she would have been even more revered because then it must have been by her sole merits and qualities—of intelligence, loyalty, beauty, etc., that Abe distinguished her.

Another hypothesis to consider is that, in moving his abode toward Canaan, Enlil must have intended to build a new temple there, and Abe was his chosen herald and envisioned High Priest for the new faith.

The Selection of the "Chosen" Descent of Abe

The new layer of additions is crystal clear in Lot's story. Through the editing and morphing processes, the princely bloodline descended from the brother of Abe to Lot was taken out and disposed of. Similarly blotted out was the union of Abe and Hagar, who, whoever she was at first, won the heart and the love of Abe, and gave him his firstborn son and heir. As Hagar's son Ishmael was only thirteen at the cornerstone events (Abe being given a new name and selected as first Patriarch of the new faith through the sole line of the promised son Isaac, on the fatal eve) he was not yet entrusted with arcane scientific and priestly knowledge as had been Lot. His case needed only, from the narrator, a downplaying and degrading of his mother (into a servant and slave) and then a total blackout from ulterior accounts.

Yet, as historian and biblical expert Gerda Lerner notes in *The Creation of Patriarchy,* in the Sumerian law (notably the Hammurabic one in effect at that time), the children of the concubine are "entitled to a lesser share in the inheritance if their father acknowledges them during his lifetime. In Ishmael's case, *Abraham had already acknowledged him as his son,* and yet God *ordered him* to expel Hagar and her son as Sarah desired, '. . . for it is through Isaac that your line shall be continued' (Gen. 21:12)" (171; my emphasis).

My hypothesis—regarding the fate of the descent of Lot and that of Hagar—is that there were some theo-political reasons belonging to the narrators themselves. With the covenant, the deity was now bound to his "Chosen" and vice-versa (and in fact, the imperative and binding character of this "contract" imposed on one ethnic group, and greatly resembling social contracts of the time, has been largely discussed by experts, among them Rivkah Kluger, as we saw). Hence the probable restructuring of some key passages to focus exclusively on one ethnic group and get rid of the other lines of descent. However, as the Book is a perfect example of it, this cannot fail to leave traces. One such story, beyond that of Lot, is of course the way Hagar is banished to the desert with Ishmael, now sixteen years old (Isaac is about three years old). What makes this story harrowing is the fact that Abraham is not even giving her and *his* son some food and water for a few days, even less so some sheep as heritage—nothing. He sends them to their death knowingly—he, the desert dweller. So let's keep that in mind.

Mayer Gruber, a social scientist, focused on what had puzzled experts, namely that "there are two consecutive narratives concerning God's rescue of Hagar from dying of thirst in the Negev desert," the second time after being expelled by Abe (172). This story highlights a grave ambiguity in Abe's psyche, just as when, in Egypt, he let their host the Pharaoh seduce his beautiful sister Sarah, not disclosing she was also his wife (the Pharaoh, on discovering it, asked them out and gave them an army and riches). A third instance of such ambiguity is of course when later he'll be willing to prove his obedience to his Deity by blindly following his order to sacrifice his and Sarah's only son, the same Isaac, a prospect that killed Sarah of grief before an angel saved the adolescent (*but not the mother,* now expendable). As Ilona Rashkow remarks pertinently in *Taboo or Not Taboo,* "Contradictions in Abraham's character may result from the psychic complexities the biblical writer imagined; or, they may result from the fact that *Abraham is an agent in a literary narrative with a highly developed system of conventions*—his traits may be more a function of the requirements of the story-line than of his personality" (2; my emphasis). This system of conventions (including beliefs, values, worldview) is precisely what I call the semantic field of a narrator, within the collective semantic field of his creed and culture at a given epoch and place. As for the aim of the tinkering and editing by late narrators, I think it is primarily to find ways to exonerate the deity of the Book. In the nuking of Sodom case, and using Abe's decent pleading to save the Righteous, it is exoneration from the immoral and unjust deed. In the so-called dismissal of Hagar case (a clear death sentence)—since it is either the Deity or Abe—the human will be sacrificed to let the divine persona show compassion. A second thread is a continuous hammering of the slave and servant status of Hagar, an aim so conspicuous as to render the doubling of the "saving" dubious at best. Let's see the story.

The first time, Hagar is pregnant and she flees to the desert because the infertile Sarai/Sarah, jealous, harasses her. An angel tells her to go back to Abe's house; he predicts she'll beget a son and gives him the name Ishmael. (Abe, let's note it, needs his firstborn son and heir.) The second time, Abe's legal heir Isaac is now three, and Sarah asks him to "throw out this slave woman and her son." Says Gruber, "God, according to Gen. 21.12, tells him [Abe] not to be distressed . . . 'As for whatever Sarah tells you, *obey her.*'"

Gruber remarks that the verb can mean either to obey or to listen, and chooses to grant the deity of the Book a kind of post-Goleman emotional intelligence—that it was a counsel to listen and talk to his wife and make her understand (175). And Gruber goes on to argue: "Since, however, throughout Gen. 16 and Gen. 21.17–20 God and God's angel show the greatest interest in Hagar and her progeny and in their survival and well-being, it makes no sense that God would tell Abraham to obey Sarah's command." Yet he did, not Sarah's specifically, but his Deity's command, and he was sure or made sure they would die. And again an angel (probably not the same one?) saved them. (Remember all Anunnaki were "angels.")

The argument above serves me well to make my point. The only question that even courageous critical biblical experts such as Ilona Gruber never consider is that the deity of the Book may have, at different epochs, different political agendas of his own (yet, his interferences in geopolitics were a fact of life for his later prophets). With a land he got as heritage, a people of devotees is what he wanted, with, at their head, a line of High Priests and/or Kings, starting with Abe's descent—given that, being brother and half sister of a royal and High Priest lineage, they were therefore demigods, partly Anunnaki. And we may then think differently about Moses, from Egypt, who, according to some experts, had horns (as in Michelangelo's sculpture, see fig. 6.1) just as the Anunnaki had horns—the one sign to surely recognize them in depictions.

Fig. 6.1. Michelangelo's famous sculpture of Moses with horns (San Pietro in Vincoli, Rome). Photograph by Jörg Bittner Unna.

With this fresh look, let's reconsider Lot's story. How fitting that he is sent to the mountain to be forlorn and alone in the whole region. How fitting that Abe is said to have moved his encampment, and thus was supposedly impossible to reach. How fitting that most of Lot's descendants in Sodom (including his heir) are eradicated in one blow, and that his wife should die—so that his male descent was said to have ended, himself brought down (in the surrealistic narrative) to utter degradation. How fitting that Lot is depicted as a vile and incestuous father, lost in sin, his sole descent left from his young daughters deemed flawed, and thus lost from memory.

How fitting that Abe was promised an heir from his legal wife Sarah just on the eve of the holocaust, before all this happened—so that in the minds of the readers, now soothed and sure to have the line of Abe preserved, the ignominious fate of Lot and all his family and his city, could be faced with a steady heart, accepted without question as the rightful punishment for dire evil deeds. How befitting, this tale composed for one people, one ethnicity only. Another firstborn evicted, another first heir dispossessed, another brother (the royal son of Terah) erased from official history.

+ 7 +

Layers in the Genesis Text

LET'S NOW CHANGE our perspective to see things more globally and sort out the distinct narrators and layers in the text (remembering also the analysis of the garden of Eden texts in *DNA of the Gods*).

The First Layer in the Text

There is a first layer in the text, and that is the sources consisting of the Informational Framework sentences, which we can trace to ancient Sumerian texts, mostly historical accounts. They are, for example, the Mesopotamian data on the wars of the gods and that of their kings, the *Tale of Adapa*, the *Erra Epos*, the *Epic of Etana*, etc.

Already, the source texts that have been selected are the ones (out of the many available in the great libraries of Sumer, such as that of Babylon) selectively adopting the perspective of Enlil, with their Moralistic Framework already emerging—such as K-3657 (the Babel tower account), and K-5001 (the nuking of the Jordan plain).

We cannot rule out, even at this point, that Enlil himself would have dictated his own version of the ancient history, and this would amply explain the biased version of the garden of Eden, including the weight of sin put on The Woman, despite the fact he knew it was all Enki's scheming—the Serpent! It could explain the plural *we,* sometimes used as an *I* by the foremost among the gods, and other times as a *we* referring to a group (his sons, or the Assembly). In my view, all the psychological traits we have unraveled fit well with Enlil's profile as shown in the tablets. This possibility fits also with some traits of the Anunnaki royals, who show a tendency (1) to aspire at being the sole god—this being of course much more sound when you are the foremost one of the time; (2) to dictate their own view of things to their scribes, or to write it themselves; (3) to demonize the brother-enemy and call "sinful" whoever (god, human, or city) is not subservient; (4) to put the responsibility for all evil events, such as events triggering wars and conflicts, on their enemy; and finally (5) they have a male-dominated hierarchy, starting with the kingship passing primarily to male heirs and their obsession with a male heir. Sexism against women is rampant and the Anunnaki society is definitely, clearly, macho, especially among the Enlilites and their natural ally Nergal.

We have seen two extracts of texts showing sentences of true Informational Framework mixed up with sentences of a clear Moralistic Framework, the latter revealing an Enlilite perspective on history. This is of immense import, because it shows that the Moralistic Framework, as biased as it is, was already existing in Sumer (and certainly as the perspective of one of the Enlilite gods), instead of being only a later addition. This is why we have to consider it as partly contained in the first layer of the text. The first layer of Genesis then becomes an IF + MF semantic field.

Let's recall these two extracts:

Text 1. The Nuking of the Jordan Plain (2024 BCE). "Lord, Bearer of the Scorcher that burnt up the adversary; who obliterated the disobedient land; who withered the life of the Evil Word's followers; who rained stones and fire upon the adversaries." (K-5001 Text, Sumerian language, with a faithful Akkadian translation.)

Text 2. The Babylon Tower (3450 BCE). "The thoughts" of this god's heart "were evil; against the Father of the Gods [Enlil] he was wicked . . . the people of Babylon he corrupted to sin," inducing "small and great to mingle on the mound ." . . . Because "they against the gods revolted with violence, violently they [were crushed and] they wept for Babylon; very much they wept." (K-3657 Text, cuneiform Akkadian; *Wars*, 198–99.)

The semantic fields of these two texts are very similar in their MF values and aims (like inspiring the fear of god), however I also detect differences.

The author of the Babel tower extract (text 2) is trying to move us and arouse emotions via a paternalistic and cheap moral instruction, while the nuking text is much more sharp and hard in its judgments. The first text's author believes he is the Great Master, almighty, and to be feared (the biographical texts in original Sumerian often shift from the use of *I* to the use of the third person, but never to the plural *we*), whereas the author of the second text believes he is a shepherd and has to teach a people who, in his opinion, can only be driven like sheep. He wants to make us weep over the terrible fate of the "disobedient" in a way very similar to the author of Lot's tale, and he allows himself (for the greater good of his teaching) quite a departure from the facts without any qualms. Same Enlilite MF and values but different images of self, and different relational styles—thus different authors. And both texts are in Akkadian (thus revealing a desire to be widely distributed in the civilized world of the time). The nuking text has one version in Sumerian, a link to the original empire before the realm of Inanna's Agade/Akkad (started around 2400 BCE), yet it speaks of the nuking holocaust happening in 2024 BCE. Whereas, the events recounted in the Babel tower text are fourteen centuries before the nuking. Both texts had to be written after Akkadian became the world language.

I would attribute the harsh, haughty, and judgmental nuking text to a Sumerian-speaking immortal Anunnaki having written a prayer of praise for his own cult—either Enlil or Nergal. And the Babel tower

238 Layers in the Genesis Text

text, I attribute to a much more recent and highly moralistic narrator, a priest—precisely, the one who concocted the story of Lot.

In fact, the author of the first layer (the source texts) could have been Enlil himself (or one of his kin or emissaries) writing or dictating to a faithful and chosen scribe. If Enlil had dictated his own version of history through devoted scribes, these scribes would have revered the text to the utmost as a divine word, or *parole,* and would have been meticulously faithful to it. We may suppose that the first layer itself is a compilation of texts, written at different periods, under the strict supervision of Enlil, as global annals of the main chapters of the history of mankind. Thus, a first scribe (of antediluvial events) could have been Enoch/Enmeduranki, the seventh antediluvial ruler/patriarch of Sumer, Adapa/Adam being the first. We know that Enoch was taken to "heaven" (Nibiru) to be taught and, on the command of the deity, he was given scribes' instruments to write down what the archangel Pravuel *would read to him from ancient books* (*Encounters,* 63). So, here we have a sound explanation for finding extracts of ancient Sumerian archives in the Book text.

Other chapters (still bearing the moralistic signature of the Enlilite semantic field) could have been written after major events occurred, by High Priests and scribes devoted to Enlil.

However, there have been definite additions to the original IF + MF version, concocted at much later times, and two layers of these can be distinguished by our semantic analysis. The story of Lot is without any doubt a fully added tale, with a Moralistic Framework so biased and so extreme that it becomes totally unrealistic—showing and exemplifying the third layer.

The Second Layer in the Text

Thus, the second layer is where we see emerging to the surface a moralistic narrator belonging to a much more recent civilization and age of Earth—let's call him Narrator 2. He is the one who doesn't know anything (anymore) about Anunnaki science and who treats the real history of the Anunnaki royals, and of their fighting, through the sole perspective of Enlil. Other gods (Enlil's family, siblings, and descent) have become either devotees and under his command (including the famous emissaries/Malakhim), or else they are framed as evil, idols, and/or fake. This more recent narrator, we have seen, was not only a city dweller, but almost certainly a temple dweller most of his life, a devoted priest who has lived in a secluded, rich, and orderly environment, far from the laypeople and the society at large. He is biased against women (just as Enlil), and while he certainly had a family and transmitted his knowledge and function to one of his sons, he nevertheless remained very haughty and remote from it. Thus, he cannot fathom a mother's or a woman's perspective, the psychology of kids, the facts of nature, or what it means to live in harsh conditions. He is overly confident and proud of his secret priestly knowledge and is teaching it to his heir and an elite. He is a well-informed scholar and priest and yet tends to dwell in strict morality, precepts of faith, and rules, and has no mental flexibility. He has not learned to exercise his mind through philosophy (as the Greeks), science (as the Egyptians and the Greeks), or by living in an open society, where all opinions and experiences diverge. From his narrow MF, we can also surmise that he has never traveled extensively, and that he has hardly ever ventured out of his temple. The persona of the narrator of the second layer is thus a priest and scholar of a temple, male—by all means, he must have been a High Priest of the descent of Abraham.

Now this persona of the second layer's narrator, viewed through the texts of the Book of Genesis, while being definitely biased and moralistic, is nevertheless a scholar of high standing, in the manner in which he respects the unavoidable source texts and their historical facts (the IF sentences)—namely the first layer (the IF + MF Enlilite version)—which were, we may assume, available to him in the original texts in Akkadian (the ancestor of Hebrew and Semitic languages in general), or their copies and translations in other Middle-Eastern languages.

This second layer, in my view, was composed at the moment of the translation from this source text (and other Middle-Eastern texts) into the (then) novel language of Hebrew (it would be the first Hebrew version). The main source text of this Narrator 2 is already reflecting an Enlilite and MF perspective on events, however he is cognizant of other texts as well—such as those of Babylon, reflecting Marduk's own sole-god perspective. A great and broad-minded scholar, cognizant of the world politics of the times, despite his extreme moralistic biases and his repugnance for the laypeople world, he will respect and keep the plural *Lords* (Elohim) and the term *men* referring to the Lords and other divine beings (thus he knows they are a human species, even if immortal). This means that Narrator 2 knew—from his source texts and the tradition transmitted to him, if not from a direct contact with the Lords—three basic truths: (1) that there had been several gods from the same royal family tree, (2) that they had fought between themselves, and (3) that these gods were men, of a human race, with wives, brothers, kids, emotions, and prone to act in fits of rage.

Now comes another set of questions for us: we may wonder about the ethics of this second layer narrator whose purpose was to make humans attach themselves to the foremost god only and abandon the other great gods, and whose two-pronged strategy for achieving this was to brand all the other royals (including the King of Heaven and father) as superstition or idolatry, and to use Enlil's wrathful acts to induce the fear of god.

Paradoxically, I do believe that one positive effect of monotheism on humanity was to prod us into a giant evolution in terms of self-consciousness, self-reference, ethics, and individualization—because (unlike the gods) we confronted our own daily sins and shortcomings and we *tried* to emulate the divine qualities of justice and/or compassion that we had projected on the one god. Not that we achieved this impossible aim, but at least the try gave us momentum for self-improvement. However, as we have analyzed so many of monotheism's dreadful effects, I believe also that the time has come for us to move on.

The Third Layer in the Text

Based on Semantic Fields Theory and psychological analysis, there is a third layer of the text from at least one author/editor—the oil slick spreading on the surface in big patches. There is, clearly so, a definite editing and wholly added narrative with extremely biased preconceptions and whose aim is to construct a dogma—religious, moral, societal (in terms of a civilized society of its kind), and ethnical. This endeavor amounts to pulling up or boot-strapping the history of one people only, the religion of one people only—through the selective focus on only one line of the descendants of Abe.

This third layer is, in my view, akin to the historical pulling up of the Catholic dogma—a whole set of beliefs tied up to form a strict corpus of dogma that will serve afterward as measures to sort out and weigh the true Catholics from the heretics, the pagans, the "not-us," and that will introduce an overlay of the contempt for women shown by the sole Deity.

Concerning the Catholic religion, this elaboration of the core doctrine took place in one unique momentous event, perfectly well documented. It happened when the Roman Emperor Constantine I called a Council—normally an assembly of *all* the bishops of the diverse Christian faiths. At this epoch in Europe and the Middle East, the religious landscape was quite variegated. Many groups of early Christians had developed their own brand of a faith with specific customs, rituals, and beliefs (such as the Gnostics). These early Christian faiths flourished in the midst of ancient Egyptian, Greek, Persian, and Roman faiths, such as the Isis Mysteries, and the cult of Mithras, the latter being the most extent faith in the world at the time. With the crowning of Constantine I, the Roman Empire had been reunified (it extended all over Europe) and the persecution of Christians had been halted; at that time, Christians formed only a tenth of its population. What is interesting is that Constantine, all his life, adhered to a monotheist brand of Roman religion called the *Sol Invicti* (linked to Apollo and Mithras) and was particularly attracted by the Arianist faith; but he had always been tolerant and wanted above all a unified religion. But a new dogma promoted by Bishop Arius had appeared in Christianity, creating a lot of dissention. The dispute was over the relationship of the Father with the Son (and the Holy Spirit). The Catholics upheld the consubstantiality—one unique essence in three different persons—and the Arianists a similar essence but not unique. It is on purely political grounds, to impose the authority of the emperor on the religion and a forced unity of the Empire, that Constantine I himself convened the Council of Nicea in 325 CE. Between 250 and 300 Catholic-prone bishops were invited, and only fourteen Arianists. Without being baptized a Christian, the Emperor nevertheless presided over the council. After days of discussion, of the fourteen Arianist bishops, only three refused to adopt the Catholic dogma, among them Arius himself—and they were excommunicated on the spot. After this crushingly positive vote of a carefully chosen and captive audience, the bishops discussed and established other articles of faith, such as the Trinity. Bizarrely, Constantine was baptized just before dying twelve years later (during one of his campaigns) but by an Arianist bishop, thus in the Arianist faith! Yet his children were raised as Catholics. The setting of the core of dogma led later on to selecting which texts among the scriptures and gospels were to become canonical. Thus came into being the approved version of the scriptures of the New Testament. And the texts that were rejected became the apocryphal gospels and texts, that is, apocryphal to (or outside of) the Catholic faith.

Indeed, the existence of apocryphal books on the fringe of the Hebrew scriptures—such as the Book of Jubilees and the Book of Enoch—which give us a lot of information in accordance with the Sumerian tablets that are absent from the Book, seems to point to such a possibility. At some point, some ancient texts became canonical, and the others were rejected, thus forming the Apocrypha.

So, with this third layer (and Narrator 3), the texts of the Book of Genesis (at least) underwent first a sorting out of the basic elements of dogma, truthful to Enlil's will as expressed in the previous layers—his semantic field, that is, his core judgments and values, especially the new monotheist mold; then an editing with additions in the text stressing his might and inducing the fear of god. The overall aim, as we have seen with the assembling of the Catholic New Testament, would have been to unify the faith, and simultaneously to make it the faith of a specific ethnic group. These additions and editing would have been grafted on the first and second layers that were already interpreting and reviewing history from the standpoint of Enlil's semantic field.

As we saw, the main transformation produced at the second layer was to cement the shift from a pantheon of gods (much too human), to the strict monotheist and moralistic framework—the sole-god faith imposed by Enlil and already developed and expounded in his writing/dictation of the first layer—thus erasing totally the family of Enlil. This is similar to how the Catholic faith erased any mention of the brothers of Jesus (save rare lapses) and of his wife of royal descent Mary Magdalena, a highly initiated apostle, morphing her into the woman "sinner"—thus from an apostle relegating her to being a prostitute. Then the texts led us to interpret her tantamount presence at the side of Jesus (that they could not expunge totally from the canonic texts) by the fact that Jesus having saved her soul, she became totally dedicated to him as a penitent, and since she was rich, by seeing to his needs.

When the third layer is being constructed, one or two millennia later, all detail about Enlil's family is already forgotten, all about the Sumerian civilization and its science (and Abe's birth and education in Nippur) having been either erased or blurred beyond recognition in the first two layers. The process has left only a few discrepancies and linguistic antics, such as the plural-made-singular *Elohim* and *us*. At this third layer's composition are added tales for the effect of patching up the strange and unexplainable discrepancies—a sound undertaking in the service of the Deity, since the narrator doesn't understand why they are there in the first place—and simultaneously taking place is a less than genuine building of a coherent and extended version to ground the corpus of dogma for one people only, using as a basis the strict MF and the religious faith and cultural context developed over centuries by this people. To accomplish this, another issue was to be settled clearly in the corpus of dogmas: Y. selected only one line of the descent of Abe . . . the other branches had to be neatly expurgated and that called for real good reasons. And thus is Lot's descent described as either slain or becoming degenerate.

The Layers Revealing a Towering God

Throughout this book, we have explored and analyzed the ancient texts from Sumer and the Middle East, as well as the Book of Genesis, using the Semantic Fields Theory's looking glass. It has led us to sort out distinct narrators, recognizable via their widely diverging semantic fields, and to pinpoint which layer in the text belonged to one or the other. The process has also permitted us to extract information pertaining to the type of civilization and time frame to which these narrators belonged.

Thus we see, with monotheism, the emergence of a totally dis-incarnated god who is neither human nor alien, but an immaterial spirit endowed (only) with positive qualities in an absolute measure—omniscient, omnipotent, creator of all that is, unfailing, absolutely righteous, etc. (And at that point real history definitely had to be erased.) But in so doing, the gap with the realistic state of the world—that is, the evil deeds, the suffering, the disorder—had to have a reason, a cause that should not originate in God the all-good and all-powerful creator. Then the entity of the devil had naturally emerged as the concept able (as we analyzed it earlier) to constellate a persona with all the opposite negative qualities similarly as extreme. This explains how the elaboration of the *semantic constellation* of the Devil, who now had a name: the Serpent, Satan. And this is how the strife between different godly worldviews was itself morphed into the new battle between God/good and the Devil/evil. All that was not strict dogma became evil, or a plot of the Devil, and punished as such.

This notwithstanding, the basic facts of the narrative (the IF in layers 1 and 2) are belying the superlative epithets to be the qualities exhibited by the wrathful god, the jealous and unjust god, governing only by command and false mercy, and trampling on human beings whenever events aroused his anger or his jealousy—whether the humans were the real culprits or not.

The Sumerians were more honest when they depicted a towering god, a giant, trampling and slaying the Earth-humans who were trying, with hopes and courage, to build their own Bond Heaven-Earth (tower)—as seen in the stone carving (see color insert, plate 14).

Where do we see Enlil or the deity of the Book really giving something to humanity in the texts we have reviewed? We are told that after a big tantrum and the curse of the Woman, the Man, and of mankind, the deity made some garments for the First Couple (how nice, after the "gift" of terrible and eternal curses that couldn't be erased!). We saw how crooked was the gift of "mercy" to Lot—as if one hand was taking back what the other one was forced to give—a gift that in the end worsened the fate of Lot (in the narrative). We saw also how the gift to Abe (the miracle of a son birthed by Sarah at a very old age) had the bitter taste of both a bargain and of a narrator's way to push out of the picture the descent of Lot, as well as that of Hagar. From this irascible and psycho-rigid supposed "father," the commands (as a prevalent style of communication) and the punishments (as a predominant style of reaction) would be somewhat understandable only in as much as he had given to mankind the most precious gift—life—that is, if he were our Creator. But if we look at things in the context of what really happened historically, he appears more like a royal heir who took over the governance as if by divine right, which it was not since his father Anu and his contender Alalu kept usurping the throne one from each other (albeit according to accepted customs and in all fairness).

Enlil as the Commander of Earth was a fact of existence, a dire fate for the young humanity that could not be turned around—if even the brilliant prince and brother and powerful contender Enki himself could not do that much.

✦ Conclusion ✦

WE COULD STILL strongly doubt that such events happened, especially the nuclear holocaust in Sumer, if only we didn't have the Sumerian tablets by the hundred thousands, if only we didn't have the discoveries of several places on Earth with rocks vitrified and unexplainable other than by evoking nuclear blasts and heat, if we didn't have the radioactive skeletons of the Indus Valley, and not least, traces of two thermonuclear explosions on Mars, and evidence of a planet lush with life that was scorched dead.

Now we can ask ourselves: Why these relentless waves of discoveries from many different scientific fields and fringe domains of research? And why now? Because despite recent devastating wars and onslaught on sacred sites by extremist brands of religions that, strangely, have targeted precisely the ancient Sumerian and Assyrian museums and artifacts, we are at the threshold of a qualitative leap in human consciousness, a leap of major proportion.

The information about intelligent civilizations in the universe, in our vicinity and able, since long ago, to visit us—this fact that comes to the forefront with such insistence and such force has been covered up for much too long. But in recent years, even the individuals at key posts and the top brass have come to know the urgency for the people of Earth to be fully cognizant of our next step ahead, that of interacting at the geopolitical level with the federation of intelligent civilizations, then of integrating its organization.

The more I'm researching the Sumerian lore, the more I'm persuaded that, despite their willingness to give us a maximum of knowledge about our origins and their home world, there was an ensemble of information that Enki, Ninmah, and Ningishzidda/Hermes didn't leak to us—and that was their own interaction with such a galactic federation. An issue I bet they mulled over and reached the conclusion that it was something that *we* had to attain by ourselves, because only then would we be fully ready to manage it.

However, it turned out that the forces that wanted to keep us as working donkeys—producing riches and metals that they would dispose of, without even paying for these or for the work—these shadow powers took all possible action to impede us from reaching this understanding, and when a few insightful individuals did, they were quick to silence them in the name of reason and good sense, of statistics and laws of nineteenth-century physics, or of religious incompatibility with their dogmas and worldviews.

We have much to learn about how the bare truth was covered, why, and what psychological incentives they used. And I hope, of course, to have triggered a degree of this awareness while doing my share of the veil lifting and decoding of traces, together with so many other researchers in this or related domains.

However, we have even more to learn by stepping fully into the new paradigm that states that life and intelligent civilizations are teeming in the universe and even at our door; that they have had contacts with us forever. Yet, predictably, there are also real bad guys out there, just as much as here—mafiosi, predators of all venues, and blind despots just like Enlil, albeit on a cosmic scale. Even if there were only decent alien civilizations, there would perforce exist cosmo-political issues with these exo-worlds so intricate and complex that we would still need to be as shrewd and insightful as we can be.

This is our time, then, for us to take this opportunity and make that leap.

✦ Bibliography ✦

A list of the ancient texts and tablets cited in this work is given
at the end of the bibliography.

Anonymous & John D. Smith. *The Mahabharata.* New York: Penguin
Classics, 2009.

Apuleius. *The Golden Ass.* New York: Penguin Classics, 1999.

Asimov, Isaac. *Foundation's Edge.* N.Y.: Doubleday & Co. Inc., 1982.

Aucker, Gene. *Guides to Biblical Scholarship.* Minneapolis, Minn.: Augsburg
Fortress, 2001.

Baigent, Michael, Richard Leigh, and Henry Lincoln. *Holy Blood, Holy
Grail.* New York: Arrow Books/Random House, 1982.

Bechtel, Lyn M. "A Feminist Reading of Genesis 19:1–11." In Brenner,
Genesis: A Feminist Companion to the Bible, 2nd series, 108–28.

———. "Rethinking the Interpretation of Genesis 2.4b–3.24." In Brenner,
Genesis: A Feminist Companion to the Bible, 1st series, 77–117.

———. "The Adam and Eve Myth as a Myth about Human Maturation." In
The 1994 Annual of Hermeneutics and Social Concern, edited by Justus
George Lawler, 152–73. New York: Continuum International Publishing
Group, 1994.

Beit-Hallahmi, Benjamin, and Michael Argyle. "God as a Father-Projection:
The Theory and the Evidence." *British Journal of Medical Psychology* 48,
no. 1 (1975): 71–75. Available online, search on DOI : 10.1111/j.2044-
8341.1975.tb02310 (accessed September 1, 2013).

Bergson, Henri. *Creative Evolution.* New York: Macmillan Co., 1911.
Kessinger Reprints, Amazon/CreateSpace, 2012.

Black Elk, Wallace, and William S. Lyon. *The Sacred Ways of a Lakota*. New York: HarperCollins, 1991.

Blyth, Caroline. *The Narrative of Rape in Genesis 34: Interpreting Dinah's Silence*. New York: Oxford University Press, 2010.

Bohm, David. *Wholeness and the Implicate Order*. London: Routledge and Kegan Paul, 1980.

Boscawen, W. S. C. Text K-3657. In *Transactions of the Society of Biblical Archaeology*, vol. 5. Oxford, England: Longmans, Green and Dyer, 1877.

Brenner, Athalya, ed. *Genesis: A Feminist Companion to the Bible*. 1st and 2nd series. Sheffield, United Kingdom: Sheffield Academic Press, 1993, 1998.

Brandenburg, John. *Beyond Einstein's Unified Field: Gravity and Electromagnetism Redefined*. Kempton, Ill.: Adventures Unlimited Press, 2011.

———. *Death on Mars: The Discovery of a Planetary Nuclear Massacre*. Kempton, Ill.: Adventures Unlimited Press, 2015.

———. *Life and Death on Mars: The New Mars Synthesis*. Kempton, Ill.: Adventures Unlimited Press, 2011.

Brin, David. *The Uplift Trilogy*. New York: Bantam Books, 1995–1998.

Brown, Dan. *The Da Vinci Code*. New York: Doubleday/Random House, 2003.

Bruns, Edgar. "Depth Psychology and the Fall." *Catholic Biblical Quarterly* 21 (1959): 78–82.

Capps, Donald. "Foreword." In Ellens, *Psychology and the Bible: A New Way to Read the Scriptures,* vol. 4.

Castaneda, Carlos. *The Fire from Within*. New York: Pocket Books, 1991.

———. *The Power of Silence*. New York: Pocket Books, 1991.

Casti, John L. *Paradigms Lost*. New York: William Morrow, 1989.

Childress, David Hatcher. *Technology of the Gods: The Incredible Sciences of the Ancients*. Kempton, Ill.: Adventures Unlimited Press, 2000.

Combs, Allan, and Mark Holland. *Synchronicity: Science, Myth, and the Trickster*. New York: Marlowe, 1995.

Cooper-White, Pamela. *The Cry of Tamar: Violence against Women and the Church's Response*. Minneapolis, Minn.: Fortress, 2012.

Cremo, Michael. *Human Devolution*. Badger, Calif.: Torchlight Publishing, 2003.

Cremo, Michael, and Richard L. Thompson. *Forbidden Archeology*. Los Angeles, Calif.: Bhaktivedanta Book Trust/Torchlight, 1998.

Csikszentmihalyi, Mihaly. *Flow: The Psychology of Optimal Experience.* New York: Harper & Row, 1990.

Delaney, Carol. *Abraham on Trial: The Social Legacy of Biblical Myth.* Princeton, N.J.: Princeton Univ. Press, 1999.

———. "Abraham and the Seeds of Patriarchy." In Brenner, *Genesis: A Feminist Companion to the Bible,* 2nd series, 129–49.

Deleuze, Gilles, and Felix Guattari. *A Thousand Plateaus.* New York: Continuum P. G., 2004.

Dennard, Linda. "The New Paradigm in Science and Public Administration." *Public Administration Review 56,* no. 15 (1996): 495–99.

Dossey, Larry. *Recovering the Soul: A Scientific and Spiritual Approach.* New York: Bantam New Age Books, 1989.

Dourley, John. *The Illness That We Are: A Jungian Critique of Christianity.* Toronto, Canada: Inner City Books, 1984.

Dunne, Carinn. "Between Two Thieves." In Stein and Moore, *Jung's Challenge to Contemporary Religion.*

Eco, Umberto. *The Name of the Rose.* Orlando, Fla.: Harcourt Brace, 1984.

———. *The Role of the Reader: Explorations in the Semiotics of Texts.* Bloomington: Indiana University Press, 1979.

Edinger, Edward. *Archetype of the Apocalypse: Divine Vengeance, Terrorism and the End of the World.* Chicago: Open Court, 2002.

———. *The New God-Image: A Study of Jung's Key Letters Concerning the Evolution of the Western God-Image.* Wilmette, Ill.: Chiron, 1996.

Eisler, Riane. *The Chalice and the Blade: Our History, Our Future.* San Francisco: Harper and Row, 1987.

———. *The Power of Partnership.* Novato, Calif.: New World Library, 2002.

———. *The Real Wealth of Nations.* San Francisco: Berrett-Koehler Pub., 2007.

Eisler, Riane, David Loye, and Kari Norgaard. *Women, Men, and the Global Quality of Life.* Pacific Grove, Calif.: Center for Partnership Studies, 1995.

Eliade, Mircea. *Myth and Reality (Religious Traditions in the World).* Long Grove, Ill.: Waveland Press, 1998.

Ellens, J. Harold. "The Psychodynamics of the Fall Story: Genesis 2.25–3.24." In Ellens and Rollins, *Psychology and the Bible,* vol. 2, From *Genesis to Apocalyptic Vision,* 23–39.

———. "Toxic Texts." In *The Destructive Power of Religion: Violence in Judaism, Christianity, and Islam,* edited by J. Harold Ellens. Westport, Conn.: Praeger/Greenwood, 2004.

Ellens, J. Harold, and Wayne G. Rollins, eds. *Psychology and the Bible: A New Way to Read the Scriptures.* 4 vols. Westport, Conn.: Praeger/Greenwood, 2004.

Erikson, Erik H. *Childhood and Society.* New York: Norton, 1950.

———. *Young Man Luther: A Study in Psychoanalysis and History.* New York: Norton, 1958.

Falkenstein, Adam, Igor M. Diakonov, Claudio Saporetti, and Mario Liverani. *The Sumerian Temple City.* Los Angeles, Calif.: Undena Publications, 1974.

Faulkner, Raymond O. *The Ancient Egyptian Pyramid Texts.* New York: Oxford Univ. Press/Clarendon Press, 1969.

Feinstein, David, and Stanley Krippner. *The Mythic Path.* New York: Tarcher/Putnam, 1997.

Fodor, A. "The Fall of Man in the Book of Genesis." *American Imago 11* (1954): 203–31.

Freeman, Walter. *Societies of Brains: A Study in the Neurosciences of Love and Hate.* Hillsdale, N.J.: Lawrence Erlbaum, 1995.

Freud, Sigmund. *Moses and Monotheism: Three Essays. The Complete Psychological Works of Sigmund Freud,* vol. 23. London, England: Hogarth, 1939.

———. *Totem and Taboo. The Complete Psychological Works of Sigmund Freud,* vol. 13. London, England: Hogarth, 1913.

Fromm, Erich. *Psychoanalysis and Religion.* New Haven, Conn.: Yale University Press, 1950.

———. *You Shall Be as Gods: A Radical Reinterpretation of the Old Testament and Its Traditions.* New York: Holt, Rinehart & Winston, 1966.

Gallo, Max. *Jeanne D'Arc, jeune fille de France brûlée vive.* Paris, France: Xo Editions, 2011.

Gardner, Laurence. *Genesis of the Grail Kings.* Gloucester, Mass.: Fair Winds Press, 2002.

Gell-Mann, Murray. *The Quark and the Jaguar.* New York: W. H. Freeman and Co., 1994.

Gleick, James. *Chaos.* New York: Viking Press, 1987.

Goleman, Daniel. *Emotional Intelligence.* New York: Bantam, 1995.

Gorbovsky, Alexander. *Riddles of Ancient History.* Moscow: Soviet Publishers, 1966.

Greven, Philip J. *Spare the Child: The Religious Roots of Punishment and the Psychological Impact of Physical Abuse.* New York: Knopf, 1991.

Grof, Stan. *Healing Our Deepest Wounds: The Holotropic Paradigm Shift.* New Castle, Wash.: Stream of Experience Productions, 2012.

Gruber, Mayer. "Genesis 21.12: A New Reading of an Ambiguous Text." In Brenner, *Genesis: A Feminist Companion to the Bible,* 2nd series, 172–179.

Guastello, Stephen. *Chaos, Catastrophe, and Human Affairs.* Mahwah, N.J.: Lawrence Erlbaum Associates, 1995.

Hallo, William W., and J. J. A. Van Dijk. *The Exaltation of Inanna.* New Haven, Conn.: Yale University Press, 1986.

Hameroff, Stuart, Alfred W. Kaszniak, and Alwyn C. Scott, eds. *Toward a Science of Consciousness.* Cambridge, Mass.: MIT Press/Bradford Books, 1996.

Hancock, Graham. *Fingerprints of the Gods: The Evidence for Earth's Lost Civilization.* Photography by Santha Faiia. New York: Three Rivers Press/Random House, 1995.

Hapgood, Charles. *Maps of the Ancient Sea-Kings: Evidence of Advanced Civilization in the Ice Age.* Kempton, Ill.: Adventures Unlimited Press, 1997. First published 1965.

Hardy, Chris H. *Cosmic DNA at the Origin: A Hyperdimension before the Big Bang: The Infinite Spiral Staircase Theory.* CreateSpace IPP, 2015.

———. *Diverging Views: On Our Way to the Galactic Club.* Delhi, India: Terra Futura, 2008.

———. *DNA of the Gods: The Anunnaki Creation of Eve and the Alien Battle for Humanity.* Rochester, Vt.: Bear & Co., 2014.

———. *Butterfly Logic: Experimental Planet Earth.* CreateSpace IPP, 2016.

———. "Nonlocal Processes and Entanglement as a Signature of a Cosmic Hyperdimension." *Journal of Consciousness Exploration & Research* (JCER) 6, no. 12, (Dec 2015). https://independent.academia.edu/ChrisHHardy/Papers

———. *The Sacred Network.* Rochester, Vt.: Inner Traditions, 2011.

Hardy, Christine. "Complex Intuitive Dynamics in a Systemic Cognitive Framework." Proceedings of the International Society for the Systems Sciences. CD-ROM. Crete, Greece, 2003.

———. *La prédiction de Jung: la métamorphose de la Terre.* Paris: Dervy/ Trédaniel, 2012.

———. *Le vécu de la transe.* Paris: Editions du Dauphin, 1995.

———. "Multilevel Webs Stretched across Time: Retroactive and Proactive Interinfluences." *Systems Research and Behavioral Science* 20, no. 2 (2003): 201–15.

———. *Networks of Meaning: A Bridge between Mind and Matter.* Westport, Conn.: Praeger, 1998.

———. "Self-organization, Self-reference and Inter-influences in Multilevel Webs: Beyond Causality and Determinism." *Journal of Cybernetics and Human Knowing* 8, no. 3 (July 2001): 35–59.

———. "Synchronicity: Interconnection through a Semantic Dimension." Presentation at Second Psi Meeting, Curitiba, Brazil, April 21–26, 2004.

Haze, Xaviant. *Aliens in Ancient Egypt.* Rochester, Vt.: Bear & Co., 2002.

Heidegger, Martin. *Being and Time.* San Francisco: Harper, 1962.

———. *The Principle of Reason.* Bloomington: Indiana Univ. Press, 1996.

Heine, Johan, and Michael Tellinger. *Adam's Calendar: Discovering the Oldest Man-Made Structure on Earth—75,000 Years Ago.* Seattle, Wash.: Compendium, 2008.

Hermes Trismegistus. *Corpus Hermeticum.* The Gnostic Society Library. Full texts online at www.gnosis.org/library.

———. "The Cup or Monad. Of Hermes to Tat." (*Corpus Hermeticum IV*). Translated by George Mead. Available at www.gnosis.org/library/ grs-mead/TGH-v2/th209.html.

———. *The Discourse on the Eighth and Ninth.* Translated by James Brashler, Peter A. Dirkse, and Douglas M. Parrott. Available at www.gnosis.org/ naghamm/discorse.html.

Hillman, James. "Psychology: Monotheistic or Polytheistic?" In *The New Polytheism: Rebirth of the Gods and the Goddesses,* edited by David L. Miller. Dallas, Tex.: Spring Publications, 1981.

Jacobsen, Thorkild. "The Reign of Ibbi-Sin." *Journal of Cuneiform Studies* 7, no. 2 (1953): 36–47.

Janssen, Frans, H. P. M. "On the Origin and Development of the so-called Lajjagauri." *South Asian Archaeology 1991,* 457–72. Stuttgart, Germany: Franz Steiner Verlag, 1993.

Jung, Carl Gustav. *Aion*. Vol. 9, *The Collected Works of C. G. Jung*.

———. *Alchemical Studies*. Vol. 13, *The Collected Works of C. G. Jung*.

———. *Answer to Job*. New York: Routledge and Kegan Paul, 1954.

———. *The Collected Works of C. G. Jung*. Edited by G. Adler and R. F. Hull. 20 vols. Bollingen Series. Princeton, N.J.: Princeton University Press, 1953–1976.

———. Commentary. *The Secret of the Golden Flower: A Chinese Book of Life*, by Richard Wilhelm. New York: Mariner Books, 1962. First published 1931.

———. *Letters*. Vol. 2. Edited by G. Adler and Aniela Jaffe. Bollingen XCV. Princeton, N.J.: Princeton University Press, 1999.

———. *Letters to the Rev. David Cox*, 25 September and 12 November 1957. Reprinted in Edinger, *The New God-Image*, 183–95. Originally published in CW 18, pars. 1648–90.

———. *Man and His Symbols*. Garden City, N.Y.: Windfall Books/ Doubleday, 1964.

———. *Memories, Dreams, Reflections*. New York: Vintage Books/Random House, 1965.

———. *Psychology and Alchemy*. Vol. 12, *The Collected Works of C. G. Jung*.

———. *Psychology and Religion: West and East*. Vol. 11, *The Collected Works of C. G. Jung*.

———. *Synchronicity: An Acausal Connecting Principle*. Vol. 8, *The Collected Works of C. G. Jung*.

———. *The Undiscovered Self*. Vol. 10, *The Collected Works of C. G. Jung*.

———. *Two Essays on Analytical Psychology*. Vol. 7, *The Collected Works of C. G. Jung*.

Jung, Carl Gustav, and Wolfgang Pauli. *The Interpretation of Nature and the Psyche*. New York: Pantheon Books, 1955.

Kane, D., S. Cheston, and J. Greer. "Perceptions of God by Survivors of Childhood Sexual Abuse: An Exploratory Study in an Under-Researched Area." *Journal of Psychology and Theology* 21 (1993): 228–37.

Kille, Andrew. "Psychological Biblical Criticism." In Aucker, *Guides to Biblical Scholarship*.

———. "The Day of the Lord from a Jungian Perspective: Amos 5:18–20. In Ellens, *Psychology and the Bible*, Vol. 2, 267–76.

King, Karen. *The Gospel of Mary of Magdala: Jesus and the First Woman*

Apostle. Santa Rosa, Calif.: Polebridge Press, 2003. Excerpt at www
.gnosis.org/library/GMary-King-Intro.html.

King, Leonard W. *Babylonian Magic and Sorcery.* Milton-Keynes, United
Kingdom: BiblioLife. Reprint of London, England: Luzac & Co.
Publishing, 1896.

———. "Legends of Babylon and Egypt in Relation to Hebrew Tradition."
The Schweich lectures, The British Academy, London, England, 1916.
Available online at www.sacred-texts.com/ane/beheb.htm (accessed
September 7, 2013).

———. *The Seven Tablets of Creation.* 1902. Reprint, Charleston, S.C.:
BiblioBazaar, 2007.

Klug, Sonja. *Kathedrale des kosmos.* Hugendubel, Germany: V. Heinrich,
2001.

Kluger, Rivkah S. *Psyche in Scripture: "The Idea of the Chosen People" and
Other Essays.* Toronto, Canada: Inner City, 1995.

Knafo, Ariel, and Tziporit Glick. "Genesis Dreams: Using a Private,
Psychological Event as a Cultural, Political Declaration." *Dreaming* 10,
no. 1 (2000): 19–30.

Knapp, Bettina L. *Manna and Mystery: A Jungian Approach to Hebrew Myth
and Legend.* Wilmette, Ill.: Chiron, 1995.

Koestler, Arthur. *The Act of Creation.* New York: Penguin, 1989.

Kramer, Daniela, and Michael Moore. "Sour Grapes: Transgenerational
Family Pathology in the Hebrew Bible." *Journal of Psychology and
Judaism* 22 (1998): 65–69.

Kramer, Samuel N. *Lamentation over the Destruction of Ur.* Vol. 12 in
Assyriological Studies. Chicago: Chicago University Press, 1940.

———. "The Oldest Literary Catalogue. A Sumerian List of Literary
Compositions Compiled about 2000 B.C." *Bulletin of the American
Schools of Oriental Research* 88 (1942): 10–19.

———. *Sumerian Mythology.* Originally published 1944, 1961. Available
online at Sacred Texts Archive, Ancient Near East: www.sacred-texts
.com/ane/sum (accessed September 7, 2013).

Kramer, Samuel N., and J. Maier. *Myths of Enki, the Crafty God.* New York:
Oxford University Press, 1989.

Krippner, Stanley, and P. Welch. *Spiritual Dimensions of Healing.* New York:
Irvington, 1992.

Lambert, W. G., and A. R. Millard. *Atrahasis, The Babylonian Story of the Flood.* New York: Oxford University Press, 1969.

Langdon, Stephen. *The Babylonian Epic of Creation.* Reprinted by Nabu Public Domain Reprints from the 1876 edition.

———. *Sumerian and Babylonian Psalms.* Paris, France, and London, England: Paul Geuthner, 1909.

———. *Sumerian Epic of Paradise, the Flood and the Fall of Man.* Publications of the Babylonian Section, Volume X. Philadelphia: University Museum, 1915.

Laszlo, Ervin. *The Akashic Experience: Science and the Cosmic Memory Field.* Rochester, Vt.: Inner Traditions, 2009.

———. *Science and the Akashic Field: An Integral Theory of Everything.* Rochester, Vt.: Inner Traditions, 2007.

Laszlo, Ervin, Stanislav Grof, and Peter Russel. *The Consciousness Revolution.* Las Vegas, Nev.: Elf Rock Productions, 2003.

Leibniz, Gottfried. *Discourse on Metaphysics and Other Essays.* Indianapolis, Ind.: Hackett Publishing Co., 1991.

Lemaire, André. "Who or What Was Yahweh's Asherah?" *Biblical Archaeology Review* 10, no. 6 (Nov. 1984), 42–51.

Lerner, Gerda. *The Creation of Patriarchy.* New York: Oxford University Press, 1986.

Lewin, Isaac. "The Psychological Theory of Dreams in the Bible." *Journal of Psychology and Judaism* 10 (1983): 73–88.

Lovelock, James. *The Ages of Gaia.* New York: Bantam Books, 1990.

Margulis, Lynn, and Dorion Sagan. *Microcosmos: Four Billion Years of Evolution from Our Microbial Ancestors.* New York: Simon and Shuster/ Summit Books, 1986.

Markale, Jean. *Carnac et l'énigme de l'Atlantide.* Paris, France: Pygmalion/ Watelet, 1987.

———. *The Druids: Celtic Priests of Nature.* Rochester, Vt.: Inner Traditions, 1999.

Marrs, Jim. *Our Occulted History: Do the Global Elite Conceal Ancient Aliens?* New York: William Morrow, 2013.

Mead, George R. S., trans. *Thrice-Greatest Hermes, Vol. 2.* Corpus Hermeticum V. (VI.) "Though Unmanifest God is Most Manifest." www.gnosis.org/library/grs-mead/TGH-v2/th211.html.

Ménard, Louis, trans. *Hermès Trismégiste*. Paris, France: Guy Trédaniel /Ed. de la Maisnie, 1977, 2004.

Mercer, S. A. B, trans. *The Pyramid Texts*. 4 vols. New York: Longmans, Green and Co., 1952.

Merkur, Daniel. "The Prophecies of Jeremiah." *American Imago* 42 (1985): 1–37.

———. "Psychotherapeutic Change in the Book of Job." In Ellens, *Psychology and the Bible,* vol. 2, 119–40.

Miles, Jack. *God, a Biography*. New York: Knopf, 1995.

Miller, David. "Attacks on Christendom." In Stein and Moore, *Jung's Challenge to Contemporary Religion*.

Mishlove, Jeffrey. *The Roots of Consciousness*. New York: Marlowe and Co., 1997.

Narby, Jeremy. *The Cosmic Serpent: DNA and the Origins of Knowledge*. New York: Tarcher/Putnam, 1999.

Pagels, Elaine. *Adam, Eve, and the Serpent*. New York: Vintage Books/ Random House, 1989.

———. *The Gnostic Gospels*. New York: Vintage Books/Random House, 1989.

———. *The Origin of Satan*. New York: Vintage Books/Random House, 1996.

Peat, David. *Synchronicity: The Bridge between Matter and Mind*. New York: Bantam Books, 1987.

Picknett, Lynn, and Clive Prince. *The Templar Revelation: Secret Guardians of the True Identity of Christ*. New York: Touchstone, 1998.

Plotinus. *The Enneads*. LP Classic Reprint Series, 1992.

Poincare, Henri. *Science and Method*. New York: Dover Publications, 1952.

Radin, Dean. *Entangled Minds*. New York: Paraview, 2006.

———. *The Conscious Universe*. San Francisco: Harper-Edge, 1997.

Rashkow, Ilona. "Daddy-Dearest and the 'Invisible Spirit of Wine.'" In Brenner, *Genesis: A Feminist Companion to the Bible,* 2nd series, 82–107.

———. *Taboo or Not Taboo: Sexuality and Family in the Hebrew Bible*. Minneapolis, Minn.: Fortress, 2000.

Ray, Paul, and Ruth Anderson. *The Cultural Creatives: How 50 Million People Are Changing the World*. New York: Harmony Books, 2000.

Ricoeur, P. "The Hermeneutical Function of Distantiation." In From *Text to Action: Essays II,* 75–88. Evanston, Ill: Northwestern Press, 1991.

————. *Interpretation Theory*. Fort Worth: Texas Christian University Press, 1976.

Robertson, Robin. *Jungian Archetypes: Jung, Gödel, and the History of Archetypes*. York Beach, Maine: Nicholas-Hays, 1995.

————. *Your Shadow*. Virginia Beach, Va.: A.R.E. Press, 1997.

Rollins, Wayne G. *Soul and Psyche: The Bible in Psychological Perspective*. Minneapolis, Minn.: Fortress, 1999.

Sandars, N. K. *The Epic of Gilgamesh*. New York: Penguin Classics, 1960.

Schwartz, Stephan. *Opening on the Infinite: The Art and Science of Non-local Awareness*. Langley, Wash.: Nemoseen Media, 2007.

————. *The Secret Vaults of Time*. Charlottesville, Va.: Hampton Roads Publishing, 2005.

Schwartz-Salant, Nathan. "Patriarchy in Transformation: Judaic, Christian, and Clinical Perspectives." In Stein and Moore, *Jung's Challenge to Contemporary Religion*.

Sen, Amartya. *Development as Freedom*. New York: Oxford University Press, 1999.

Sheldrake, Rupert. *Morphic Resonance: The Nature of Formative Causation*. Rochester, Vt.: Park Street Press, 2009.

Singer, June. "Jung's Gnosticism and Contemporary Gnosis." In Stein and Moore, *Jung's Challenge to Contemporary Religion*.

Sitchin, Zecharia. *The Cosmic Code*. New York: Harper, 2007.

————. *Divine Encounters*. New York: Avon, 1996.

————. *The End of Days*. New York: Harper, 2008.

————. *Genesis Revisited*. New York: Avon, 1990.

————. *The Lost Book of Enki*. Rochester, Vt.: Bear & Co., 2002.

————. *The Lost Realms*. New York: Harper, 2007.

————. *There Were Giants Upon the Earth*. Rochester, Vt.: Bear & Co., 2010.

————. *The Stairway to Heaven*. New York: Harper, 2007.

————. *The 12th Planet*. New York: Harper, 2007.

————. *The Wars of Gods and Men*. New York: Harper, 2007.

————. *When Time Began*. New York: Harper, 2007.

Sjöberg, Ake W., Eugen Bergmann, and Gene B. Gragg, eds. *The Collection of the Sumerian Temple Hymns*. Vol. 3 of *Texts from Cuneiform Sources*, 3–154. Locust Valley, N.Y.: J. J. Augustin, 1969. Available at The

Electronic Text Corpus of Sumerian Literature page, http://etcsl.orinst
.ox.ac.uk/section4/tr4801.htm (accessed January 20, 2016).

Smith, George. *The Chaldean Account of Genesis*. London, England: Sampson
Law, et al., 1876. Reprinted by Nau Public Domain Reprints. Available at
http://sacred-texts.com/ane/caog/index.htm (accessed January 20, 2016).

Stein, Murray. "Jung's Green Christ: A Healing Symbol for Christianity." In
Stein and Moore, *Jung's Challenge to Contemporary Religion*.

———. *Jung's Treatment of Christianity: The Psychotherapy of a Religious
Tradition*. Wilmette, Ill.: Chiron, 1985.

Stein, Murray, and Robert L. Moore. *Jung's Challenge to Contemporary
Religion*. Wilmette, Ill.: Chiron, 1987.

Teilhard de Chardin, Pierre. *Phenomenon of Man*. New York: Harper Torch
Book, 1965.

Tellinger, Michael. *Slave Species of the Gods: The Secret History of the
Anunnaki and Their Mission on Earth*. Rochester, Vt.: Bear & Co., 2012.

Temple, Robert. *The Sirius Mystery*. London, England: Sidgwick and
Jackson, 1976.

Trible, Phyllis. *Texts of Terror*. Minneapolis, Minn.: Fortress Press, 1984.

Waite, Arthur Edward, ed. *Hermetic and Alchemical Writings of Paracelsus*.
Boston: Shambhala, 1976.

Waters, Frank. *The Book of the Hopi*. New York: Viking/Penguin, 1963.

West, John Anthony. *Serpent in the Sky: The High Wisdom of Ancient Egypt*.
New York: Quest Books, 1993.

Wilson, Colin. *From Atlantis to the Sphinx*. New York: Virgin Books, 1997.

Mesopotamian Tablets

Creation of Man by the Mother Goddess

The Curse of Agade

Epic of Creation (Enuma Elish)

Epic of Gilgamesh

Epic of Etana

Erra Epic (Erra Epos)

The Exaltation of Inanna

Hymn to Enlil the All-Beneficent

Hymn to Eridu
Inanna's Descent to the Underworld
Khedorlaomer Texts
Kingship in Heaven
The Kuthean Legend of Naram-Sin
Myths of Enki
The Myth of the Pickax
The Myth of Zu
Tale of Adapa (Generations of Adapa)
Tales of the Magicians
Text CT-XVI, 44–6
Text K-3657, first translated by George Smith; retranslated by W. S. C. Boscawen
Text K-5001, in *Oxford Editions of Cuneiform Texts,* vol. 6
When the Gods as Men

Hebrew Apocrypha

The Book of Enoch
The Book of Jubilees

Christian Apocrypha/Nag Hammadi Texts

The Authoritative Teaching (translated by George W. MacRae). Available at http://gnosis.org/naghamm/autho.html (accessed February 27, 2016).
The Gnostic Society Library (website). Index of Nag Hamadi texts (translations online) Index. www.gnosis.org/naghamm/nhlalpha.html (accessed February 27, 2016).
The Gospel of Mary. Available at www.gnosis.org/library/marygosp.htm
The Gospel of Philip (translated by Marvin Meyer). Available at http://gnosis.org/naghamm/GPhilip-Meyer.html (accessed February 27, 2016).
The Gospel of Thomas (translated by Thomas O. Lambdin). Available at www.gnosis.org/naghamm/gthlamb.html (accessed February 27, 2016).

Hypostasis of the Archons: See The Reality of the Rulers.

Library Codices: Index of all 52 Nag Hammadi texts. Includes the gnostic gospels. Available at The Gnostic Society Library, http://gnosis.org/naghamm/nhlcodex.html (accessed September 7, 2013).

The Nag Hammadi Library in English. Edited by James M. Robinson, San Francisco: HarperCollins, 1990 (revised edition; first published 1977).

The Nag Hammadi Texts. Integral research version in English and French, at Laval University, Quebec, www.naghammadi.org/traductions/traductions .aspx?lang=eng (accessed September 7, 2013).

The Reality of the Rulers (The Hypostasis of the Archons) (translated by Willis Barnstone and Marvin Meyer). Available at http://gnosis.org/naghamm/Hypostas-Barnstone.html (accessed February 27, 2016).

The Secret Book of John (The Apocryphon of John) (translated by Stevan Davies). Available at www.gnosis.org/naghamm/apocjn-davies.html (accessed February 27, 2016).

The Sophia of Jesus Christ (translated by Douglas M. Parrott). Available at www.gnosis.org/naghamm/sjc.html (accessed February 27, 2016).

The Thunder, Perfect Mind (translated by George W. MacRae). Available at www.gnosis.org/naghamm/thunder.html (accessed February 27, 2016).

Writing without Title. Text NH II , 5; XIII , 2. In the Nag Hammadi Texts. Louis Painchaud's integral research translation in French, at Laval University, Quebec, www.naghammadi.org/traductions/textes/ecrit_sans_titre.asp (accessed September 7, 2013).

✦ About the Author ✦

SYSTEMS THEORIST and cognitive scientist, Ph.D. in psychological anthropology, and former researcher at Princeton's Psychophysical Research Laboratories, Chris H. Hardy has spent the past two decades investigating nonlocal consciousness and thought-provoking mind potentials. Author of more than sixty papers and seventeen books on these subjects, she is an authority in the domain both in scientific terms and as an author and workshop facilitator.

In her book *Networks of Meaning: A Bridge Between Mind and Matter* she developed a cognitive theory, posing a nonlocal consciousness, of which professor and author Allan Leslie Combs said, "This book may well be the first step to an entirely new and deeply human understanding of the mind." She recently expanded this into a cosmological theory positing consciousness as a cosmic web in *Cosmic DNA at the Origin*.

Hardy spends a lot of time traveling and exploring various knowledge systems and cultures, maintaining a keen interest in Eastern religions, shamanism, and esoterica. She presents regularly at various international conferences and is a member of several scientific societies exploring system theory, chaos theory, parapsychology, consciousness studies, and the new mind-matter paradigm in physics.

For more information (e.g., data on the historicity of the Sumerian tablets, recent astronomical discoveries supporting Sumer's data, etc.), visit her blog at http://chris-h-hardy-dna-of-the-gods.blogspot.fr.

✦ Index ✦

Page numbers in *italics* refer to illustrations.